I0541963

OFF the Merry-Go-Round and ON with Your Life!

POWER HOUSE

OFF the Merry-Go-Round and ON with Your Life!

GO FROM SPINNING TO WINNING AS YOUR NEW WAY OF LIVING

DANA MARIE ECKLUND

© Dana Marie Ecklund, 2022

All rights reserved. This book is protected by the copyright laws of the United States of America. This book may not be copied or reprinted for commercial gain or profit. The use of short quotations or occasional page copying for personal study is permitted and encouraged, provided proper citations and credits are acknowledged. Permission will be granted upon request for appropriate usage.

Unless otherwise identified, scripture quotations are from the New King James Version® (NKJV). Copyright © 1982 by Thomas Nelson. Used by permission. All rights reserved. Scripture quotations marked (MEV) are taken from THE HOLY BIBLE, MODERN ENGLISH VERSION. Copyright© 2014 by Military Bible Association. Published and distributed by Charisma House. Scripture quotations marked (AMPC) are taken from the AMPLIFIED® BIBLE, Copyright© 1954, 1958, 1962, 1964, 1965, 1987 by the Lockman Foundation. Scripture quotations marked (AMP) are taken from the Amplified® Bible, Copyright © 2015 by The Lockman Foundation. Used by permission. www.lockman. org. Scripture quotations marked (NIV) are taken from the Holy Bible, New International Version®, NIV®. Copyright © 1973, 1978, 1984, 2011 by Biblica, Inc.™ Used by permission of Zondervan. All rights reserved worldwide. www.zondervan.com. The "NIV" and "New International Version" are trademarks registered in the United States Patent and Trademark Office by Biblica, Inc.™ Scripture quotations marked (ESV) are from The ESV® Bible (The Holy Bible, English Standard Version®), copyright © 2001 by Crossway, a publishing ministry of Good News Publishers. Used by permission. All rights reserved. Scriptures marked (KJV) are taken from the KING JAMES VERSION (KJV): KING JAMES VERSION, public domain. Scripture quotations marked (CEB) are taken from the COMMON ENGLISH BIBLE. © Copyright 2011 COMMON ENGLISH BIBLE. All rights reserved. Used by permission. (www.CommonEnglishBible.com). Scriptures marked (TLB) are taken from THE LIVING BIBLE (TLB), copyright© 1971. Used by permission of Tyndale House Publishers, Inc., Carol Stream, Illinois 60188. All rights reserved. Scripture quotations marked (GNT) are from the Good News Translation in Today's English Version- Second Edition Copyright © 1992 by American Bible Society. Used by Permission. Scripture quotations marked (NASB) are from the (NASB®) New American Standard Bible®, Copyright © 1960, 1971, 1977, 1995, 2020 by The Lockman Foundation. Used by permission. All rights reserved. www.lockman.org

Please note that Power House Studios, LLC.'s publishing style capitalizes certain pronouns in Scripture and text that refer to the Father, Son, and Holy Spirit, which may differ from some Bible publishers' styles. Similarly, the name satan is intentionally not capitalized, even if that may violate traditional publishing or grammatical rules. Additionally, this book's author has chosen that select words of Biblical significance shall also be capitalized.

Original art and illustrations by Ryon Lee Media, Inc., ryonleemedia.com.

Published by: POWER HOUSE, An imprint of Power House Studios, LLC. thepowerhousestudio.com

ISBN#979-8-9853756-2-6 (Paperback)
ISBN# 979-8-9853756-3-3 (eBook)
ISBN# 979-8-9853756-8-8 (Workbook)
ISBN# 979-8-9853756-7-1 (On With Your Life Journal)

Printed in the United States of America.

DEDICATION

I dedicate this book to my husband, children, and family, who told me, "Go for it!"

And, to my brothers and sisters in the Lord Jesus Christ who live in this world but have decided to not be a part of this world's way of doing things;

To those who will boldly say, "The Lord is my helper; I will not fear. I'm moving forward, no matter what man thinks or does to me;"

To those who have decided to be KINGDOM minded and are willing to do whatever it takes to get off every merry-go-round in life and avoid any new ones;

Take the information and insights you receive from this book and use them to get off your own merry-go-rounds, leading the way for others to get off also.

CONTENTS

ACKNOWLEDGMENTS

I thank my husband, children, and family for being so very patient and supportive, excited to get this book published, and for believing with me that it will help many people.

To my pastors, teachers, and spiritual leaders who have imparted spiritual truths to me at every level throughout my life thus far: Hearing these truths caused me to receive revelation. Faith came, and freedom followed.

I'm sending a big "SHOUT OUT" to my oldest daughter, Jessica Kate Marie, for doing most of the content editing and writing this book's foreword. Your expertise and insight inspired me to dig deep into my life and share with others my real-life stories and the truths from God's Word that helped me in my journey. Thanks, Jess!!

Thanks to one of my personal cheerleaders, Michelle Everett, I joined the "*Power House Blueprint*™ – *The 90-Days Vision into Sight*" program through Power House Studio, LLC. This gave me the kick in the pants I needed to finish and launch this book!

Most importantly, to my Good Father God, Who is helping me do my part in accomplishing His plan for my life. My desire is that I point people to Jesus and that You, Lord, get all the glory for every helpful thing people receive out of this book.

FOREWORD

God: "You have dwelt at this mountain long enough."

That's what He told His children (the Israelites) way back in the Old Testament (Deuteronomy 1:6) when they were stalling to obey His command to go and possess the land of Canaan. God was ready for them to begin the journey to inherit the land He promised them. They didn't make the connection, but they had been in the same ol' rut, circling the same ol' mountain, doing the same ol' things for long enough! God had already given them this land of promise, and all that was left for them to do was to go in and take it.

It's not God's plan for any of His children to stay too long in the same place in their spiritual walk. Our God is a God of forward movement—He is a God of real progress. He said in 1 Timothy 4:15 that our progress should be noticeable to all. He also said in Proverbs 4:18 that the path of the just grows brighter and brighter. That's a perfect example of the God-kind of progress! The path begins dimly lit, but if you will begin to take steps forward to obey God, doing what you know to do, the brighter this path will become.

In the same way God was ready for His Israelite children to take a step and begin the journey to receive the land He had given them, He is also ready for you to get moving forward to the good land He has for you. In the Old Covenant (Old Testament), the Promised Land was a physical place of blessing and abundance. Today, in the New Covenant (New Testament), we've been given the same blessings and promises, along with much more! God already knows what steps you should take. In order to possess your promised land—your wealthy place of rich fulfillment in every good thing—you must begin to take your first step and simply do what God wants you to do right now, "while it is called 'Today'" (Hebrews 3:13). It's up to you to move ahead and take what's yours. Don't expect the plan of God to fall into your lap. "'For I know the plans I have for you,' declares the Lord, 'plans to prosper you and not to harm you, plans to give you hope and a future'" (Jeremiah 29:11 NIV).

In order to progress, we must be obedient to BEGIN. I've heard an elder in the faith say many times: "If you don't start where you are, you'll stay where you are." Doing the plan of God starts with a step. You can either begin on the path God has for you—starting where you are and putting one foot in front of the other, one step at a time—or you can stay in the same place, doing the same thing over and over and over. Spinning on a never-ending cycle of monotony—never changing and never going forward and upward—is not what we were born to do.

God has placed in each one of our hearts a vision and dream to do what He's called and planned for us to do—one of excitement and fulfillment; but we will never reach those dreams and plans unless we begin to take obedient steps forward. As you read this book, you will see it is my mother's heart, and I know the Lord's desire as well, that none of us wake up when we are well-aged and sadly realize that we never did what we were purposed to do. We should no longer be at ease or satisfied to let another day go by where we do not take a step forward in the plan of God for our lives.

In this book, my mother introduces a parallel that exists between an ever-spinning merry-go-round on the playground and a type of merry-go-round in various life situations. Although it was not God's perfect plan for her to have lived with so many different hurts and pains (from all those years of jumping on and off merry-go-rounds), she has been obedient to make her life an open book. She has exposed very personal events in expectation that every reader will begin to see the truth about what's going "around" in their lives. As they realize the enemy's tactics against them and God's plan of action for them, they will be motivated and empowered to get off their own merry-go-rounds.

On any of the different merry-go-rounds in life, you may think you are making some good, forward movement. You might make some changes, make new friendships, renew some commitments, and possibly even promise some New Year's resolutions (Ha-ha!). But the truth is, if you are not walking with the Lord and on His path for your life, you are more than likely going to get right back on that same ol' merry-go-round, allowing something else to spin you...around and around and around. Going in circles—around and around—is not God's kind of progress. You will only have true progress when there is some purposeful, forward movement in God's plan.

If in life we stop taking steps forward towards fulfilling God's plan, the enemy, who is the playground bully, will say to you, "Welcome aboard the merry-go-round!" as he continually spins you silly until you aren't able to get off, or walk straight when you do (like those times from grade school).

Reading this, you may have begun to realize that you, like the Israelites, have awakened every day in the same place, doing the same things, day in and day out. The Bible instructs us to be alert and awake regarding what is going on in our lives (Ephesians 5:14-17) so that we stop to evaluate what we are doing and who we are doing it with. Along with that, 2 Timothy 3:8-9 says that when we resist the truth, we progress no further. We must be honest with ourselves: Is there forward movement in my life? Or, should I admit there are only circles?

Just like God said to the Israelites, I can still hear Him saying to us today: "Son, Daughter, you have dwelt at this mountain long enough. It's time to move forward."

-Jessica-

INTRODUCTION

In the writing of this book, I really endeavored to share the life-changing message with humor, transparency, and true-life examples. I have also included some powerful tools that I know will help you. You will see how they have helped me, my family, and others in the pages ahead.

READ IT!
1 John 4 & 1 Corinthians 13
Who Love is, what Love does

You will see special "Read It" prompts throughout the book, like the one above. I've included these to teach you helpful patterns and allow you to use your own personal effort and action to move forward. The extra reading in these sections will help you understand the key points more deeply. God wants you to receive revelation from His Word so that you can go on with your life with real progress. These extra bonus passages will be instrumental in making life changes, so watch for these along the way and make time to look them up and read them in your Bible.

You will also see "Stop the Spin!" prompts throughout the book like the example below. These sections are added nuggets of wisdom and instruction

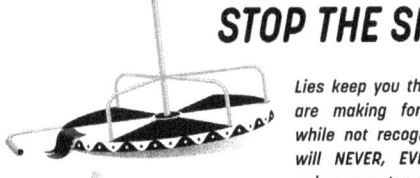

STOP THE SPIN!

Lies keep you thinking that you are making forward progress while not recognizing that you will NEVER, EVER go forward unless you stop and get off.

Instead of yielding to lies, believe in God's truth about your situation. See with the eyes of faith and believe His promises are true.

to help nail down the revelation and develop new responses. I hope that these will especially stick out in your thoughts and be deeply rooted in your memory for you to draw on later.

To complement the tools found in the book itself, I am also making the coordinating journal and workbook available. (You can order them both at: https://onwithyourlife.com) These are specifically designed to give you the most help and permanent results from your journey as you get *"Off the Merry-Go-Round and On With Your Life!"*

The *On With Your Life Journal* is designed to use while you read the book. As you read through the book, write the things that stand out to you in your journal. I list suggestions and give you prompts in the journal.

After reading the book, you can use the *OFF the Merry-Go-Round and ON With Your Life Workbook.* If you use the journal while reading, you can refer to your journal entries to help you remember your thoughts as you go through the workbook. This will greatly help you get off life's merry-go-rounds and on to your God-provided path in life.

This is not a one-time read-through book, and then you're done. This book will challenge you to use the help included in the text. But you have what you need on every page to stop spinning and start winning! This book will stir up hope in you. When you have read it and journaled, I am convinced you will desire to start right away using the workbook and making your way off life's merry-go-rounds.

I'm excited for you and your journey to a new way of living!

ONE

THE TEXT MESSAGE

I'LL NEVER FORGET the most intimate and vulnerable text message I think I've ever received from my beautiful second-born daughter, Courtney. It was on a Sunday afternoon, during Christmastime of 2016. I had just left our church in Branson, Missouri, and I could feel the festive holiday atmosphere Branson is known for. We had our traditional children's play at church, and then our pastor spoke a Christmas message that made me think of the first time I ever really did believe in Jesus.

When I got home, I began wondering if Courtney, who had just turned thirty-one years old, had been able to watch the church service online. As I was preparing to do some shopping, I heard my phone chime. It was her!

"Do you believe?"

That was the beginning of a text conversation with Courtney. She was in a rough place at the time. Her husband was sitting in the county jail, and she was under a lot of stress. She seemed to be continuously under the stress of her life, just running in circles, always trying to figure things out. It seemed she was getting worn down by constantly living in fix-it and survival mode. I was especially curious to see what else she was going to text. I stopped everything and entered into what seemed to be a once-in-a-lifetime text message from her to me:

(ME) I really do believe!

(COURTNEY) Me too!!

(ME) Ya know, Court, ever since I first heard as a child, I really did believe. I got sidetracked several times and got off and on like on a non-stop merry-go-round. Finally, I decided as a teen—Sr. in high school—to get off the merry-go-round. I asked myself if this was what I was going to do my whole life … get off and on. I started looking at people around me and realized I needed to make a choice. I could be an example for God or against God. Up to that point, I showed my friends that you could take God or leave Him whenever you wanted, and it was ok. They only saw hypocrisy in me because I went to church each week and then partied around with them. I was wrong. I hurt people.

Then I heard about being hot or cold rather than lukewarm. I decided that for the sake of changing the course to the rest of my life and for the sake of my friends, I would finally make a stand and never waiver again what I believed about God having a plan for my life. I decided to drop my pride and give my life to God and take the risk of persecution and rejection to find out what my life could do for God—my Creator. I realized faith and believing without acting on it was just dead faith and really not believing at all.

2

From that day forward, I had to wake up each day and take a step toward the persecution and not turn and run back. It was action. It hurt. It was lonely for a long time. God then was able to start lining things up for me. Then He was able to answer some of my heart's desires. Peace led me through the loneliness. I knew it wouldn't last forever. Giving up my life wasn't the end of the world. It was the beginning.

Courtney, your husband and kids are not what your life is all about. They are a piece. They will never, ever, ever be able to replace those pieces of your life you have ignored and been running from. You will only lead your husband and your kids astray and away from you if you do not turn permanently and stop this back-and-forth, jumping on and off the merry-go-round.

The movement of the merry-go-round is deceiving. Making you think you are really going somewhere and you aren't. Decide if any lukewarm is in you in any way. Decide what you will do once and for all and stick to it. Get off of the pointless round and round and round. This is a new day and a new beginning. The choice is yours today, again. Mom

(COURTNEY) That's good, Mom! I'm tired of wavering! I've done it for far too long! [Sends image]

(ME) Wow, that pic is something I want on my wall. It's good, Baby!

Be all in or get all out. There is no halfway.

That was a good word I wrote that could be for your husband, also. He's been talking too long and not really surrendered.

(COURTNEY) Yes, I will read it to him when he calls. It was very good. We keep letting life and temptations pull us back in. But I'm ready to live the real life! LOL. That's funny you sent all that because I got that thing on someone's Facebook last night. I saw it and screenshot it.

(ME) Cool. You and your husband have been doing the same thing I did for years. In the summer, when school was out, I was forced not to be around friends every day. I went to summer church camp and got involved in youth. I recommitted my life to God every summer and then went back to school, not even planning to seriously resist. I didn't take the precautions I should have and didn't live on God's daily bread, His Word. I got depleted spiritually. And then weak. Pretty soon, I said, 'What's the use? I'm already back in all this.'

I was fooled. I had the Greater One inside me. He was my strength. I was using my own. Dumb. I failed every year. When you and your husband are forced (incarcerated) to focus and re-route your life, it's easier. But when back in real life around the same places and people, it happened all over again because there weren't any daily precautions taken. I can only say these things to you guys because I admit I did it myself. I can also rightfully share with you how to stay out of it because I did it myself. I am totally and forever surrendered to Him. He is my heart's desire before your dad and before my children. Even if I stand alone and live alone for God, I will—I've been alone before, and He would help me again if it came to that. But it wouldn't change my belief in Him. I will be forever eternally with Him. I'm preparing for that time right now. It's real to me. Mom

...

Courtney? Where'd you go? You went offline, LOL.

(COURTNEY) Sorry I got sidetracked. Now I'm at Walmart. I will read it in a bit.

This was not the only time I shared my testimony with one of my children. My four children have all heard this from me in person—not just through a text. This time, it was the timing. Her husband was in jail, her heart was open, and she had watched the church service online. The message stirred in her heart. It challenged her life direction and revealed how tiring and wearying her lifestyle was on her.

Her reaching out to me in the spontaneous text message also revealed that she was thinking of whether she really did believe in Jesus or not. Her heart heard my words and testimony in this simple yet serious text message, and she began to turn from spinning to winning. That day, she decided to get off the merry-go-round and on with her life. In her heart, she chose to BE ALL IN. Sure, she had steps to walk out, but her decision had been made: BE ALL IN.

Why don't most people BE ALL IN when they decide to follow Jesus? I can tell you that I was ALL IN for years, but for only as deep as the water was. Obviously, you cannot go out into deeper water if the water never *gets* deeper.

My daughter really does believe this 2016 Christmas message, as she said. I'd say that she really is ALL IN. That's why she liked the meme so much. Our pastor's message that day was about Jesus loving us so much that He came to Earth as our Messiah to save us. You can't even be a real Christian believer unless you believe this. My daughter asked me if I believed this. Yes, I most certainly do.

Back to the question, **"Why don't most Christians BE ALL IN and forever follow after Jesus?"** And, why do so many Christians still keep repeating the same bad decisions? From my own experience, I can say that the answer to these questions is simple:

They don't understand what happened to them when they were born again.

Nobody introduced them to the *new man,* so they keep identifying with their old nature and way of living life. Because they weren't mentored or discipled correctly, or maybe not at all, they continually go back into their OLD lifestyle and get the same bad results. Often, new believers were never taught anything more than to "believe in Him." They might have learned that the Bible says, "For God so loved the world that He gave His only begotten Son, that whoever believes in Him should not perish but have everlasting life" (John 3:16). But that's as deep as the water got for them.

More than likely, they never heard about how they were *given* the mind of Christ and a completely *new nature—God's nature—*when they received Jesus as their Lord and Savior. God's Holy Spirit came inside them and gave them a completely new spirit. They might not understand that they don't even have that *old nature/old man* anymore.

Many Christians, including myself, were mistakenly taught there is a battle between their *old man* and the *new man.* This teaching has caused so much confusion among Christians. The truth is, conflict can only be between their new man and their fleshly, old habits and ways they previously lived their life. Thanks to receiving Jesus, the *old man, the old nature,* is history (Romans 6:6). Here's the deal, though. The *new man is* ALL IN. The *old man* is entirely ALL OUT. (This would be a good time to let out a big SHOUT!)

The Bible says *old things* are passed away, and all things have become *new:* "Therefore, if anyone is in Christ, he is a new creation; old things have passed away; behold, all things have become new" (2 Corinthians 5:17).

In fact, as you read, you will see that the majority of the New Testament is written to show born-again believers who they are *as new creations* in Christ Jesus. It's not just to show us how to stay away from sin and *act like* a Christian.

The New Testament is our mirror—the mirror we look in to see Jesus and the new *us*. The truth is that our redeemed *new man* can't even sin! "Whoever has been born of God does not sin, for His seed remains in him; and he cannot sin, because he has been born of God" (1 John 3:9).

Our flesh still wants to sin because, for some people, the flesh has been practicing sinning for years. The new "us" is forever sinless, like Jesus. Remember, we're talking about the NEW us on the *inside* is who can't sin any longer. It's just a matter of reprogramming our soul (mind, will, and emotions) to believe and receive revelation about our *new identity* as a *new creation*.

Our new identity—who we are in Christ—is now the TRUE identity. It is the identity we are supposed to be living by.

When Christians realize that God now sees them as righteous, holy, and pure once they've been born again, their desires will change, and they'll want to line up with how God now sees them. Automatically desires begin to change as they renew their mind with the Holy Word of God (Ephesians 4:20–24). They will stop resisting God and start running to God. The repetitive bad-decision making will stop, and new, good decisions will stop the merry-go-rounds. That's a lot easier than trying to change your old man. That only leads to frustration and dead works, which causes Christians to be unhappy and want to give up and quit!

You must remember this: Your old man ain't changing! The war is between your *new nature* versus your old nature. But that war has already been won by Jesus. Now, that's GOOD NEWS! That's the TRUTH of the Gospel that makes us free. When you believed in Jesus Christ and decided to follow after Him, it was just the beginning. Afterward is when you start learning who you really are now. You can start living from the inside out, letting the nature of Christ live through you!

It's meant to be very simple! I hope to help you see things differently as you read through this book. I'm going to take you through many things some of you have never even heard before. We cannot believe what we have never heard before. So, as we look at God's Word, we will shine the light on religious legalism and see what God says about unbelief.

My story is just that. I went from hearing one thing about God to the next thing to the next thing. I had an opportunity to believe (or reject) each thing AS I HEARD IT. Every time I was taught something new in the Bible, it was as if the water got deeper, and I moved forward instead of spinning in circles.

READ IT!
Romans Chapter 6
Dead to Sin but Alive in Christ

I was given the opportunity to believe and *go deeper* or stay in unbelief—in the shallow water. **God wants to provide you with that same opportunity to believe and go deeper**. Allowing God's Word to develop our minds to line up with the mind of Christ is the most important thing we will ever do after receiving Salvation. Learning about this foundational truth—who we are in Christ—will take us from spinning to winning as our new way of living. It can be the difference between life and death for all of us, between moving forward and going in circles, like a merry-go-round.

> But what does it say? "**The word is near you**, in your mouth and in your heart" (that is, the word of faith which we preach): that if you confess with your mouth the Lord Jesus and believe in your heart that God has raised Him from the dead, you will be saved.
>
> For with the heart one believes unto righteousness, and with the mouth confession is made unto salvation.
>
> For the Scripture says, "Whoever believes on Him will not be put to shame." For there is no distinction between Jew and Greek, for the same Lord over all is rich to all who call upon

Him. For "**whoever calls on the name of the LORD shall be saved.**"

How then shall they call on Him in whom they have not believed? And how shall they believe in Him of whom they have not heard? And how shall they hear without a preacher? And how shall they preach unless they are sent? As it is written:

"How beautiful are the feet of those who preach the gospel of peace, who bring glad tidings of good things!"

But they have not all obeyed the gospel. For Isaiah says, "LORD, who has believed our report?" So then faith *comes* by hearing, and hearing by the word of God (Romans 10:8–17; emphasis added).

If faith comes by hearing and hearing by the Word of God, we must first *hear* the taught Word of God regarding Jesus, right?

So, first things first … what about those Scriptures we just read? Have you called on Him? Have you heard of my Jesus? Do you know Him as Lord, Savior, Redeemer? If not, that is the first step *off the merry-go-round and on with your life!* I have included a prayer in the back portion of this book to help you take that step to a new life. Why not pause to turn to that page in the appendix and settle that forever? Receive Him as Lord and Savior today. If you were born-again sometime in the past but have been away from the Lord, you can use the prayers in the appendix to draw near again.

God so loved the world that He sent His only begotten Son …

And, well, after we hear the initial invitation of John 3:16 in the Word of God, there's more!

Let's talk about it.

TWO

MERRY-GO-ROUNDS GO ROUND AND ROUND

Part One: A Fool Repeats His Folly

I F YOU'VE EVER been on a merry-go-round, you know it can make you sick if you ride it too long. When I was around twelve, some friends and I went to an amusement park. They had a *Silly Silo*. WOW! Yeah, it's like a merry-go-round. It looked like a blast! So, I got in. It's basically a merry-go-round with walls. You stand along the walls as the silo starts to turn. While it's spinning, it feels like a vacuum is sucking you against the wall really tight so you can't fall.

You have NO CLUE that once it stops, you will get out and fall on your face! It was sure deceiving! We were all laughing like crazy and felt great *at first*. THEN, it hit us. All that spinning *round* and *round* and *round* was nuts! I mean, who in the world invented that?! *Now,* I actually think of it as torture or something! The crazy part of this story is that I didn't do it just once. I got right back in line and did it a second time, even when I was beginning to feel *off-balance*. But I couldn't be the wimpy kid, now could I? Seriously?

What a prime example of not stopping to think before you do something—and then doing it over and over again with your peeps!

That Silly Silo experience pretty much soured me for merry-go-rounds—especially after my throwing-up episode at the end when I got off the ride the *second* time. As an adult, I am still aware of things that have that repetitive turning and how much I really, really don't like it. Just remembering that throbbing headache and the humiliation of losing my lunch in front of the huge crowd that day is enough to keep *me* from getting on a merry-go-round again.

Even the slow-moving carousels don't appeal to me. When you are going that slow, it is sort of boring and feels like everything is in slow-motion on your way to nowhere! While you don't really have the awful side-effects you would get from the speed of the faster merry-go-rounds, they both have the same unpurposed motion.

When you are on a merry-go-round, you only think about one of two things: "Go faster!" Or, "Stop!" The thrill is only for a minute until you are topped out on the speed. If the other kids don't want to stop the merry-go-round, you have no choice but to stay on unless you jump off cold turkey! And, if you jump off while really going fast, you could experience some injuries. The pain and suffering resulting from jumping off will probably require some Band-Aids and a healing period. Ha!

I'm seriously not trying to slam merry-go-rounds, but they remind me of wasted movement. I get it. They do go fast, and since the playgrounds at schools and parks aren't large enough to have a big racetrack around them, they at least meet that need for speed that some kids have. It's pretty deceiving when you think about it. Screaming out "faster, faster" makes you *think* you are really zooming forward and going somewhere. Then the merry-go-round stops, and you realize how dizzy you are. You couldn't even think straight while you were on the silly thing! I am reminded of this Scripture in Proverbs 26:11, *"As a dog returns to his own vomit, So a fool repeats his folly."* YUCK!

Merriam-Webster Dictionary defines *folly* as a <u>lack of good sense or normal prudence and foresight</u>.[1] And it defines *foolish* as <u>having or showing a lack of good sense, judgment, or discretion</u>.[2]

So, is it safe to say that if we keep repeating the same folly over and over that we are being foolish and lacking common sense? Yeah, I'm pretty sure God never designed us to just repeatedly spin around and around.

Part Two: A Merry-Go-*What?*

The definition for *merry-go-round* by Oxford English Dictionary is (emphasis mine):

- a <u>revolving</u> machine with model horses or other animals on which people ride for amusement;

- a large <u>revolving</u> device in a playground for children to ride on;

- a <u>continuous cycle</u> of activities or events, especially when perceived as having no purpose or producing no result.[3]

My definition of a merry-go-round is simply:

- ❖ wasted time doing something aimlessly with no purposeful movement, which hinders one from doing what they are supposed to do;

- ❖ a distraction to the big picture;

- ❖ deceitful; gives the impression, because of the movement, that you are doing something productive, but you really aren't;

- ❖ a frustrating system.

Have you noticed there are very few merry-go-rounds in the public parks and schools compared to how many there used to be? Yeah, I'm sure it's because someone who has decision-making power in this area has realized a few key things:

1. Merry-go-rounds are DANGEROUS!! The number of merry-go-round accidents is crazy high! (I know they were at my school.)

2. Merry-go-rounds are high maintenance. And the upkeep is a hassle, keeping it oiled, balanced, and free from rust.

3. Merry-go-rounds were famous for kids falling off, getting stuck underneath, getting hit when trying to jump on, throwing up, and having their heads throb from spinning round and round.

And those are just to name a few! It's the same with the personal merry-go-rounds in our lives: They are dangerous! They are high maintenance! You get stuck! And it is usually painful to get off!

The Nuts and Bolts of Physical Merry-Go-Rounds:

Let's look at the components, structure, and design of physical merry-go-rounds on the playground or at the fair:

❖ <u>The Center Post</u>: The center post is what holds it in place. This post **alone** is what keeps the merry-go-round attached *so it can spin*. There is just one single post—one strong-rooted support.

❖ The Base: The base sits over the top of the center post and is tightly bolted onto it. The base or floor of the merry-go-round gives someone something to sit on or hold on to while it turns in circles.

❖ The Decorative Fixtures and Handlebars: The decorative fixtures and handlebars are attached to the base of the merry-go-round. These decorative fixtures are designed to appeal to the riders and are what make kids jump up and down, begging their parents to let them ride one. The decorations give the children the impression they are doing something they really *aren't*, like riding a real horse. The handlebars appeal to the riders' sense of security, giving them the impression the ride is safe or harmless fun.

❖ The End Result: The outcome is the thrill you get *for the first few minutes* until you start feeling dizzy and nauseous and can't see straight.

The Merry-Go-Rounds of Life

Now, let's look at the components, structure, and design of the merry-go-rounds of life. These relationship, life-event, or activity merry-go-rounds have similar components as physical merry-go-rounds:

❖ The Center Post: The center post of every merry-go-round relationship or activity in our lives is the same: UNBELIEF / BELIEVING THE LIE. This lie, the center post (the ROOT support), is responsible for keeping the whole thing spinning. The center post could be that you don't believe there is a better option. It might be that you don't believe you could ever change or ever do something different. Or, perhaps, you do not believe you can really do God's plan for your life or ever will. Whatever the unbelief is, the anchor for that post is that you (we) <u>are not hearing and believing the truth of how God sees you through Jesus and how much God loves you.</u>

❖ <u>The Base</u>: The base of every merry-go-round relationship or activity is our comfort zone. This is the lie we are sitting or standing on while we are DOING THE SAME THING OVER AND OVER AGAIN. (Most of the time, we do it without even thinking.)

❖ <u>The Decorative Fixtures and Handlebars</u>: The fixtures and handlebars of every merry-go-round relationship or activity are the things or patterns that people hold onto in life. These fixtures, or *holds*, in life have something decorative that draws people in, keeping them hooked. They are APPEALING TO FLESHLY DESIRES—something we know we should let go of but that we don't hate bad enough *yet*. It is a part of our life that we haven't been willing to surrender to the Lord.

❖ <u>The End Result</u>: Every merry-go-round relationship or activity starts with a thrill and ends with a negative result. At first, you can't see the negative end result, the resulting feelings, and the consequences. But that doesn't last long. The end result of every merry-go-round relationship or activity in our lives is the same. It is HURT, CONFUSION, FEAR, STRIFE, DEAD-END— WASTED TIME NEVER GOING WHERE YOU ARE SUP- POSED TO GO.

As you read this book, I will be sharing the merry-go-rounds of my life as I expose my life's mistakes and victories. I hope my testimony will help you recognize the merry-go-rounds in your life. As I give you simple answers from the Word of God, I hope that will cause a desire to get off any merry-go-round that you are on and never get back on again.

All the merry-go-rounds from my life have had the same common structure as a physical merry-go-round:

1. They all had a center post of unbelief and lies that kept them in place and spinning.

2. They all had a revolving base or platform, allowing me to do the same thing over and over again, never doing something different to see a change.

3. They all had decorative fixtures and handlebars that appealed to my flesh, attracted me, drew me in, and gave me something to hold on to while riding.

4. They all had a negative end result or consequence.

All merry-go-rounds in our lives stay in place by unbelief—either unbelief as a result of *never hearing* the Truth or unbelief resulting from *not believing* the Truth we have heard. What happens if, suddenly, when we hear the Word of God, we choose to BELIEVE in His Goodness and His good plan for YOU and me? As we believe, His promises would become active and real in our lives, and we would surely fly off those merry-go-rounds!

As we make an effort to open a Bible and read it for ourselves, believing what it says about who God says we are as born-again believers, we will want to live our lives according to that new identity. We will no longer "go round and round the mulberry bush" every other day! We won't be dizzy and confused as we keep our eyes looking straight ahead and on the Lord. We can trust His love for us so much that we will *want* to follow Him in everything we do. As we grow in believing His Word and His love, we will begin to move forward. We will be single-minded and clear. That is when we really begin acting on the wisdom and insight He has given us to overcome difficulties! **We can change from being a merry-go-round *rider* to a merry-go-round *avoider*.**

THREE

THE DEADLIEST PART OF A MERRY-GO-ROUND: UNBELIEF

Part One: The Spin of Unbelief

WHY IS UNBELIEF the deadliest part of a merry-go-round? Because <u>unbelief</u> is the only thing that will keep us from receiving and walking in all that Christ's finished work on the Cross provided for us. We don't receive His finished work automatically. His grace provided it, but faith—believing—is what releases it into our lives. God designed it like this so everyone could be on the same playing field, making it fair.

It's a matter of life and death that we truly believe and rest in the *finished work* of Christ, ONLY, and not also in our own efforts. Our faith must be in His grace (what He provided for us) and not in ourselves. Our faith must be in the right thing. We must not put faith and trust in ourselves and our efforts to live victoriously. Why? *Because trusting in ourselves and our own effort is doing it wrong.* That won't bring the right results, and we eventually stop believing and trusting God's Word if we never get the right results. *Not trusting God and His Word is unbelief.*

Here's the truth: If we are born-again believers in Jesus Christ, we have already been *made free.*

We are free from the merry-go-round lifestyle, but many Christians don't even know it! They are *ignorant* to it, just like I was for years. It's the truth, though—and it's what we must renew our natural mind to so that we can believe the right things and start going through our lives enjoying this freedom.

Christ set us free, and we are well able to walk in that liberty that He provided for us. It's imperative we don't have unbelief regarding our new nature and identity as an adopted child of God (Romans 8:15). We must believe that when we invited Christ into our hearts, He really did move in, right then! God became our Heavenly Father right then, and Christ became our Savior and brother right then. We immediately became adopted into God's family, now having access to the Father ourselves. We received the same inheritance as our brother, Christ (John 16:15). Christ packed up everything the Father gave Him and brought it with Him to live in our spirit, now as one with us (1 John 4:17). *If we don't believe this*, we will always be trying to live free by using our own natural human faith, strength, and abilities to receive God's promises, change our circumstances, and live free from merry-go-rounds. We will quickly burn out!

READ IT!
Galatians 2:16-20 KJV
Living by the faith of Jesus

Before we can recognize unbelief and understand how it works, we first need to understand how the God-kind of faith works. When we became born again, God gave each of us THE measure of faith we need to believe with and receive with (Romans 12:3). *That* measure of faith is the same faith we are supposed to use every day. The measure of faith He gave us is not like our natural human faith based on our five natural senses. His faith is based on who He is—Truth and Light— and is the only thing that will run off any unbelief we might have.

The faith OF Jesus is the God kind of faith that we use to believe IN Jesus. That same faith is how we believe who we are now in Christ, and it's what we now live by.

Jesus gave us His faith—so if He gave it to us, it's ours, and now we get to call His faith *our faith,* right? People confuse this by saying they are using *their faith,* but unless their faith is founded in and on the work Jesus did, not in their own works, it is called *dead works.*

If He already gave His faith to us through His grace, where is it located? Is it out there somewhere waiting for us to make it come *to* us? No—it's inside our new, born-again spirit, resting in the same place with everything we need that pertains to life and Godly living. It's in the same place where we know all things and the mind of Christ is located. It's in the same place where the finished work of Christ and all the promises of God reside—right along with the Spirit of God and our new spirit—*all sealed up* (2 Corinthians 1:22, Ephesians 1:13–14). We are now the temple of God's Holy Spirit. He lives inside every one of us who believes.

If we have read or heard the Scriptures that talk about the things I just mentioned and don't believe them, <u>we are in UN-belief</u>. God gave us the faith of Jesus to use as a bridge that will take us from living in our old natural ways over into the spiritual realm where we can live from our new life in Christ and receive the spiritual blessings that He gave us. It's how God set it up for us to be able to live after we are born-again new creatures.

God provided an awesome life in the Spirit for us. We can now access that awesome life here in the natural realm using the measure of faith we've been given. We can use it to walk daily in the victory Jesus provided for us through His death, burial, and resurrection. I've heard this way of living referred to as *living from the inside out.* Again—in our newly created spirit is where we have His faith, and it's where we have been given all things that pertain to life and Godliness. We must now live out of our spirits instead of our natural-born ways. We must begin using what we are now equipped with.

There is a thing called natural human faith, but it is not the same as spiritual faith which comes from God. <u>Natural faith</u> can only believe what is heard and what is seen. For example, Abraham believed God because he heard what God audibly said to him. The four Gospels (Matthew, Mark, Luke, and John) talk about how Jesus went about doing miracles while He was physically here on Earth. People believed what they *heard* Jesus audibly say, what they *saw* Him do, and what reports they heard from others. When Jesus was resurrected and went back to Heaven, He was no longer here physically talking to us and physically showing us signs and wonders.

After the four Gospels and beginning in Acts, we see how we must now believe according to the New Covenant way. We no longer have His physical presence to see and believe nor His audible voice to hear and believe. Now we have God's *written* Word and the *voice of His Spirit* to teach us and remind us what Jesus said (John 14:26). When we *hear* His Word and hear His voice inside us, this causes <u>His faith</u> to come up out of us, we believe, and that's when we will receive. Now, at any time of any day, we can use His faith to believe.

We are not relying on our five natural, physical senses to believe. Our five natural senses can easily fake faith. They make us *think* and believe we have a genuine God kind of faith when actually we don't. Getting this right will stop the begging and crying out to God in unbelief. How do we know we are being led by these deceiving imposters—our physical senses? We don't get God kind of results.

What if the reason we don't believe (disbelief, unbelief) is because of <u>ignorance</u>—lack of knowledge about it? What we haven't heard, we don't have knowledge of, and we stay operating in ignorance. What we don't know the truth about, we can't believe. So, **what if we don't believe because we were <u>taught wrong</u> about certain passages of Scripture?** That's harder to overcome because we first have to erase the wrong teaching and beliefs before we can learn new, correct teaching to believe. Don't worry. Both of these types of unbelief can be fixed by being taught Truth.

What if your unbelief comes from a <u>hard heart that is rebellious toward God and Truth?</u> (This is the type of unbelief the Israelites had while wandering around in the wilderness.) This unbelief will continue until the person decides to allow God's love into their life and soften their heart to Truth.

And lastly, what if you have *natural unbelief* **based on our five** *physical* **senses?** (Natural unbelief is the opposite of the natural faith I talked about earlier, but neither is spiritual.) This unbelief is connected to what we see, hear, smell, taste, and feel. This unbelief came with our flesh life and can only be overcome when we begin to sense and live from the spiritual realm more than we live from our natural fleshly realm.

Jesus is the Word, and if He lives inside our spirits, we have God's Word, Truth, and Light in us, right? So, it's a matter of getting our minds to come into agreement with what's in our spirits. We must get into agreement with God! It's so important that we get in God's Word until His Word GETS INTO OUR MINDS. As it does, it washes clean our old carnal ways of thinking, lining up our thoughts with His thoughts toward us and revealing to us the new identity we've been given.

READ IT!
Romans Chapter 10
Salvation and faith comes through God's Word

When we hear God's Word, our minds gets renewed to the truths I'm speaking of, and faith comes up (is released) out of us (our spirits) and causes God's Word to be alive and active in our lives here in the natural realm.

Faith really does come! The unseen becomes the seen at this point. If we want to live the victorious Christian life, free from merry-go-rounds, we MUST renew our minds to who we are now IN CHRIST so that faith can come and make a bridge for our spirits' new life to cross over into our outward physical life where we live while here on Earth.

God made it easy for us. He did all the work. He provided everything we need. All we need to do is renew our minds to these truths. I'm going to bring out more of these Bible truths as we go, giving you opportunities to make a choice to believe them or not. If you choose to believe them, unbelief will not have a place to stay. If we use the faith of Jesus (which we have already been given), we can enjoy the Godly life Jesus paid the price for us to live. This is such an exciting subject to keep talking about, but we'll save it for the rest of the journey through this book!

For years, *I tried* to live a Christ-like life and have victory in my marriage while in the *spin of unbelief.* During that time, I didn't think I was in unbelief; but the truth is, if you <u>really believe</u> something, you will act on it and get results. I wasn't acting on God's instructions concerning how I treated my husband, David. So, in truth, I didn't trust God and didn't <u>genuinely believe</u> that He would work in my marriage without *my help.* Funny, huh?

I thought my husband *needed to be reminded* that change needed to occur in our marriage and that it would come through *him* doing some things differently. I ignored that God had told *me* to do some things differently: keep quiet, pray Bible Scriptures over him, speak in faith about our situation, and stop with the bad, unbelieving fearful attitude which kept me trapped, meditating on the negative things going on.

I wasn't trusting in God's love for my husband and me, nor in His grace to cause change to come. If we ignore the truth of God's love and don't walk in the revelation of the love that God has for us personally, then we won't be using real God-pleasing faith to believe things will change. My revelation of God's love for my husband and me was limited to the religious teachings of man—which was a very performance-based, conditional, and condemning love. My expectations for him were huge, and if he didn't meet these expectations, I didn't "feel" love for him. He operated the same way toward me.

Because we were so confused about God's *agape* (selfless) love for us, we were definitely confused about how to truly love each other (or anyone else, as far as that goes). Because we didn't understand the unconditional love God has FOR US, David and I were frustrated with each other. If we are frustrated and do not understand God's non-condemning love and forgiveness, we won't be walking in faith, trusting Him to answer our prayers. Our faith works by the revelation of God's love (Galatians 5:6).

Things stayed the same until I chose to believe God, walk in love toward my husband the same way God unconditionally loves me, and do the things God had instructed me. Standing in God's grace and walking in the *genuine* love and faith of God will *loose us* from unbelief. Then, we are able to move forward.

STOP THE SPIN!

Are you doing what I did? There were many times when I tried using faith based on how I saw someone else pray and get results. Boy! That is frustrating to believe the lie that you are praying in faith when you are actually just imitating what you saw and heard someone else do.

There were times when I tried living off of someone else's revelation and didn't genuinely trust God for myself. I never got results that way, and you won't either. Instead, hear from God for yourself.

Spend time with God for yourself, so you can receive your own revelation. Then you will have personal revelation born from a personal relationship with God. Once we have that, we can find out from God specifically what we should believe Him for, stand on that, and see real results!

Trying to make things move forward while in unbelief won't work. I had to take responsibility for my own revelation of faith and love-walk and stop being frustrated. I had to stop "waiting on God" to do something. I had to stop *insisting* that God do things my way instead of me doing things His way—which is always through love and faith.

Love and faith are the two MUSTS because God IS love, and it's impossible to please Him without genuine <u>faith in His love</u>. It's how He designed it to work.

So, what is this *spin of unbelief?* Unbelief is <u>*not believing*</u>. Unbelief in what? What are you not believing? Are you not believing that you really might be living your life on a merry-go-round? Do you not believe that what you are doing hurts you and others? Are you not believing that God's will for you is that you stop repeating something negative or harmful over and over again? Are you not believing in God's love for you and His good plan for your life? Are you not believing <u>*you*</u> have some responsibility to seek and find out what He has put in your heart to do and then do it?

Possibly the First Merry-Go-Round Riders

Think about the Israelites for a minute. They could very well be considered the first merry-go-round riders on Earth. If you have been in church any length of time, you have most likely heard many stories about Moses. He lived with the first-generation Israelites in the desert, wandering around aimlessly for forty years because of their unbelief in God's promise. One day they believed, and the next, they didn't. They believed part of God's Word spoken through Moses, but part of it they didn't. Their wasted time spent in the desert is in the Bible as an example of what we are NOT SUPPOSED TO DO!

By his own admission, my husband shares that he did this for most of the first thirty-nine years of our marriage BUT didn't even realize it. David says he could preach about how the Israelites wandered around doing the same thing over and over and never made it into the Promised Land. BUT, he said, there came a moment when *he realized HE was doing the same thing!*

David says he was one of those Christians who knew he would have gone to Heaven if he had died at that time. But he also admits that was as far as he got toward receiving that "life more abundantly" through receiving Jesus as his Savior, which he had read about in John 10:10. At the time, my husband didn't believe we had to put any effort into possessing the Promised Land, the place where we live in all God has planned for us. *If God wants me in the Promised Land, by His grace, He will put me in there*, David thought to himself, *I shouldn't have to do anything to possess it.* He wasn't alone. Many other Christians believe this also. So, he waited and wasted many years, just *wandering* aimlessly with no plan to reach his goals. The truth is, we are not waiting on God. God is waiting on us to boldly stand up and take action toward making our vision and purpose in life a reality. I mean, seriously … how bad do we want it?!

The teachings of *man* created that belief (which is really unbelief). It has since spread throughout the Church in every generation. I thank God that He heard our hearts' cry and the prayers of people who loved us. I thank God for the day when my husband and I finally allowed ourselves to believe and do something different than what we heard growing up. We started believing there is a Promised Land in the here and now, available to every Christian willing to do what it takes to possess it and enter in.

Let's look at these unbelieving Israelites and the twelve men who were sent to spy out the Promised Land before they entered it:

God told Moses to "send men to spy out the land of Canaan, which I am giving to the children of Israel" (Numbers 13:2). This land was their Promised Land. God had already told Moses and the people—multiple times before this—that He had given them this good land flowing with milk and honey. So, these twelve men (Joshua, Caleb, and ten other men) were sent out to see what this Promised Land was all about.

And they returned from spying out the land after forty days.
Now they departed and came back to Moses and Aaron and

all the congregation of the children of Israel in the Wilderness of Paran, at Kadesh; they brought back word to them and to all the congregation, and showed them the fruit of the land. Then they told him, and said: "We went to the land where you sent us. It truly flows with milk and honey, and this is its fruit. Nevertheless the people who dwell in the land are strong; the cities are fortified and very large; moreover we saw the descendants of Anak there."

Then Caleb quieted the people before Moses, and said, "Let us go up at once and take possession, for WE ARE WELL ABLE to overcome it."

But the men who had gone up with him said, "We are NOT ABLE to go up against the people, for they are stronger than we." And they gave the children of Israel a bad report of the land which they had spied out, saying, "The land through which we have gone as spies is a land that devours its inhabitants, and all the people whom we saw in it are men of great stature. There we saw the giants (the descendants of Anak came from the giants); and we were like grasshoppers in our own sight, and so we were in their sight" (Numbers 13:25–28, 30–33; emphasis added).

Joshua and Caleb chose to look at this land with eyes of faith, believing they could possess it <u>simply because GOD SAID it was THEIR land</u>. The other ten men chose to look at this land through eyes of unbelief and fear, choosing to believe the lie that they couldn't possess this land because of what they saw, the giants.

These unbelieving men *recognized the truth* about the land. They told Moses the land truly does flow with milk and honey, and they brought back the big fruit to show him. Even though they saw it for themselves, they chose to believe something else instead. The fear they were experiencing and the disbelief in God helping them take the land was beating down on their thoughts. Their unbelief and resulting emotions were so strong that they caved into unbelief and lost all hope of entering the Promised Land. Caleb reported, "we are *well able* to overcome it" (Numbers 13:30; emphasis added). But ten men filled with <u>doubt, unbelief, and fear</u> infected the entire nation because *they decided* they were *"not able"* to obey and step out in faith.

I give these men a thumbs down who gave an evil report, discouraging the Israelites through fear. These ten men said it was a land that *eats up the inhabitants*. The people there were giants, and, compared to them, the ten considered themselves like *grasshoppers*. I guess they forgot about how God walked them through the Red Sea on dry land! I guess they forgot how God dropped them delicious bread from the sky and fresh quail in the middle of nowhere. I guess they forgot how He poured ice-cold water from a hot desert rock when they were thirsty!

This is how far the report of fear and unbelief went. The unbelieving spies got the whole congregation of Israelites so worked up that they all lifted up their voices and cried and wept all night! (That is found in Numbers 14.)

Can you picture this? Can you hear the cries of fear throughout the whole land? Can you see how this might also be happening today in our day and age? There will always be some people acting in fear because they believe reports which are based on lies. The people who are not acting in fear are the ones who are believing reports that come from an honest and truthful source. Sometimes the bad report sounds louder than the truthful report and can be confusing unless we recognize truth over lies.

Then, the multitudes talked and complained against Moses and Aaron. They were so confused and gripped with fear that they started talking crazy! They began talking about falling by the sword and how their wives and children would become prey. They said it would be better to have died in Egypt or the wilderness or even return to Egypt! WHAT?!

The Israelite people decided to follow the *logic* of ten men who had unbelief and fear instead of believing the two men who *relied on* the <u>integrity of God's Word to back them up</u>! They decided to believe what man said over what God said. This unbelief and fear were rebellion-based and paralyzed them! It confused them and clouded their thinking! How many of us can relate? How many of us, paralyzed by fear, have not taken what God has already promised us? We have all done this in one form or another. Instead of judging, let's learn from their actions of unbelief.

STOP THE SPIN!

Lies keep you thinking that you are making forward progress while not recognizing that you will NEVER, EVER go forward unless you stop and get off.

Instead of yielding to lies, believe in God's truth about your situation. See with the eyes of faith and believe His promises are true.

They did not enter the Promised Land because they chose not to believe what God said, which led to their lack of obedience. Instead of having faith in God's Word, love, and ability, which is His grace toward us, they rebelled against God. Our lack of faith in God can actually be rebellion toward Him too. He wanted to give them victory over those giants! He wanted to see them eating those BIG GRAPES! Their time was at hand to step in and receive their new life of freedom, but instead, they died—never seeing God's promises manifest in their lives. Yikes—not for me!

I'm sure the Father's heart was hurt because the Israelites, His people, <u>did not trust</u> His Word or promises. They <u>did not value</u> all the miracles and wonderful things He had already done for them. Worst of all, <u>they hardened their hearts to the truth and questioned God's integrity by not believing what He told them</u>. They eventually realized they messed up and decided to obey, but it was too late. Even the New Testament warns us to not repeat that group's mistakes:

> Today, if you will hear His voice, DO NOT HARDEN your hearts as in the rebellion (Hebrews 3:15; emphasis added).

> So we see that they COULD NOT ENTER IN because of unbelief (Hebrews 3:19; emphasis added).

> But the word which they heard did not profit them, <u>not being mixed with faith</u> in those who heard it (Hebrews 4:2; emphasis added).

Let's look at the flip side of this scenario: The ones who BELIEVED what God said and were unafraid to obey were those who RECEIVED what God said! That would be Caleb and Joshua. This next generation of Israelites, led by Joshua and Caleb, refused to get on the merry-go-round of griping and complaining. They didn't get caught up in the fear and confusion, spinning around the camps like crazy. This awesome, faith-in-God, fearless, believing group went forward and lived in the Promised Land!

Yippee!! Caleb and Joshua are my heroes!! Real cheerleaders for freedom!! Like them, in order to possess God's promises and go forward, we must choose, at some point, to believe God's Word *is true*.

> Then Caleb quieted the people before Moses, and said, "<u>Let us go up at once and take possession, for we are well able to overcome it</u>" (Numbers 13:30; emphasis added).

Caleb said they were *well able* to overcome it. It sounds like he had a revelation of God's grace to me! Joshua and Caleb knew that if the Lord told them to go take the Promised Land, He would equip them and back them to do it. They believed God had their backs!

> But My servant Caleb, because <u>he had a different spirit with him and followed Me fully</u>, I will bring him into the land where he went, and his seed will possess it (Numbers 14:24 MEV; emphasis added).

> On the seventh time, the priests blew the trumpets, and Joshua said to the people, "Shout the battle cry, <u>for the LORD has given you the city</u>" (Joshua 6:16 MEV; emphasis added).

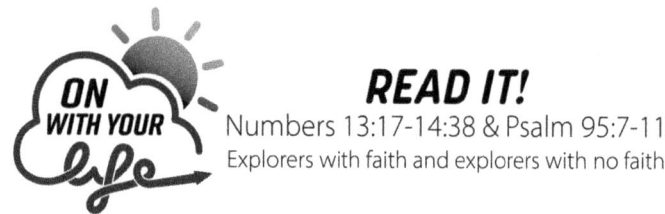

READ IT!
Numbers 13:17-14:38 & Psalm 95:7-11
Explorers with faith and explorers with no faith

High-five to Caleb and Joshua! They followed the instructions the Lord gave them. They were rewarded for their faith and obedience and received the prize of the Promised Land! Let's follow Joshua and Caleb's example of faith by trusting God and His love for us and the good plan He has for us.

Unbelief is the deadliest part of a merry-go-round! Unbelief *kept the Israelites from* going forward and *receiving* God's promise and Blessing! Unbelief is what caused them to die in the wilderness! It wasn't unbelief due to not having a word from God. He gave them words of instruction. It wasn't unbelief due to being taught wrong about God—like He will not help them. They had already witnessed His miracles, goodness, and help several times before, so they knew He would. It WAS unbelief that came from being rebellious and resisting truth. Why do we *not* want to get on any kind of merry-go-round while living our life? Because it is unbelief fueled by fear. <u>Unbelief goes around in circles, staying in the same place, becoming more confused, and unable to think or see straight ahead.</u>

The faithless Israelite merry-go-round turned out to be not very merry after all. These Israelites believed in their hearts and confessed with their mouths that they would never go into the Promised Land and would just die in the wilderness! And so, it was!

Up to one million unbelievers[4] (minus two believers) died and never entered their promised land, and it wasn't God's fault. The sin they committed was the sin of UNBELIEF. This sin of unbelief perverted God's promise and prevented it from ever coming to pass in their lives. They never got off their merry-go-round and on with their life!

However, unlike unbelief, faith moves forward. So, let's find out what the Bible says about unbelieving, unbelievers, and unbelief so that we are sure to have no part in it! I don't want you to just believe my word and what I am saying without seeing it in God's Word. His Word is the <u>final authority</u>.

Look up the following verses and entire passages for YOURSELF! There is something eye-opening about us making our *own effort* to open the Bible. When we see it with our *own eyes* and read it out loud, so our *own ears* hear it, it causes faith to come up from inside and then out of our own mouths. This is what's called *revelation and understanding*. This is when we REALLY start believing.

Exposing Our Own Unbelief

> He <u>could not do</u> any miracles there, except that He laid His hands on a few sick people and healed them. And He was amazed because of their unbelief (Mark 6:5–6 MEV; emphasis added).

Jesus *couldn't* do many mighty works there; Scripture doesn't say he *wouldn't*. That sure goes against some religious teachings.

So Jesus said to them, "Because of YOUR unbelief" (Matthew 17:20; emphasis added).

This Scripture reveals that we have a responsibility ourselves.

Jesus said to him, "IF you can believe, all things are possible to him who believes." Immediately the father of the child cried out and said with tears, "Lord, I believe; help my unbelief" (Mark 9:23–24; emphasis added).

We can have faith in our hearts but still have thoughts and feelings of unbelief in our heads.

Later He [Jesus] appeared to the eleven as they sat at the table; and He rebuked their unbelief and hardness of heart, because they did not believe those who had seen Him after He had risen (Mark 16:14).

Can we get a hard heart when we choose not to believe certain things Jesus did?

What if some did not believe? Would their unbelief nullify the faithfulness of God? God forbid! Let God be true, and every man a liar (Romans 3:3–4 MEV).

God's truths remain true whether we believe them or not. Are we wavering when we are not fully convinced of God's promises? Can we have unbelief because of ignorance and not even realize it?

He did not waver at the promise of God through unbelief, but was strong in faith, giving glory to God, and being fully persuaded that what God had promised, He was able to perform (Romans 4:20–21 MEV; emphasis added).

Although I was formerly a blasphemer, a persecutor, and an insolent man; but I obtained mercy because I did it ignorantly in unbelief (1 Timothy 1:13).

Can unbelief stop Christians from living in God's promises for them right here on Earth? That answer is in Hebrews 3:19, "So we see that they could not enter in because of unbelief." And again in Hebrews 4:6 (MEV), "Since therefore it remains for some to enter it, and they to whom it was first preached did not enter due to unbelief."

Let's stop patterning our lives after this group of unbelieving Israelites, ok? As we are instructed in Hebrews 4:11 (MEV), "Let us labor therefore to enter that rest, lest anyone fall by the same pattern of unbelief."

God doesn't want us to have any unbelief so that we can enter into His rest!

Unbelievers and Unbelieving

Be attentive, brothers, lest there be in any of you an evil, unbelieving heart, and you depart from the living God (Hebrews 3:12 MEV).

The word *brothers* in Hebrews 3:12 indicates it is written to Christians. *Right?* Apparently, Christians can choose an evil heart of unbelief. Paul warned them (and us) in 2 Corinthians 6:14 (MEV), "Do not be unequally yoked together with unbelievers." And he asks, "For what fellowship has righteousness with unrighteousness? What communion has light with darkness?"

We can still be a witness to unbelievers without fellowshipping with their darkness. But be aware! In Acts 14:2 (MEV), the Bible says that "the unbelieving Jews stirred up the Gentiles and embittered their minds against the brothers." It appears that unbelievers infected the believers' minds with evil. When we are *unbelieving*, we do not see things as they truly are.

> To the pure, all things are pure. But to those who are defiled and unbelieving, nothing is pure. Even their minds and consciences are defiled. They profess that they know God, but in their deeds they deny Him, being abominable, disobedient, and worthless for every good work (Titus 1:15–16 MEV).

> But the cowardly, unbelieving, abominable, murderers, sexually immoral, sorcerers, idolaters, and all liars shall have their part in the lake which burns with fire and brimstone (Revelation 21:8).

YIKES! (Expressing shock and alarm.) And … WOW!! The Bible has a lot to say about unbelief, unbelievers, and unbelieving. There are many more verses that I didn't even mention. But **it's a BIG DEAL!**

Part Two: Unbelieving Christians

What is keeping all merry-go-rounds spinning *for Christians?* Their unbelief in what God's Word says as a whole. As we read the Word of God, we find out about the full *Salvation Package*—who we are and what we have in Jesus. With that being said, the unbelief problem in this area is two-sided. Either we outright don't believe what we see in the Bible, or we just plain haven't renewed our mind to the truth of the Word. When our mind is *unrenewed* to the Word in an area, we are walking in darkness and have not yet come into agreement with our new identity in that area.

With this in mind, we see that there *can* be an *unbelieving Christian*. There can be a professing Christian still walking in some unbelieving darkness because they have *some* unbelief for *parts* of God's Word. So, *unbelievers* can actually be Christian OR unsaved people. For example, an unbelieving Christian may believe that Jesus went to the Cross and paid for their sin, BUT they are limited to that. The unbelieving limitations will vary from person to person.

What did Jesus have to say to His own disciple, who some have called *Doubting Thomas*?

> Then He said to Thomas, "Put your finger here, and look at My hands. Put your hand here and place it in My side. Do not be faithless, but believing." Thomas answered Him, "My Lord and my God!" Jesus said to him, "Thomas, because you have seen Me, you have believed. Blessed are those who have not seen, and have yet believed" (John 20:27–29 MEV; emphasis added).

How does someone receive salvation from Jesus? Through hearing <u>what God's Word says, **believing it** in their *heart*, and confessing it with their mouth.</u> (That is found in Romans 10:9–10.) How does someone receive all other promises in the Bible given to us through what Jesus did on the Cross? *The same way*.

You must read/hear from the Word what He has promised, **believe it** *in your heart*, and *confess it* with your mouth. *Jesus, by His grace, already did everything needed to redeem us from the whole Curse. But He won't do our believing and receiving for us.*

Believers Believe

A *believer* is someone who is firmly persuaded in someone or something without needing physical proof. *Let's face it—everyone believes something. We all have beliefs we live our life by.* However, when I use the word *believer* in this book, I am referring to *Christian believers* (unless otherwise noted). A *Christian believer* is someone who has confidently accepted the existence of God as their Creator and Jesus—the Son of God—as their Savior. They believe in and serve the One True God, Jesus, even though they cannot see Him. They believe that when Jesus left the Earth and went back up to Heaven, He left His Holy Spirit here with us to take His place. They believe in living their lives through and for Christ instead of their own passions and desires.

Believers have confidence that "greater is He that is in you [us] than he that is in the world" (1 John 4:4) simply because God said it. Because of this, we can experience victory over all the works of the enemy and live blessed and victorious lives no matter what is going on around us. We look to what the Bible says Jesus did on the Cross as our standard for belief, *not what man says.*

We believe that John 10:10 is true: **"The thief does not come except to steal, and to kill, and to destroy. I have come that they may have life, and that they may have it more abundantly."**

There was a time in my life when I did not fully believe Scriptures like John 10:10. I was a Christian, but I had not come to fully believe every part of the Word because my mind had not been renewed to the Word by reading the Word. Also, I had not heard the full teaching of the Word, so I was unaware; therefore, I was walking in some level of ignorance. In any area that we have not yet renewed our minds to what the Word says, whether on purpose or in ignorance, we are walking in unbelief and darkness.

I remember wondering about verses like these also:

God made Him who knew no sin to be sin for us, that we might become the righteousness of God in Him (2 Corinthians 5:21 MEV).

For you know the grace of our Lord Jesus Christ, that though He was rich, yet for your sakes He became poor, that you through His poverty might become rich (2 Corinthians 8:9).

Most assuredly, I say to you, he who believes in Me, the works that I do he will do also; and greater works than these he will do, because I go to My Father. And whatever you ask in My name, that I will do, that the Father may be glorified in the Son. If you ask any thing in My name, I will do it (John 14:12–14).

Ask, and it will be given to you; seek, and you will find; knock, and it will be opened to you. For everyone who asks receives, and he who seeks finds, and to him who knocks it will be opened. Or what man is there among you who, if his son asks for bread, will give him a stone? Or if he asks for a fish, will he give him a serpent? If you then, being evil, know how to give good gifts to your children, how much more will your Father who is in heaven give good things to those who ask Him (Matthew 7:7–11).

This is the confidence that we have in Him, that if we ask anything according to His will, He hears us. So if we know that He hears whatever we ask, we know that we have whatever we asked of Him (1 John 5:14–15 MEV).

These signs will accompany those who believe: In My name they will cast out demons; they will speak with new tongues; they will take up serpents; if they drink any deadly thing, it will not hurt them; they will lay hands on the sick, and they will recover (Mark 16:17–18 MEV).

Give, and it will be given to you: good measure, pressed down, shaken together, and running over will be put into your bosom. For with the same measure that you use, it will be measured back to you (Luke 6:38).

Jesus answered them, "Have faith in God. For truly I say to you, whoever says to this mountain, 'Be removed and be thrown into the sea,' and does not doubt in his heart, but believes that what he says will come to pass, he will have whatever he says. Therefore I say to you, whatever things you ask when you pray, believe that you will receive them, and you will have them. And when you stand praying, forgive if you have anything against anyone, so that your Father who is in heaven may also forgive you your sins. But if you do not forgive, neither will your Father who is in heaven forgive your sins" (Mark 11:22–26 MEV).

There are so many other verses I was curious about but never got real answers on. Many, many times, I was told the things that happened in the Book of Acts (the results of the work of God's Holy Spirit) were only for that time period. I was told not to take all the verses in the Bible *literally*—especially Scriptures that sound like I myself would have some responsibility for an outcome of a situation or Scriptures that sound like I personally might be trying to use the authority that they said only Jesus had while here on Earth. This is a lie believed by many church-goers.

The only promise in the Bible I was taught we could believe and ***receive*** was the promise of forgiveness for sins. Later, I found out I had to believe and ***receive*** <u>all</u> of God's promises and blessings the same way. By God's grace, He provided those promises, and through faith—by believing them—I was able to ***receive*** them.

READ IT!
Do a study on the word **Receive** in the Bible to see what I mean!

This is how I was *initially* taught to know the will of God: If the door opened, then that was God's will; if the door stayed shut, then I was probably knocking at the wrong door; if something bad happened to me, then it was God's will for me. I was taught that you don't really ask God for things and expect to get them. He might say *yes* sometimes, and He might say *no* sometimes. Basically, if my prayers weren't answered, I found a reason that always put the responsibility back on God and never on me.

Believing this way didn't give responsibility to me at all. Believing this way didn't take into account that someone else's actions might be trying to interfere with God's plan for me. God was blamed and given good or bad credit for anything that happened.

I was taught that if I wasn't receiving God's best, then it was because God didn't want me to have His best: *Some people just draw the little straw, and some people draw the big straw.* That comment really doesn't line up with the Word of God, does it? No. The Word says:

> For all the promises of God in Him are Yes, and in Him Amen,
> to the glory of God through us (2 Corinthians 1:20).

God does not sometimes give a *yes* and sometimes a *maybe.* Do you know why He always says *"Yes,"* to His promises? One reason is that He gets glory when His promises come to pass in our lives. Every single time, God says *yes* to every single one of His promises to us. Is there a stipulation or requirement? *Yes.* You must believe it and receive it. You must come into agreement with God and say, "AMEN!" (Which means, "So be it!") When we renew our minds by reading and meditating on His promises, we are able to fully walk in them because we believe them.

Of course, I know that hearing about *believing and receiving Salvation through Jesus Christ* is the most important thing, but it's not the only thing. Many Christian groups and churches have dared to venture further out into the deeper water. Many no longer teach only about sin and how to get to Heaven but also teach about signs and wonders from doing the Great Commission. They teach us to believe and receive all of God's promises in the Bible and that it's not by anything WE can do, but because we are IN HIM—just like 2 Corinthians 1:20 says. They teach how we can ask God for things and receive from Him. They preach about God's will being done through Jesus while He was here on Earth and how we are to continue doing these great works, and even more.

These are the groups who are experiencing signs and wonders and miracles. **These people live *life more abundantly* because they believe and receive what John 10:10 says**! *Who are their biggest persecutors, though? The unbelieving saints!* The biggest persecutors are Christians who refuse to believe that the New Testament signs and wonders we read about can still happen today by Jesus working *THROUGH US*. These persecutors refuse to believe ALL of God's Word. How do I know? I USED TO BE ONE OF THEM!

I remember saying these exact words over twenty-eight years ago: "I've been to the mountain top! If there is anything more to *understand* or *receive* from God, He would have shown me through the teachings I have heard through my church denomination." How arrogant and closed-minded to have such a denominational pride!! Makes me nauseous and embarrassed to even think about it, and quite humbling to think I ever believed that logic and said it out of my mouth! Wow! Thank God for His mercy and for opening my eyes!

I was like many Christians who do not know about the *complete work* of the Cross. This complete work of the Cross has been referred to as ***The Great Exchange***. The Great Exchange describes all that Jesus took of ours, having nailed it to the Cross with Him, and what He gave us in exchange. He came from Heaven to Earth and did this so while we live here on Earth, we can have Heaven ON Earth. Now, we can ask and pray in Jesus' name and receive all we need from Father God by faith in what Jesus did.

The Great Exchange

These are just SOME of the wonderful exchanges Jesus made for us through what He did for us on the Cross that we can choose to believe or not:

> Jesus became a curse *for us*, removing any reason for us to be cursed. (Galatians 3:13)

> Jesus became guilty of sin, so we could become innocent of sin. (Isaiah 53:10–11)

Jesus was judged for our unrighteousness, so we could <u>receive the righteousness of God</u> by faith in Jesus. (2 Corinthians 5:21)

Jesus became everything that was wrong with mankind since the fall of Adam, so mankind could <u>become everything He is</u>. (Colossians 2:13–14, Ephesians 1)

Jesus became poor, so we could <u>become rich</u>. (2 Corinthians 8:9)

Jesus took our sickness and disease, so we could <u>be healed</u>. (Isaiah 53:5, 1 Peter 2:24, Psalm 103:3)

Jesus took our anxieties and fears, so we could <u>have His peace</u>. (Isaiah 53:5, John 14:27)

Jesus took our failures, so we could <u>have His abilities and succeed</u>. (Philippians 4:13, Jeremiah 29:11)

Jesus died and was raised again, so we could <u>live</u>. (2 Corinthians 5:15)

We only get *one shot* at this short time here on Earth, and since time is passing anyway, let's make the most of it by at least being *willing* to believe in <u>ALL of God's Word</u>. Is there anything in God's Word that will harm us or keep us from victory? NO WAY! His Word is for us to understand and is not complicated or confusing. So, suppose we hear something totally different from what we have ever heard before. In that case, we should go ahead and get our Bible out, read it, and <u>be open</u> to *seeing* something different in the Holy Scriptures.

We should pray and ask Holy Spirit to show us verses that will answer our questions about controversial topics in God's Word. We should let the entire Word of God answer our questions instead of just taking a couple of Scriptures

STOP THE SPIN!

Maybe, like me, God has been trying to show you something different.

Maybe you haven't been willing to drop denominational and religious pride so you can actually believe it. Ask the Lord if there is anything you haven't been willing to see that He wants you to see and believe. Try reading the Bible a different way. Read it without thinking of how you were taught the Scriptures through man, or man's traditions, or your own experiences. Just read the Bible, believing what HE says—not adding to it, or taking away from it, or twisting what it straight up says.

out of context and regarding them over dozens of other Scriptures. As we receive revelation from ALL of God's Word, we will have an *everyday victory* here on Earth and <u>MOVE FORWARD</u> into God's plan for our lives.

Let's not make it difficult, but simply believe what God says and get off the spin of unbelief—get off the merry-go-rounds and on with life!

Part Three: Society's Spin

Throughout many generations, we can see where the enemy (through the world) has taken the words *believe*, *believers*, and *believing* and downplayed them. The world has dishonored them so much that now they have very little impact when heard. As a result, when Christians use the phrases *faith in God* or *believing in God*, the power and authority are not sensed along with it. Collectively, the Christian church body at large (which I simply refer to as *the Church* most of the time) has allowed the worldly use of these words to mix with how they apply Biblical truths.

Why am I even mentioning these things in this section? Because the enemy has *subtly led* many to *dishonor* God and devalue His Word, most people don't even recognize they have jumped onto a merry-go-round of thinking the way the world thinks.

Society has taken these words and applied them for everything *except* toward Jesus, God's Word, and the promises in His Word. These words are now being used flippantly in worldly advertising campaigns to even promote the seasons and celebrations of the year. For example, believers of a *santa claus*; believers of an *Easter bunny*; believers of a *tooth fairy*; believers of *ghosts*; believers of *cupid*; believers of *karma*, etc. Now, the Church has accepted these watered-down definitions and has taken part in sabotaging what are supposed to be holy holidays and celebrations! This has gone so far that Christians even support Hollywood movies and entertainment that totally change the whole meaning of why we have Christmas! (Not cool!)

> And they shall teach My people the difference between the holy
> and the unholy, and cause them to discern between the unclean
> and the clean (Ezekiel 44:23).

The *Church* has been so infected and desensitized with the misuse of these words they now have a hard time wrapping their head around the truths in the Bible. They have joined the world and even decided that it is ok to lie *like the devil* to their children, promoting these characters and celebrations—mixing the holy with the profane in the Church.

Half the time, the children can't figure out why they get in trouble for lying, and the parents can't figure out why their kids don't believe their words OR God's Word! They tell their kids that *santa* won't come to their house on Christmas Eve and give them gifts if they are bad. Sooooo, at an early age, they teach their kids it's OK to lie about certain things. Just as damaging is how they teach them to *perform* and do good works to get gifts; otherwise, they will be on the *naughty list!* Then, eventually, it seems OK to tell them Jesus might not be very happy with them either if they are bad. Hmmmmm! Do you see how we have actually helped the devil create this philosophy that we can only

STOP THE SPIN!

How about we get off this merry-go-round of lies and tell the kids the truth about the real reason for Christmas and Resurrection Day (Easter) and that these other things are just fun things we like to do? Let them know who is really giving them the gifts and who is really eating the cookies and milk. Let them know who is really moving the little elf around the house and who is filling and hiding their Easter baskets. Let them know that God does not keep a "naughty list."

Once they know the real truth about the celebrations and activities, they can just have fun. And you won't be tempted to lie and make up stories every year to keep a twisted belief rooted inside them. They will respect you for being honest with them and for not training them to act like the father of lies, the devil. EEEK!

We shouldn't be pressured to lie to our children. Take the pressure off, tell the truth, and JUST HAVE FUN with the kids, openly knowing that you are all just pretending. This will honor God instead of honoring the ways of the world.

receive from God based on our performances? These are lies that, if believed, will keep you from going forward into a holy and prosperous life as a Christian.

The *world* chooses to make a bigger effort to promote and believe characters like a santa claus and an Easter bunny *more* than they choose to believe and promote the <u>*real meaning*</u> of the holidays. They believe these cartoon characters to be real and the stories in the Bible to be fictional. So it's understandable why they are confused and have a hard time believing in Jesus and God's love for them! They even believe a santa claus gives better gifts than the One who gave them the gift of life!

Is it just me, or does this sound twisted to you?

All of this has been *a worldly merry-go-round of unbelief* in the real meaning of Christmas and the Resurrection. (The holiday that most call Easter.) This is one merry-go-round the Church has jumped on, without even thinking about how it might cause confusion regarding who and what we should believe in.

Are we still friends?

Society's Spin on *Love*

The enemy, through the world, has done the same thing with spinning the word *love.* And, sadly, the Church has accepted it and now plays along, also. (The devil thinks it's awesome!)

READ IT!
1 John 4 & 1 Corinthians 13
Who Love is, what Love does

The world and the Church have allowed the word *love* to be used so flippantly that if you tell someone that you love them, it often doesn't impact them. They don't feel any more special than pizza! Many Christians have patterned their lives after relationships they see in movies and television shows, letting their emotions determine if they *love* someone or not. One day they see someone and have feelings to *fall in* love with them, and the next day they see a different side of them and *fall out of* love with them. Fake people (actors) on a show in a fake life are enticing them to believe lies about love. What they are actually *falling for* is infatuation—not love.

The world has desensitized the word *love* and down-graded it to say they "love" everything, EXCEPT God! They love their house. They love their boat. They love their job. They love ice cream. They love coffee … and the list goes on. I see in the Bible that it tells us to *love God, love people,* and *love His Word*.

We can *really like* our *stuff*. And, we can *really appreciate* our house and car and boat. We can be *so thankful* for our job. But we shouldn't *LOVE* any of that stuff. Why can't we just use the word *like* instead of *love* for all those *things*?

I know this may sound extreme to some of you, but according to 1 John 4: 8, 16, *GOD is love*. We are also shown in 1 Corinthians 13:4–7 all the attributes of love. If we are born again, we have these attributes *inside of us* because God's Holy Spirit is inside of us. We aren't commanded to *love* things. But we are commanded to love God and people:

> A new commandment I give to you, that you love one another, even as I have loved you, that you also love one another (John 13:34 MEV).

> Jesus said to him, "You shall love the Lord your God with all your heart, and with all your soul, and with all your mind. This is the first and great commandment. And the second is like it: You shall love your neighbor as yourself" (Matthew 22:37–39 MEV).

You've probably heard trendy phrases that come and go throughout society, like one I recently heard, "Love is love." *What? Love is love?* Is that like, "Pie is pie," or "Hate is hate"? (Shaking my head.) The world will always come up with something new or trendy, but the real love, God's love, remains the same.

Let's draw a line in the sand and keep **the value** of the words *BELIEVE* and *LOVE* where it should be. Let's believe and live in the Biblical Love, Who is God—and honor Love (God) by keeping it separate. Let's not be so quick to jump right into these subtle traps and schemes the devil uses to detour people away from how vitally essential these words are in honoring God. Let's live victoriously here on this Earth, off merry-go-rounds and on with real life. It's no wonder the world isn't running toward God and His goodness! Let God's Word be your standard. Remember: Faith and love are a dynamic duo in the Kingdom of God, and He gave us both! His love and His faith!

Part Four: The Fuel of Unbelief Is Fear

Unbelief and fear go hand in hand. Both are deadly to the plan of God for our life. Unbelief is the spinning merry-go-round, and fear is the fuel that keeps unbelief spinning. It stops us from going forward, paralyzing us from doing what we have in our hearts to do. We saw what fear did with the Israelites—kept them wandering around and around the wilderness with no purpose—and it will do the same to us if we remain in it.

> Do not fear, for I am with you; do not be dismayed, for I am your God. I will strengthen you, I will help you, yes, I will uphold you with My righteous right hand (Isaiah 41:10 MEV).

Fear is not of God—fear is the enemy's invention, based on his lies, and is used to keep people from believing God's Word. As a result of not believing the love God has for us and the truth of His Word, fear can work its way into every area of our life if we allow it, and it will run right over our trust and faith in God.

Fear is an enemy to our faith! Both fear and unbelief are tactics the enemy of our soul uses. These tactics are meant to keep Christians from moving forward into victorious living here and now, the kind of onward living which gives glory to God and draws people to Jesus. "The thief does not come except to steal, and to kill, and to destroy," but Jesus said, "I have come that they may have life, and that they may have it more abundantly" (John 10:10).

Jesus came not only to give us life but to give us life *more abundantly*. The enemy's primary goal is to keep us from finding out about this abundant life that Salvation has given us through Jesus Christ as our Lord and Savior. How does he do it? By fear, lies, and twisting and perverting the teachings of the "Acts of the Holy Spirit," the "Great Commission," the "Redemptive Work of Jesus," and most importantly, "Our New Identity in Christ Jesus."

The devil doesn't want people to know about the whole Salvation Package available to us through Jesus. He doesn't want you to get the full revelation of what Jesus did on the Cross. He doesn't want you to know how Jesus' death, burial, and resurrection gave us *more* than just forgiveness of sin and a ticket to Heaven for eternity. That's why it is so necessary for us to read and study God's Word, so our minds get renewed, and we can recognize his perversions and twistings.

Fear and Faith Both Expect Something

Fear is faith corrupted. Fear is faith perverted. Fear EXPECTS to have something bad happen because it believes the report of what is *seen* in the natural—just like the Israelites did. Faith EXPECTS something good to happen because it believes the *unseen* report of the Lord—whatever the Bible says. Fear will fuel your unbelief—just like it did with the Israelites—and it will stop you from moving forward—just like it did with the Israelites!

If we ARE NOT learning and believing God's truths, we will have a bigger tendency to believe the devil's lies. We won't be able to tell if something is coming from God or the enemy. So, "be sober and watchful, because your adversary the devil walks around as a roaring lion, seeking whom he may devour" (1 Peter 5:8 MEV).

Suppose we ARE NOT intentionally alert and awake to the devil's schemes and aware of his deceiving tactics. *That* is how we will fall into his traps and snares and require miracles from God to get us out!

A few years back, David traveled a lot out of town for his job. When he would leave, I would be home alone. At first, it took me quite a bit of resisting feelings and imaginations of fearful thoughts that would try to come on me every time he left. But I found things to keep myself busy and productive instead of entertaining those thoughts and feelings. I could stay at home, walk the dog at night, go down to my basement at night, sit outside at night, etc., and it never bothered me.

During one of those times when David was out of town, I received a phone call that could have been very alarming to me, yet I had absolutely no fear about it. BUT THEN, not long after, the enemy's *temptations to fear* started in on me again. I continued resisting the spirit of fear, thanking God for His goodness in my life.

A week went by. David was home but getting ready to leave out of town again, and suddenly I started *feeling* dread (which is fear) about him leaving this time. This feeling of dread caught me off guard. I had plenty of stuff to do with my business and writing my book. I was actually very excited about getting much-needed things done around the house and yard too. I was also looking forward to spending time preparing for some awesome things we had planned for when he got back home. We had a week of marriage conference meetings coming up at church. Then, we were headed to Colorado for a week-long business and vision conference right after that. This would be the first time in over thirty-three years of marriage that we were focused completely on God's vision and purpose for our marriage and life together. I didn't want anything to interfere with my time to prepare my heart and mind for these next few weeks. I was at a new height of joy and excitement for the future and sensed in my spirit wonderful things coming. So I wondered, *why did I suddenly start feeling dread?* It wasn't long before I knew the answer to that.

The morning he left out, I began getting phone calls from people about something going on in our second-born daughter's life. The enemy was hitting me with fearful thoughts, on top of the natural *mommy emotions*. I knew in my heart that this time she didn't need the natural mommy like before. *This time* she needed a strong, spiritually-awake mommy, one who would not cave into emotional pressures. I knew what she needed most was for me to allow God to do what He wanted in this situation without my interfering. There was a time in the past for me to reach out to her, but not this time. (Yes, we can step in and sabotage God's help if we insist on doing things our own way.)

I will fill in more details about the circumstances in chapter five, but for now, let me just stay with these main thoughts of fear and dread. Sadly, within one day, I found myself stepping right back on that old merry-go-round I thought I would NEVER get back on again. My heart became heavy. My joy was now gone, and confusion took over regarding all the things I wanted to get done before David got back home. I found myself entertaining thoughts of depression and fear of loneliness. Wow! I honestly shocked myself that I could go backwards so fast. *How did this happen so quickly?* The devil is sneaky, and we must stay alert to his ways. Instead of resisting thoughts of fear and dread, I allowed myself to dwell on negative outcomes that *could* take place in this specific situation.

By the time I realized it and put a stop to allowing myself to get sucked up into the middle of a garbage merry-go-round, I was worn down. I had wasted two full days of my life being fearful because of the lying thoughts and emotions. Then it took me a couple more days of getting into God's Word, renewing my mind, and singing praises to Him. I had to force myself to look around and stir up thankfulness again for everything He was doing in my life and get back on track.

The enemy's schemes and distractions to detour us are real and always rooted in fear and unbelief. The Word of God in 2 Corinthians 2:11 reveals this saying, "lest satan should take advantage of us; for we are not ignorant of his devices."

With God's help, we can spot those schemes and distractions and deal with the situations in a super-naturally effective way. Doing things God's way is what will take us off the enemy's merry-go-round of fear that tries to paralyze us from going forward. I was so thankful God helped me recognize the enemy in this! This happened right before we were about to take a huge jump of forward movement in our marriage and life. His grace was there for me to overcome it. (I'll share more later about this trip to Colorado so that you'll understand why the devil was trying so hard to interfere with us going *that week*.)

STOP THE SPIN!

People have allowed themselves to become desensitized to fear and lies. Some people believe more in what they see in Hollywood movies than in God's Word. Hollywood horror movies are meant to portray evil in a way that makes people think they don't have any help or strength inside them to stand up against the power of darkness.

The devil is behind many of these movies and especially likes it when Christians watch them. Children's cartoons are slipping in fear to our children, as well. They even say it's ok to have some fear.

Are you going to allow that junk into the minds of your kids? They shouldn't be afraid to cross the street; they should be cautious and aware of vehicles when crossing the street. They shouldn't be afraid of the water and drowning; they should learn how to swim in the water, to be aware of where they are swimming, and understand their abilities and limitations while swimming. Being afraid of simple things like bees, snakes, spiders, sharks, water, storms, heights, etc. opens the door to fear having a place in other areas of our lives, as well.

If the devil can keep us sidetracked from spending time in God's Word and prevent us from renewing our minds to God and His truths, then he can keep us living in a constant state of fear. His goal is to cause us to never accomplish anything we have in our hearts to do for the Lord. He definitely doesn't want us to believe we have power over him and his works.

But Jesus gave us a response! He said, "Look, I give you authority to trample on serpents and scorpions, and over all the power of the enemy. And nothing shall by any means hurt you" (Luke 10:19 MEV).

The enemy's works are intended to steal God's Word-seed from our heart before it can take root. He wants to kill any growth that has begun in our love walk. He desires to destroy any work or advancement of God's Kingdom here on Earth. Any attack from the enemy is an attack with a goal to get us to lose faith in God and His goodness.

We should be so *aware* of the fear that when we see an area of our life with a foundation built on fear and lies, we also see a huge RED FLASHING LIGHT telling us, "Stop! Don't go there! Don't believe it! Change that! Don't participate in it!"

Give No Place to Fear

Fear can be more than just a fear of the dark or fear of monsters or ghosts. Fear is more likely to show up as intimidation or anxiety from thoughts of being rejected or failing. Fear can manifest when you go to a job interview or stand up to speak in front of a crowd. It can make you think something bad will happen to you or your family. Fear can stop you from asking your teachers questions or asking them to explain something you don't understand—ask me how I know that [smiles]. It can even show up when you are praying, and then suddenly, you are afraid that God is not hearing you or that God won't keep His Word and promises toward *you*.

If we openly expose our heart, thoughts, and emotions to any kind or amount of fear, then we will be more aware of, sensitive to, and rattled by things we shouldn't be frightened about at all. Fear of any kind or level is still fear. According to what we are told in the Bible, it is not okay to have any amount of fear. *God has big reasons for telling us not to fear or be afraid.*

> Are not two sparrows sold for a copper coin? And not one of them falls to the ground apart from your Father's will. But the very hairs of your head are all numbered. <u>Do not fear</u> therefore; <u>you are of more value than many sparrows</u> (Matthew 10:29–31; emphasis added).

Fear is based on lies straight from the enemy. Believing God's TRUTH is what will set us free from all fear. For every lie from the enemy, there is a TRUTH from God's Word that will set us free. We gain victory over enemy lies by being *in-tune* with our Good Shepherd, Who tells us we are valued to Him. The closer we get to the Lord (the TRUTH), the further we get from fear, lies, and darkness. The closer we stay to the Lord and His Word, the easier it is to resist the enemy's lies.

We have clear instructions in God's Word about abiding in Truth and hearing His voice. Spend time with Him just *sitting on His lap*, so to speak, listening and learning of Him. Just imagine yourself sitting on the knee of Lincoln's huge memorial. Think about how big Lincoln's knee is compared to you. You, and what you are dealing with, are so small compared to how big God is and how much He values you.

The Lord doesn't want us to receive Him and then flounder around helplessly the rest of our lives. He already made provision for us to have the victory manifest in our lives. To move forward in faith—taking this victory by faith, off the spin of unbelief—we must take an honest look at our lives and see where fear has been allowed to run rampant. Unrecognized and uncontrolled fear can quickly multiply and snowball. Once you are afraid of one thing, eventually, you are afraid of other things. Unless you take an *honest look* in the mirror of your life, at your motives and reasons as to why you aren't doing what you know in your heart you are to be doing, you won't see it.

Why aren't you taking steps toward accomplishing the vision and desires of your heart?

Why won't you let yourself *see* further than the city limits you live in?

Why are you watching the weather and news constantly?

Why won't you forgive that person?

Why won't you ask your spouse the *scary* question?

Why do you want to *know it all* and never want to be wrong?

Why don't you want to take a trip by airplane or cruise ship?

The root behind all these kinds of issues is fear and unbelief. Recognizing where fear has held our life captive is the first step to receiving victory. "For God has not given us a spirit of fear, but of power and of love and of a sound mind" (2 Timothy 1:7).

If it didn't come from Jesus, I don't want it! I won't accept it! If God didn't give me fear, I don't want it! If He gave me power, love, and a sound mind—then I receive that!

We see that God is limited to what He can do in our lives if we have unbelief and fear, which we know comes from the enemy. Fear limits us! Eventually, whatever we believe in is drawn to us and manifested in this natural realm. In regard to fear, it will be like a magnet if we let it:

For the thing which I greatly feared has happened to me, and that which I dreaded has come to me (Job 3:25 MEV).

We will attract what we fear because we think on it so much and then allow it to stick to our minds, thus *allowing* the very thing we fear to manifest in our lives.

Faith is also a magnet: you attract what you have faith in. If we believe in God and His goodness, and as we meditate on those things, we will live in and attract His goodness. Even King David in the Old Testament knew this when he said, "Surely goodness and mercy shall *follow me* all the days of my life" (Psalm 23:6).

The Bible says, "For as he thinks in his heart, so is he" (Proverbs 23:7).

So … faith or fear? We get to choose how we respond and the kind of life we live.

We have a choice to strengthen our faith or strengthen fear by what we meditate on and allow our thoughts, eyes, ears, and feelings to believe. When we truly believe, once and for all, the truth of God's Word and of His love for us, working in us and through us, then we will see victory over every fear. The Bible makes it very clear as to what CASTS OUT fear:

> No one has seen God at any time. If we love one another, God dwells in us, and His love is perfected in us. We know that we live in Him, and He in us, because He has given us His Spirit. And we have seen and testify that the Father sent the Son to be the Savior of the world. Whoever confesses that Jesus is the Son of God, God lives in him, and he in God. And we have come to know and to believe the love that God has for us. God is love. Whoever lives in love lives in God, and God in him. In this way God's love is perfected in us, so that we may have boldness on the Day of Judgment, because as He is, so are we in this world. There is no fear in love, but perfect love casts out fear, because fear has to do with punishment. Whoever fears is not perfect in love. We love Him because He first loved us (1 John 4:12–19 MEV; emphasis added).

Perfect love casts out fear. Romans 5:8 tells us, "But God demonstrates His own love toward us, in that while we were still sinners, Christ died for us." Knowing in your heart that God loved you, even while you were still a sinner, is huge! Christ didn't wait to die for us until after we were perfect and stopped sinning. His love for us was perfect and complete BEFORE we ever believed in Him and received Him. Getting this revelation and believing in His perfect, unconditional love for us will outweigh (overrule, veto, or supersede) every fear in our lives. This also causes us to love our brother unconditionally. His love will just easily come out of us as we yield to it.

If you aren't experiencing God's goodness, it could be you are living in fear and not really knowing God, Who is Love. Knowing and *believing* His love for you is the beginning key to being fear-free! Believing *in your heart* His perfect love for you is what will drive out all fear. The more perfect (complete) you are made through believing in *His* love for *you*, the more every fear in your life will be cast out.

READ IT!
1 John & Romans
Know God's love and give
no place to fear!

The more we believe in God's love for us, the more we will stop being afraid of rejection from man and the condemnation we might receive from failing at something. We will be totally free from fear and able to enjoy all the benefits of God's love for us. We will be unstoppable to do everything the Lord has for us to do!

Revelation and everyday life application of these next three Scriptures are enough to get us off any merry-go-round:

> Do not be conformed to this world, but be transformed by the renewing of your mind (Romans 12:2; emphasis added).

But you did not learn about Christ in this manner, if indeed you have heard Him and have been taught by Him, as the truth is in Jesus: that you put off the former way of life in the old nature, which is corrupt according to the deceitful lusts, and be renewed in the spirit of your mind; and that you put on the new nature, which was created according to God in righteousness and true holiness (Ephesians 4:20–24 MEV; emphasis added).

Receive with meekness the implanted word, which is able to save your souls [minds] (James 1:21; emphasis added).

STOP THE SPIN!

Problems involving any of the four types of unbelief will leave if you follow the instructions of the Scriptures. The Scriptures on the previous pages are especially helpful.

As you do, you won't have unbelief due to ignorance because you will now have heard and know the full Gospel of Jesus Christ. And, you won't have unbelief due to wrong teaching because you will be hearing the truth of the Gospel—and the Gospel will make you free. The revelation of God's love will soften your hard, unbelieving heart, and you won't walk in rebellion toward God any longer. You will recognize natural unbelief (which involves your five physical senses) and get rid of it by being more spiritually led than fleshly led.

Following the instructions given in the three Scriptures on the previous pages is enough to send the spin of unbelief to its death and make Bible-based believing a new way of living for you!

FOUR

RELIGIOUS & CHURCH-GOING MERRY-GO-ROUNDS

Part One: "La-La-Land"

MY RELIGIOUS MERRY-GO-ROUND experience is about me just doing what everyone else in all my different church groups was doing. Just picture a line of cattle thoughtlessly following each other, unaware of their surroundings! I call this my "La-La-Land" years. I named them La-La-Land because it was a season of years where I didn't think for myself regarding truths in the Bible and my relationship with Jesus.

Before I jump into this very sensitive chapter, let me give you a part of my background story. I hope this will help you understand why I feel like I am even partly qualified to write this chapter. *Here we go …*

First, let me make this very clear: I am not saying that going to church is a *merry-go-round*. However, my church-going journey was not normal and resembled the characteristics of a merry-go-round! Going to church to gather with other believers is a good thing—something the Bible tells us to do—and when done right, it is necessary for every Christian. Going to church should be about becoming a disciple of Jesus Christ and not about becoming a disciple of the pastor or the people in the congregation. So often, it seems, that the *unspoken yet well-known* emphasis is to conform to the image of the people and personality of the group rather than to the image of Christ.

READ IT!

Hebrews 10:24-25, Matthew 28:19-20, & Acts 11:25-26

Gather with other Believers

It was easy for me to conform to the image of these groups because I was very insecure and both easily influenced and easily intimidated. Because of dealing with rejection and feelings rooted in my dad abandoning our family, I was always looking for acceptance and approval anywhere I could get it. Because church-goers were my new group of peeps, I looked for it through them.

I have had lots of exposure to many different church denominational influences over my, so far, fifty-eight years, as seen in this list (some of these churches I personally attended and some of the influence came through people who I knew attended there): Nazarene, Catholic, Methodist, Presbyterian, Community Bible Churches, Apostolic, several different Baptist churches, Baptist Bible College, Evangel Bible Church, Home Church, Mennonite, Word of Life Church, Christian Centers, Full Gospel Churches, Charismatic churches, Street Church (for the homeless), Word and Faith Churches, Charis Bible College. (And, it's possible that I may have left some out!) Whew!!!

You might be thinking, "That's not normal! How awful!" Yet, I'm thankful that this exposure helps me relate with a lot more people and get where they are coming from when talking to them about spiritual and Biblical topics.

From the time I was a baby, I have been in one church or another. I have been a member of at least a dozen different churches and visited dozens more. Growing up, I mostly only knew people who went to a church of one denomination or another. And, if they didn't go every Sunday, I can guarantee you that *everyone* I knew stepped inside the church building for at least Christmas, Easter, weddings, and funerals.

After I turned ten years old, I was surrounded by mostly church-goers. They were all people who seemed like they really loved God. If I met someone new, one of the first things we would ask each other is, "What church do you go to?" It seemed like the focus was more about going to church than it was about our personal relationship with Father God, Jesus Christ, and Holy Spirit, which should be the whole reason we go to church.

I knew church-going people from one end of the denominational spectrum to the other. I knew super-legalistic, attend-every-day-of-the-week church-goers. I also knew Sunday-only church-goers and Saturday-night-confession, get-it-off-your-chest church-goers. For some, their outward appearance showed they were obviously a church-goer because they only wore long dresses and wore their hair up in a bun (or their parents did). Others, it was just the opposite. These probably couldn't be identified as a church-goer until time for church service. Then, suddenly, they were completely transformed into the perfect person or family, wearing their Sunday best. They were taught to be good actors and actresses. Hopefully, nobody would catch them off guard or stop by unannounced!

My mother's parents were Nazarene. My mother was raised in that denomination. I was dedicated to the Lord as a baby in the Nazarene church. Whenever my sisters and I visited my grandparents, we would go to the Nazarene church, and we did whatever they did. I learned how to sit perfectly quiet as my grandmother would smile and bribe us with gum or candy to occupy us during service. You could tell my grandparents had it in their hearts to be there because they always looked happy, which made us feel happy. The best memories I have of going to that church was how my grandma made sure my sisters and I got all dolled up in our "Sunday best" each time we went. We got a good bath the night before, and our hair was nicely combed before we walked inside. I looked forward to going because the people were so nice to us cute little girls.

On the other hand, my father's parents were stout Catholics. Whenever I stayed with them over a weekend, I remember they would NEVER miss a Saturday or Sunday mass service. It did not matter where they were or what they were doing. In their minds, *it was the law, and breaking this particular law was the worst!* Memories of going with my paternal grandparents to this church are totally opposite to my memories of attending the Nazarene church. Because my parents were not members of the Catholic Church, my sisters and I were not allowed to participate or do anything they did in the service. We were warned not to touch the holy water, not allowed to stand up when the others did or sing the songs, and scolded if we didn't sit perfectly quiet until it was over. I remember feeling ashamed and not accepted there. I didn't look forward to the feeling I got as a little girl when I went there. This is all my grandparents knew, so I don't blame them. They honestly had it in their hearts to be members of this organization. And being a member of this organization required them to do certain things each week.

If I wasn't at one of my grandparents' churches, my parents would still make sure my sisters and I went to church in the town where we lived. In this small town of 300 people, there was a Methodist church that my cousins were involved in, so my mom would drop us off there almost every Sunday when we were home. At the time, I thought this church did some really fun things! One of those was that they hosted the town's Annual Haunted House in the church basement each year. True story!

What an event! It was one of the scariest haunted houses I had ever been in. People would come from everywhere to the Methodist Church haunted house. It was their major fundraiser! People would line up and down the street to get in and cars parked for blocks. After it was over, I remember feeling a little bit leery of going downstairs to my Sunday School class, though. (Now, this church might be what some consider *the opposite side of the spectrum*.) The haunted house and other activities were the traditions of this particular Methodist church. Because we went there, we thoughtlessly accepted and participated in these traditions.

When I was ten years old, my mom and dad separated. That was when my mom decided to start going to church too, instead of just dropping us off. She took my sisters and me thirty minutes away to a Community Bible church in another small town. I was a member of this church and attended two to three times a week, mostly by force of my mother while I was in high school. Even though I didn't live up to their standards, this church still drilled in me that if I was going to be a Christian, I had to be totally separate from the world. Since I was mostly living *for* the world, every time I went to church, I felt ashamed—like totally exposed with a spotlight on me. I felt like I became their prayer project, the *help Dana get her life on track* project, so she will do what we all do.

In the second half of my senior year of high school, 1982, I decided to live my life only following after Jesus. Anyway, that's what was in my heart to do. But the thing is, I didn't know what following Jesus *looked like* except for the lives I saw in the church groups I was associated with. After graduation, at the suggestion of someone at my church, I decided to go to Bible college. I wanted to get myself even more grounded in my new life decision to follow Jesus. It was four hours away, and someone paid my way to this private Christian college. We all agreed it was the best thing for me at that time.

This Bible college was the extreme opposite of the lifestyle I had just come out of. This new group of people seemed to be set in their ways regarding certain rules they required the students to keep. In my spirit, I recognized some things right away that didn't seem correct; but at that time, I didn't know any other thing to do except to be there. I thought it was better to be there than back at home with the potential of never getting out of that town and possibly falling back into my old, destructive lifestyle.

I never really felt like I belonged there or fit in at this college. I was a small-town girl exposed to almost every kind of evil, perversion, and outlaw thing in this world. The entire year I felt like a *black sheep*. My heart desired to be with people who weren't quite so *sheltered*, but I was thankful I at least had a couple of roommates who could relate to me. We were always close to breaking this school's legalistic rules—mostly those rules that made no sense to us. (And, you definitely didn't question the rules.) For example, we were given a list of *approved* churches we could attend, which contained only churches connected to or in the same denominational association as this Bible college.

My friends and I found out about a church group (one *not* on the list) that got together on Friday nights and went to downtown Des Moines to do street witnessing. I loved street witnessing! I felt totally comfortable with all the prostitutes, pimps, drug and alcohol addicts, and homeless people. One Friday night, my friends and I decided to join this *not-on-the-list group* of Christians and go with them out to the city streets and tell people about Jesus. Before we broke up into groups and went out, we all sat in a circle and prayed. As they were praying, I heard some of them speaking softly in a different language. I thought I was hearing things, so I just ignored it. I could feel something different about the people in this group, but it wasn't scary. *It was Love.* I wanted to go back again, but I couldn't because someone at the school found out and subtly warned us we could be expelled.

Years later, I realized this *outsider* group was *spirit-filled* and spoke in tongues—something I had never heard about at that time. They also believed in the works of the Holy Spirit as described in the Book of Acts. They believed they could lay hands on people on the streets while praying for them, and they honestly expected them to be healed, set free, and delivered from the works of the enemy. Ohhhhhh … so now I knew why we were prohibited from joining them! My school and church groups didn't believe those Acts of the Holy Spirit were for today, so they didn't want us exposed to it! (SAD!)

This college highly influenced the students toward its man-made rules. Actually, it demanded a lot of performance and behavior modification. I wondered where they got the *Christian Rules of Conduct and Dress Code* that we were expected to keep. I wondered why we could only go to the churches on the school's *approved* list. I'm pretty sure everyone received that list when they enrolled, but if not, it was definitely a well-known and talked about list.

I wasn't there long before I was already really trying to conform to the image of this school. I learned some *Christianese*. This makes me laugh now. Some of you know what I'm talking about. Christianese is a church-goer's language, and each church has a different dialect. I dropped most of my CHRISTIAN music cold-turkey for this school, also. We weren't allowed to listen to music classified as *Christian* if it had what they considered as a worldly beat to it. They didn't even take into account that the words being said in the songs were genuinely praising God and speaking only about His goodness. It wasn't *acceptable* music if the tempo sounded like the world. I'm not even talking about heavy metal music. These unallowed songs were ones you could totally hear and understand the lyrics that would actually draw you into worshipping the Lord.

One evening, my friends and I took music albums, broke them all up, and threw them into the trash. We sat around and talked about how demonic they were. That was the end of music with a beat for me!!

I attended there for a year before getting married and moving to California. It was my husband David who later introduced me to Keith Green. Wow, the beautiful and peaceful feeling I got from listening to this music. I had never heard such music before. It was very anointed, and he sang from a heart who loved Jesus. His music actually helped me love Jesus more. But how could that be? He had long hair and looked rebellious. His music didn't sound like it would be approved by the college. I had to get past feelings of condemnation because his music had a beat. I also had to get past the way this musician *looked*. It's nuts, but because of his long hair touching his shirt collar, I could just imagine the leaders of my Bible college shaking their heads and fingers at me. Call it vain imaginations if you want, but that was how I perceived them.

This might be a slight RABBIT TRAIL, but I want to include that *Christian music has really changed since I was in that Bible college. But surprisingly, most of what has changed is how the Church now accepts <u>every song</u> on the Christian radio station as Christian. It seems like the Church has gone from one ditch to the other ditch regarding Christian music. I have gotten very picky about what I listen to, especially in the Christian category. I'm not judging them by their beat, but I do judge the <u>**lyrics**</u>. A lot of songs misrepresent God. This must hurt the Father's heart to be so misinterpreted and blamed for so many bad things mentioned in these songs.*

So, here's a funny: We also *weren't allowed to go to the movie theatre or even play cards* because these were all activities and entertainment the world did. *Swimming with guys around? Forget it!!* Yep—I was pretty much limited to ping-pong!

This kind of stuff is still happening in some churches, and we wonder why this generation doesn't want our God or to be around church-going people. I admit, I needed a life of discipline and a boot camp experience, but can you just picture me coming out of the worldly, partying lifestyle, and then all of a sudden, I have to wear long dresses and act super-spiritual?

All I knew was that I loved Jesus and was thankful to Him for dying on the Cross for my sins. Because of what He did for me, I thought the least I could do for Him was sacrifice my old clothes and start dressing weirdly. *They didn't want us to dress like the world*, but they made us dress in such a way that we stuck out like a *sore thumb* in the world.

The legalism *actually caused me to want to break the rules*. Were all of the outward changes wrong? *No, not necessarily, but they weren't changes made from my own heart*. Had they taught me to renew my mind to God's Word first, had they taught me to focus on my heart change first, then many of the outward changes (the ones that were truly God-inspired) would have followed—*from the heart*.

I got to the place where I couldn't wait to leave, but at the same time, I felt like I was such a bad girl for still feeling like a *black sheep* and never truly becoming *one of them*. Even though attending there was the best thing for me to do at the time, it left me confused in so many ways. I remained in a battle over whether to keep their rules even after leaving the school.

I knew I didn't want to be *churchy*, but at that time, I didn't know any different way for a Christian to act, so I followed the rules and looked like they wanted me to look and acted like they wanted me to act.

Embarrassingly, I admit, I followed thoughtlessly just doing this FOR YEARS! **I thought I was on the winning team, but I was actually on the spinning team!**

Why did this religious school, and other religious organizations, add these *performance* rules to the liberty we have in Christ? It brought me heaviness and corrupted my mind. Satan alone wasn't confusing me; man-made traditions and legalism were confusing me!

Why do we continue to do *man-made* religious and traditional acts? Why do we keep believing these acts make us more spiritual, believing they bring us closer to God?

He answered and said to them, "Well did Isaiah prophesy of you hypocrites, as it is written: 'This people honors Me with their lips, But their heart is far from Me. And in vain they worship Me, *Teaching as doctrines the commandments of men.*' For laying aside the commandment of God, *you hold the tradition of men*" … He said to them, "All too well you reject the commandment of God, that you may keep your tradition. … making the word of God of no effect through your tradition which you have handed down" (Mark 7:6–9, 13; emphasis added).

You ran well. *Who hindered you from obeying the truth?* This persuasion does not come from Him who calls you (Galatians 5:7–8; emphasis mine).

Beware lest anyone cheat you through philosophy and empty deceit, *according to the tradition of men, according to the basic principles of the world*, and not according to Christ (Colossians 2:8; emphasis added).

Religious traditions of men and legalism are the workings of *self-righteousness and self-effort.* The religious tradition of men teaches that we get our *right standing* through Christ when we are born again but then mixes in man-made rules afterward. <u>Whether they knew it or not, this religious organization was teaching us to have a *behavior relationship* with God and not a personal-from-the-heart, *faith relationship* with Him.</u> If you were to ask them, I know they would say that our Christian life should be based on a personal relationship with Jesus. Still, at the same time, they only taught things in the Bible that lined up with how *they thought* that personal relationship with Jesus should look.

I missed a whole lot of Holy Spirit-inspired Bible teaching in that Bible college. I was a young Christian with an UNRENEWED mind and given all kinds of rules and regulations that seemed <u>more binding than the lifestyle I just came out of</u>! This religious, legalistic influence seemed way more burdensome and detrimental to me than any influence I was exposed to in my previous lifestyle.

STOP THE SPIN!

Religious, legalistic influences can be way more burdensome and detrimental to people than many influences they might have been exposed to in a previous lifestyle.

We should be taking the burden away from people NOT giving them more burdens through do's and don'ts.

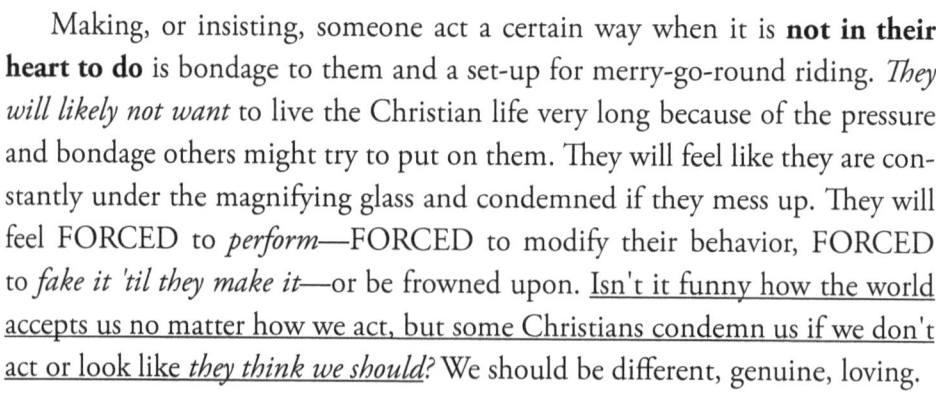

Making, or insisting, someone act a certain way when it is **not in their heart to do** is bondage to them and a set-up for merry-go-round riding. *They will likely not want* to live the Christian life very long because of the pressure and bondage others might try to put on them. They will feel like they are constantly under the magnifying glass and condemned if they mess up. They will feel FORCED to *perform*—FORCED to modify their behavior, FORCED to *fake it 'til they make it*—or be frowned upon. <u>Isn't it funny how the world accepts us no matter how we act, but some Christians condemn us if we don't act or look like *they think we should*?</u> We should be different, genuine, loving.

There was a time when David and I had some neighbors who were of the Mennonite denomination. They would pop in a lot of times like good neighbors do. We had a dairy farm, so we were always doing work outside, and I mean A LOT of work. The Mennonite man and his wife were nice to us, but you could tell we were their *good neighbor project.*

One super-hot summer day, I was outside mowing, and they saw me and stopped by. Guess what I was wearing? Yep, of course, my worst fear had come upon me! They saw me wearing shorts and a tank top outside. I cringed when I saw them pull up. I immediately felt naked and ashamed! Was this Holy Spirit telling me I was doing something wrong? Well, I honestly wasn't sure. The woman—dressed all totally covered from head to toe on this super-hot summer day—walked over to me. As I was standing next to the lawnmower, sweating and feeling naked, she began to share about … *the Proverbs 31 woman.* Yep—she went there! I was cringing inside! I was so mad at her, I wanted to unleash some hate speech on her! But I didn't.

Feeling totally degraded and condemned after it was over, I decided that from then on, I should be aware of who was watching me, and I should change for them. I was hoping to have a friendship with these neighbors. I started trying to find longer shorts (which at that time was almost impossible). And I tried to find more modest, shoulder-covering shirts, hoping to gain at least some approval from this religious woman. Well, it honestly didn't seem to make a difference. She always seemed very unhappy and bitter toward me no matter what I was wearing. I'm sure it would have pleased her if I had joined her denomination, burned my pagan clothes, and began to wear the religious costumes they all wore.

(Can you picture this? There I am, standing in my front yard, wearing my short shorts and tank top, being lectured by a woman in a long dress, a covering on her head, and a triple covering over her breast area. I can laugh super hard about this now, but it was not funny at the time. This wasn't neighborly love. I was being bullied by this bitter religious woman.)

The sad thing is that this woman's only focus was on how I looked. I really don't think everyone in that denomination would have treated me like that.

Her husband certainly didn't treat my husband in a preachy and condemning way. But it can be hard not to put them all in a box together because of how she represented them.

The Scripture clearly says God is looking at our hearts. First Samuel 16:7 plainly says, "For the LORD does not see as man sees; for man looks at the outward appearance, but the LORD looks at the heart" (emphasis added). We need to get this straight, and the foundation needs to be taught correctly to new believers. Once we get that squared away, we have established a strong foundation on which to build our relationship with God. When we get our hearts right, the rest will naturally develop. As we are discipled CORRECTLY, we begin to live out our new nature being born again.

We also had some other neighbors who would stop by regularly during this time. They were down to earth as much as you could get, chewing tobacco—both the husband and wife—and cussing up a storm. F-bombs were just part of the husband's vocabulary. They were in constant strife with each other and finally separated.

BUT THEN ... one day out of the blue, they showed back up at our place, hardly recognizable. They even walked differently. No more chewing tobacco or drinking. No more cussing. And they were back together. All they talked about was Jesus, how they had become born again, and how they were changed. Well, I could definitely see the outward change in them. Oh boy! The wife was wearing a long dress and had her hair pulled back. It wasn't the Mennonite denomination they had joined, but a different one that also required a dress code.

It wasn't long after this that the man told us he was now the pastor at a small church in the area. Shazam! All of a sudden, he was ready to minister as a pastor. Well, I gotta give him credit for the passion he had. But the saddest part of this whole story is that he and his wife were never FIRST discipled before they became shepherds of a flock of sheep. They never received the foundational truths about their new identity and what happened to them in their spirit when they became born again. To this day, I think of them and wonder how long they lasted trying to keep up with this performance!

I have wondered if religious traditions of man immediately came and stole their freedom in Christ. It seemed like they never even had a chance to build a personal relationship with Jesus based on their new identity. These people wanted to be accepted by this church-going group so badly that they were willing to conform to the group's image before being transformed by renewing their minds.

How this reminds me of my own Salvation transition! I was raised around people with very little morals and followed that path throughout my high school years. Then I got saved and quickly jumped off that path and straight to another one! Now my only influencers were people who were all about outward appearances and acting the part of a holy person.

I didn't realize it right away, but I had jumped onto a merry-go-round by being discipled at that particular Bible college! I went from one ditch to the other—from the *world* to *religion*. Merry-go-round jumping ... now that's definitely dangerous!

The new friends at college were more concerned about how we looked and acted than they were about our heart issues. I was stuck on this legalistic externally-focused merry-go-round because of its hold on me, and it took years to get off. For example, if you ask my husband, he will tell you that I felt so guilty if I ever left the house without *tracts* (small pamphlets of religious materials) in my purse. It irritated me, and I started to condemn myself and act mad at everyone because I was mad. I was mad at myself!

I had allowed myself to become so deeply rooted in man's religious traditions by following the poor examples of Christ-like influences in my life. I stayed on that legalistic religious merry-go-round for so long that I helped cause our family to be stuck on it too! I became ugly to some of my family members, and instead of drawing them TO CHRIST, I ran them off! It hurts my heart to think about it! I was so messed up, and messed up my husband and kids too!

Even though I was so defensive and protective of this denomination for twenty years, the whole time, I had a battle going on inside me. I wasn't clear as to what this battle was, but now I know **I was in an identity battle**—*I didn't know who I was IN Christ.*

I honestly had a personal relationship with Jesus. But because of how I was taught, it was a limited relationship with other things added to it. I filtered my relationship with Jesus through everything I learned. Still, unfortunately, these were man-made rules that were added to my relationship with Jesus. Whole parts of the Bible were not even taught. I became more performance-based (legalistic and religious) in my relationship with Jesus in so many ways. I constantly tried to please God and spiritual leaders with my words and works rather than living from a heart of faith and love.

As I look back, it seems like man-made religion was literally following me around for much of my life. After David and I stopped going to that type of denominational church a few years later, we got deeply involved in yet another denomination, complete with it's own set of *man-made religious rules.*

We were so hungry to have spiritual parents take us under their wing and train us to be a good and proper Christian family. It makes me laugh now how I tried so hard to fit in yet still felt like I was never enough, never doing it right. At first, I made the pastor's wife my role model for what a Christian wife, mother, and minister should be like. It was a real struggle to conform to her image. I battled the *real me* and stuffed Dana down so deep that it has taken years for *the real Dana* to come back out.

We actually became youth pastors at this church for five years. We were young, had teens ourselves, and were very energetic, and we were on fire for God. Soon, the battle to conform to this group's acceptable image was rubbing hard against what was in our hearts as believers. We were so fired up to reach unchurched kids, but we lived in a town with very few unchurched people—there was a church on almost every corner. Every time we had an event to reach unchurched and unsaved teens, it seemed like a huge success. However, it wasn't long until we began to see that those showing up were teens or members of other churches in town. Basically, we all just attended and supported each other's youth rallies and events. Very few newcomers came. Our heart for the unchurched was still there—David and I had a heart for who might be considered "the dirty kids." I'm sure we were drawn to them because we used to be one. We weren't intimidated by them like some sheltered Christians who might not be able to relate to these kids.

We started a bus ministry and began to go into the hills of Arkansas to pick up these backwoods, unwanted kids and bring them to church. We absolutely loved them so much. We could relate to their home life and what their parents were dealing with. Of course, when you bring *misfit* kids into your group, you also bring in their personalities, dysfunctions, and bad habits. Soon enough, David and I were confronted by the leaders about these kids' actions. The real hard kicker was this: One day, they asked us to start finding kids from other backgrounds—other than the *misfits*—to bring to the youth group. The leaders wanted us to focus on bringing kids whose parents would also come and contribute financially to the church. On top of that, we were scolded for unknowingly allowing these teens to smoke outside the youth building and do whatever the leader's imaginations thought we were allowing them to do.

This was the beginning of the end for David and me at this church. We really had a hard time with it—could not even wrap our heads around what we had just heard. Now, I know I am writing this from our vantage point. I also admit, we copped a bad attitude. We were finally fed up with man-made religion, so we did not make it easy on these leaders.

By this time, David and I realized our own kids were being affected by the surrounding religious atmosphere in this church and the Christian school they attended there. We felt like our children were more damaged by the religious people there than they were affected by the *dirty kids* we brought in. We knew we needed to get all of us out of there. If this is how the church leaders wanted their church, we knew it was no longer the place for us. The Lord had actually dealt with us to leave on our own about a year prior, but we didn't, for reasons I won't share right now.

Well, it didn't end well for them or us. It went south pretty quickly when lies were told about us, and we were wrongly accused and confronted. Again, I admit we weren't perfect. I admit we should have left when we had the prompting to do so a year before, so we take responsibility for our part in this bad ending. The sad thing is that we were hurt, the teens who no longer had a youth group were hurt, and the church leaders were hurt—all because of nasty man-made religious thinking and acting. They thought they were walking in love when actually religion, legalism, condemnation, and shame were running the show.

They didn't want us to leave after we were asked to step down as youth leaders. They hoped we would stay at the church and receive correction from them, get our act together, and start acting like them. They must have been out of their minds if they seriously thought we would stay there a minute longer and continue to expose our children to the religious condemnation and legalism running the place. They didn't see it, but it doesn't mean it wasn't there. It took years for all of us to heal from this situation. I know most of you readers have experienced something like this.

Growing Up

Until we all come into the unity of the faith and of the knowledge of the Son of God, into a complete man, to the measure of the stature of the fullness of Christ, so we may no longer be children, tossed here and there by waves and carried about with every wind of doctrine by the trickery of men, by craftiness with deceitful scheming. But, speaking the truth in love, we may grow up in all things into Him, who is the head, Christ Himself (Ephesians 4:13–15 MEV).

After getting married and church-hopping a few times, I began allowing myself to listen to other preachers from a different "*bubble*." I finally found some truths I had never heard before. These teachings lined up with the Bible and answered the many questions I had but could never get answered. The Bible started to make sense to me and no longer sounded like God was confused. It seemed like every church my husband and I went to had revelation different than the other churches we visited. Some fed us one thing, and another fed us another thing.

I remember the very first time I ever heard something *deep* and *meaty* being preached. I wasn't quite ready to digest what I was hearing. I remember *choking on it*. It took a few more years of growth and mind renewal before I was able to digest and absorb deeper, spiritual truths of the Bible, most of which I had not heard before. I finally realized there are more than just a couple of great truths in the Bible, and I wanted to find out and *gobble up* every great truth I had never been spiritually fed before.

> Brothers, I could not speak to you as to spiritual men, but as to worldly, even as to babes in Christ. I have fed you with milk and not with solid food. For to this day, you were not able to endure it. Nor are you able now (1 Corinthians 3:1–2 MEV).

Attending a church where they <u>only</u> preach and teach a couple things, like forgiveness of sin and Christian conduct, is like eating the same thing every day, over and over. Yes, definitely, the forgiveness of sin through the redeeming work of Jesus should be the first meal received and digested. But after eating that several times? When do the *next courses* ever get introduced? When do we learn how to grow and progress further in our lives by allowing Christ to live through us? And I don't mean learn how to modify our behavior! When do we hear about being redeemed from the *Curse of the Law*? When do we learn how we are supposed to be living in the Blessing of the Lord because Jesus restored and gave the blessed life back to us? Aren't these churches noticing how the same people are going forward each week *re-committing* their lives to God because that's all they are hearing? Didn't they notice me and others running to the altar each week and think maybe something was wrong with that?

When do we actually learn to live in victory over fleshly habits and bad circumstances that happen to us so we can move forward and get past them? Does God really want us to only experience full victory *when* we get to Heaven? That doesn't really line up with Love, does it?

As I grew, I discovered that I desired and craved to hear more than only about sin. I just didn't know there was anything else to hear. (This made me mad, later, when I found out there really was more to Christianity.) Now I know that being sin-focused, Law-focused, and behavior-modification-focused are not New Testament principles at all! Unlike the Old Testament times, when man had no option to have a personal relationship with God or live with His Spirit inside them, the New Testament is about a restored relationship with God through Jesus. Mankind was separated from being able to <u>personally</u> commune with Him before the sacrifice of Jesus. The sacrifice of Jesus broke down the wall between God and man. Before Jesus, man could only go through the priests (man) to hear from God. Now, because of what Jesus did for us, we can go straight to the Father and communicate and be led by Him ourselves (Hebrews 4:16).

For the first twenty years of my Christian walk, I only heard the teachings from one certain circle of denominations. Because of that, I felt like the idea of victorious Christian living was basically a gamble. I was not taught anything about being able to live in the Kingdom of God *here on Earth*. I was taught that we do not have authority over the devil and that miracles and acts of the Holy Spirit have stopped among the believers. Based on that, I never understood why Jesus told the disciples to go *make disciples* if they weren't supposed to teach others what they knew and did themselves.

HELLO?? <u>Aren't we supposed to be *followers of Christ*</u>? Do we just throw out and ignore the Scriptures that talk about authority, power, and spiritual weapons <u>given to us to walk in the victory Jesus gave us</u>? No, but instead, we can believe these Scriptures are for us, for this time, and we can use them daily!

> Yet in all these things <u>we are more than conquerors</u> through Him who loved us (Romans 8:37; emphasis added).

> Because you are strong, and the word of God abides in you, And <u>you have overcome the wicked one</u> (1 John 2:14; emphasis added).

> You are of God, little children, and <u>have overcome them</u>, be-
> cause He who is in you is greater than he who is in the world
> (1 John 4:4; emphasis added).

For most of us, there was never any point in our Christian life when we were given the opportunity to hear, *through the pulpit*, Biblical truths that would really help us in life. If we don't hear, then how will we believe? That's why it's so important we get into God's Word and read it and hear it ourselves. If we do, we will see these truths and Scriptures for ourselves and have the opportunity to believe them and live them out.

Thankfully, this journey caused me to dig into God's Word myself and get Biblical answers to my hundreds of questions. I thank the Lord that He heard my prayers and led my path to intersect with other Christians who could give me some answers from the Bible, as well. Instead of just believing teachings that came from man's traditions and experiences, I found Scriptures that said differently.

> And you shall know the truth, and the truth shall make you
> free. ... Therefore, if the Son makes you free, you shall be free
> indeed (John 8:32, 36).

I am so thankful I stopped *feeling* like I was just an old sinner saved by grace who still had to rededicate their life to God every time there was an altar call. I remember how hard it was for me to stop feeling condemned if I didn't have a stack of tracts in my purse at all times, ready to leave with a waitress or on a street bench. I am so thankful God has opened my eyes to legalism. I am thankful that I no longer feel I have to perform religious acts just because everyone else is.

I choose to live my life AS A WITNESS. I choose to come boldly to the throne of grace for help every day and be led every day by God's Spirit inside me. I choose to live my life without the condemnation of man and the enemy.

It was a good day when I started to believe God's Word over man's traditions and got off that merry-go-round!

Changing What I Heard—Getting out of La-La-Land

My husband and I were involved in a church in Branson, Missouri, for twelve years before we left the area. We liked to go whenever the doors were open. Did people wonder if we were caught in a religious trap or think we were weird for going so much—especially when we used to drive an hour each way to go to church? Maybe. Can we not even dedicate a few hours from our 168-hour week to worship, be discipled, and focus ONLY on God? My husband and I value Him enough to do that.

We were starved spiritually for so many years before! So when we finally found a solid Bible-teaching church, it seemed like we were eating from a smorgasbord of the great food we had never tasted before! The teachings of God's Word fed us like we had never imagined. For us, going to church two to three times a week was not a religious act. It was a matter of life and death because of all the junk we were dealing with in our lives! This was our pain-med—our go-to drug of choice, so to speak. Except, faithfully adding this to our lives saved our minds and lives!

In 2017, I was able to re-do my Bible college experience. This time, with my husband, at Charis Bible College in Woodland Park, Colorado. What a completely different Christian discipling and Bible teaching experience! This three-year journey took us to a whole new level in how we see Christianity and live the Christian life. I am so thankful we took the leap of faith and left our new home and location near our family and exchanged it for the best thing we've ever done as a married couple.

Now, back in Southern California, David and I are involved in a church that believes being pro-active in society is part of the Church's role in fulfilling the Great Commission given to us by Jesus. The leaders of this church are so bold as to even say from the pulpit, "We will not tolerate religion [*man-made religion*] in this church!" These are things very important to us. We had this on our priority list when looking for our new church here in California. When we heard this, we jumped in with both feet, joined a service team, became connect group leaders, and are doing our part to help spread the Gospel of Jesus Christ in our areas of influence.

Have I come full circle? Let's say that I'm at least the closest I've ever been [smiles]. Have we found the PERFECT church? Not at all, and I have learned that I should never limit God by saying, "This is it! I've finally found the group of believers who is the most *right-on* scripturally and 100% religion-free." We are *all* still growing.

Through different denominations and Christian circles, the steps I've taken in my Christian walk have brought me from revelation to new revelation. I'm thankful I'm not still stuck in one church-going denomination, feeling like I would be a traitor if I attended somewhere else or listened to a different teacher. I live my Christian life based on God's Spirit and God's Word leading me, not a religious organization or specific circle of people influencing me. How freeing!

Please note: I don't share this to hurt any particular group of church-goers. This is only my personal church-going journey. The whole point is that we each have a responsibility for our own actions and revelation. We each need to evaluate our own motives and reasons why we are doing what we are doing. We should think about whether God put it in our hearts. Or, did man put a tradition in front of us, *heavily suggesting* that these actions came from God to us <u>through them</u>? I hope some eyes are opening. ***Honoring God and His leadings should always trump honoring man's ideas and leadings.***

If you have had negative church-going experiences like I have shared, I encourage you not to quit going to church altogether. I'm thankful my husband and I could recognize that the failures of people were not failures of God toward us. We never stopped going to church.

The more I renew my mind by reading and studying the Word of God for myself, the more I see how <u>I had previously established my identity with whichever Christian group I was involved in</u>. I was only modifying my behavior and thoughts to what they said and did. I was only IMITATING what I saw other Christians doing—even as an adult—in hopes of gaining their approval and acceptance. I was not thinking for myself—thus, I lived for years in a man-made religious La-La-Land. I thank God my eyes were opened to see the man-made traditions infecting both the Body of Christ and me.

STOP THE SPIN!

Man-made religion causes you to ACT (to perform). Relationship empowers you to BE.

With the Lord's help, we can stop acting to impress man. We can be totally free. We can choose and live out the intimate personal relationship we have with our Heavenly Father, Jesus our Lord, and His Holy Spirit inside of us. We can live from our hearts! We can live by the revelation of who we are IN CHRIST and the relationship that gave us with God. It is definitely a lot more fulfilling and rewarding to go to church on purpose, serve at church on purpose, and feed on God's Word on purpose.

When I began genuinely believing everything in His Word, I also began to recognize religious traditions made by man. I was set free from the legalistic merry-go-round I rode for many years.

I went from spinning in religion to winning in my relationship with Jesus, and you can, too!

Religious & Church-Going

Let's examine the components of *Religious & Church-Going Merry-Go-Rounds*:

- ❖ <u>The Center Post</u>: The lie that keeps this merry-go-round spinning is believing that man-made religious rules and traditions really come from God. It is cemented in fear of believing and doing something different.

- ❖ <u>The Base</u>: The platform that supports this ride is living your Christian life the same as others, robotically, never seeking God and His Word for yourself. Its nature is outward changes that are not born from the heart.

- ❖ <u>The Decorative Fixtures and Handlebars</u>: The approval and acceptance from other Christian church-goers are the appealing fixtures and handlebars that tempt us to hold on and keep spinning.

- ❖ <u>The End Result</u>: After the initial thrill of approval from others, the end result finds one with no personal identity IN CHRIST; stuck, not going forward into God's plan for you as an individual.

Part Two: Giving Honor to Whom Honor Is Due

At this point, I feel it would be a good place to give honor to a pastor we had in 1988. This denominational pastor, in my opinion, got off the familiar, religious merry-go-round. He did something he had never done before and risked persecution. This pastor came out of his rigid denominational box (the same box I was in for years). He actually became open to doing something he saw in the Word of God but didn't understand himself. He humbled himself and showed me that he valued the Word of God more than the traditions he was familiar with from his Biblical training.

When David and I had our third child, Cassie Jo, she was basically born with a death sentence due to a health issue. (I will share it in detail later in chapter six.) When she was eight months old, she was scheduled to go for another surgery. We were going to this denominational church at the time. One day, during my regular Bible reading and praying time, I was reading in the book of James. I had read James 5:13–18 (about meeting specific needs) many times. On this day, verses 13–16 seemed to catch my attention.

I know this is weird, but I had to resist feeling guilty for even being open to studying the subject of healing! Healing is something very specific in the Bible that Jesus talked about over and over, and I felt like I couldn't *go there*!! I was determined not to lose my daughter through this health issue. I was so determined that I was willing to be like the Canaanite woman who came to Jesus and bugged Him until she got what she asked Him for.

READ IT!
Matthew 15:21-28
The Story of the Canaanite Woman

I asked my husband about the passage of Scripture in James. At the time, he didn't have clear answers either, but he and I both agreed that God put it in there for us to do. He said we should ask our pastor about it, so we built up the courage and asked him if he would come over and answer some questions we had. He and his wife graciously came over to our house to visit with us.

> Is anyone among you suffering? Let him pray. Is anyone cheer-ful? Let him sing psalms. Is anyone among you sick? <u>Let him call for the elders of the church, and let them pray over him, anointing him with oil in the name of the Lord. And the prayer of faith will save the sick, and the Lord will raise him up.</u> And if he has committed sins, he will be forgiven. Confess your trespasses to one another, and pray for one another, that you may be healed. The effective, fervent prayer of a righteous man avails much (James 5:13–16; emphasis added).

We asked him about this passage. Our pastor didn't get defensive or bow up. He didn't fear it either, that I could tell. He said, "I'm honestly not really sure what this passage means, but I do know that it is something the Bible says to do. I have never done this before, but I don't see why we can't do it. I will get the elders from our church together, and we will come and do this before your daughter has her surgery."

Our pastor postponed doing this a couple of times. I found out why later: he couldn't get the elders of the church to come with him and do it! The day I was to leave and take my daughter back down to Little Rock to the Arkansas Children's Hospital for the surgery, he and his wife showed up at our house. (David was a full-time student at a Christian university at the time and was away at class.)

Pastor apologized that the elders were not with him. He seemed a little em-barrassed because he knew I was expecting the whole group. I thought it was strange and actually had my feelings hurt a little bit. Because the elders did not show up, the devil tried to discourage me and my faith regarding doing what this passage says. *I mean, why wouldn't they come? Were we doing something wrong? Does Jesus need to PHYSICALLY come back here to lay hands on people? Aren't we His hands?*

Our pastor and his wife boldly prayed. They admitted to God that they really didn't understand this passage but were doing it in faith. They believed they were being obedient to His Word and the request of my husband and me.

(Think about this: Suppose I never spent personal time in the Bible? I would have never come across James 5! I would have never asked about it! And maybe this would have never happened! I am so thankful I was in the Word that day!)

They anointed our baby with oil, laid their hands on her, prayed for healing to take place, and for God to protect her from any infections. I was so touched. It gave me hope. This was my first experience praying and believing God for the healing of one of our children. ***Thank God our pastor and his wife chose to believe this and act on it.*** I CERTAINLY BELIEVED IT!! Why shouldn't we? It's something the Bible tells us to do!

This pastor was a gem. Here is another out-of-the-traditional-box thing he did for us because he believed he was supposed to do it. The first Sunday we went back to church after our daughter was born was hard. It was the first weekend I couldn't be at the hospital with her because we didn't have money for me to go. Our car had four bald tires. We had two little girls at home, and I wasn't working anymore. David was in school full time, so he could only work part-time. While sitting in church, all I could do was think about how I was ever going to be able to get back down to Little Rock, four hours away, to see our baby. My heart was hurting so badly, and I asked God for help.

God used our pastor to do something that, at that time, I personally had never seen done before in a church. After the service, but before he dismissed everyone, he asked the people to give an offering to our family. *(I had seen several pastors ask for offerings after service before, but it was always for the missionary or evangelist who was visiting.)* That small church took up an offering and gave us $1,200! Over thirty-three years ago, that was a lot of money to me back then!

Our pastor heard and obeyed God, even though it might have made him uncomfortable, especially since I'm pretty sure he didn't get *pre-authorized* permission from the elders. He had to believe what he heard in his heart and act on it. He had to trust the leading of the God's Spirit inside of him.

I put the money in an envelope and treasured what the Lord had done for us. We bought new tires for the car, and then the rest of the money was spread out over the next fifteen weekends. That weekend was the only weekend I ever missed getting to go visit our baby. The money lasted me exactly four months until she was released to come home from the hospital. I would go to Little Rock for two to three days and then back home to be with my husband and our other two daughters. Every weekend, I always had the money for gas and food **because our pastor did something off the normal spin.**

I'm still thankful! How life-changing would it be, for them and for others, if all pastors in the Body of Christ would be willing to be led BY GOD and not by a denominational association? That is TRUE LOVE FOR THE SHEEP. **He stepped off the denominational merry-go-round and helped influence my trust in God!**

FIVE

SOMEONE ELSE'S MERRY-GO-ROUND

Part One: Recognizing It

HAS YOUR HEART ever gone out to someone so much that you begin to take it upon yourself to fix their life, and before you know it, you are *all caught up?* Thinking back over my life and everything I have been involved in, I can really see where I got *caught up* in the spin of other people's lives when the Lord never led me to. The temptation to want to help people and *care* for them, way past the leading of the Lord, was a big one for me.

From PTA and Chamber of Commerce to county fairs, community events, countless church projects, and many other volunteer groups, I've had plenty of opportunities to take other people's problems home with me rather than casting them onto the Lord. This is not even counting the times I've spent in hospitals listening to what people were going through and trying to fix them.

We all know it's not wrong to want to help people and to care for them—those desires come from the love of God in our hearts. Yet, it's important to recognize—by the leading of the Holy Spirit on the inside of us—our part in outside situations going on in other's lives. Jesus clarified these parts for us in the following verse. He shows us how there are people who pray for laborers, and then there are laborers—and neither are the *Lord of the Harvest*:

> But when He saw the crowds, He was moved with compassion for them, because they fainted and were scattered, like sheep without a shepherd. Then He said to His disciples, "The harvest truly is plentiful, but the laborers are few. Therefore, pray to the Lord of the harvest, that He will send out laborers into His harvest" (Matthew 9:36–38 MEV).

Like Jesus, being *moved with compassion* means we do something, but that "doing something" may not always be what we think it should be. It is important we get our "doings" from the "Lord of the Harvest"—Jesus—by Holy Spirit. Sometimes, when our heart is moved for someone we see in town or on the side of the road, He will lead us to simply pray a faith-filled prayer from a heart of love, asking God to send the right person (laborer) across their path. And then other times, He will grace us in such a way that we will know that WE are their laborer, and we will know exactly what to do.

In both cases, we lean on the Lord of the Harvest, not taking any care, as we follow His leadings. However, where I've messed up, and where many other Christians have messed up, is that I was unknowingly acting **as** "Lord of the Harvest." I was taking their problem on as if I was their savior, healer, caretaker, joy and peace giver, etc. Doing this puts a burden on us that we are not built to carry.

READ IT!
Philippians 4:6 & 1 Peter 5:7
Giving it to God

Jesus is the only Lord of the Harvest. He is the only Savior and the only Healer. Jesus is the only One who can truly take every care from every one of us, once and for all, and actually do something about it that lasts. Yes, He uses us to help each other and others, but all the help comes *from* Him and *by* Him, and this help always leads people TO Him.

When we step outside of His leadings to "help" someone, we get outside of His strength, grace, and ability. It can be easy to do this when we see other people hurting because it seems too hard to resist the desire to take on the care of what they are dealing with. Even just listening to someone you don't know while at the grocery store can weigh you down if you let it. In previous years, there were many times I was already spinning on a couple of my own merry-go-rounds. I was very aware that I could not afford to take a ride on someone else's, so most of that time, I kept my distance and avoided a lot of close conversations with people.

Too often, in our effort to help, we end up jumping on someone's merry-go-round by letting their problems in. On someone else's merry-go-round, you feel what they are feeling, react how they are reacting, respond how they are responding. And, you have the same outcome they are having—only to do it all over again and never reach a real destination of victory. That which is happening in their life is now controlling yours. What you set out to do—help them—is not what you ended up doing.

If you allow people to unload on you every time they see you and use you as their sounding board, it will eventually pull you right into the middle of it. You will be tempted to "jump on their bandwagon" and let everyone else know what's going on too. It will appear that you have a real *reason* to be involved when, in reality, you don't. Over time, it will become a heavy load for you. Your emotions will get stirred up, and frustration will arise. For what? Do you have that much time and energy to waste? OUCH!

Here is an example of how I was off someone else's merry-go-round and then got back on. I dropped my guard and got distracted long enough to let the enemy score a point—so to speak. (It was a good wake-up call to me, and with God's help, I won't let someone else's merry-go-round become my merry-go-round ever again.)

Remember the story I told earlier in chapter three when the feelings of dread suddenly came over me just as David was leaving town? And then right after he left, we got a phone call about our daughter? (It was in the section about fear.) Well, she was back in jail. Let me tell you the rest of it.

A couple days after I had received the victory over all the dread, fear, and depression that I had allowed to come on me through that time, I asked the Lord why it seemed to have happened so fast, like it caught me off guard. He *spoke to my heart,* and I knew it was due to me not immediately turning to Him for help, wisdom, and peace. Instead, I had taken the care of it on myself and all the emotions that came with the situation. He gave me a visual revelation of what happened. This is what I heard and saw:

> *I saw myself on a clear glass elevator and below the ground floor. I saw the dark shaft the elevator was in. I saw the sad, depressed look on my face. The elevator was slowly going down, down, down.*

> *Above me were the ground floor and light. Green plants, color, and life were everywhere. Life is LOVE, Who is God. I just looked up at it with a sad face. I asked the Lord how I got down there, below ground level, when just the other day, I was at a higher level of joy and faith and expectation like I've never been before.*

> *He said that I allowed the enemy to "push my emotional/hormonal down button," and it was my choice to either keep riding down, or get ahold of myself and push the "up" button. He said the tempter (the enemy) tried to get me through my emotions, which triggered a huge hormonal upset and actually tested my faith in God. It tested me as to whether I would let all that junk get into my heart and jump on that merry-go-round full force, or would I resist those*

fleshly emotional temptations and fight to get back my joy and strength and walk by love and faith again.

I knew, of course, my Father was right. He told me I should never have gotten involved, even a little bit, with all the drama back and forth between my daughter and son-in-law. They were both in different states and locked up in county jails at the time. I told Him that I was surprised I went "down" so fast. He then reminded me of everything I learned previously in my life and had just put in this book. (Yikes!! Ouch!!)

He said now I needed to practice what I have been preaching! He reminded me about not letting the enemy steal my joy, staying thankful, and praising Him. He reminded me about keeping my eyes only on Him, using His Word to combat the enemy's temptations the same way Jesus did, and using Love—Who is God. He said I got away from His love and into my "heady—natural" kind of love, all based on emotions and not on what HE/LOVE is. The Lord also said that I pushed aside the warnings I had from Him about staying out of it and about ignoring my daughter's reaching out to me until things had settled down. He said He will tell me the next time when it is right to reach out to her and that at that time, I should listen to Him. He said He is always trying to protect me from any detours that could take me away from His plan for me, but I interfered with His help by getting involved anyway.

I gratefully received the correction from my good Father and intentionally and purposefully pressed through the *blah feelings* I had. I made myself do something productive to get my mind off it all. Thankfully, I didn't beat myself up and let condemnation come in. Thankfully, I took my own advice and did what the Lord said, and my mind cleared up. Joy and strength came back, but it wasn't without some effort. *I plan to pay attention* better and obey His

Word the next time these temptations come. I plan to recognize any *heaviness* coming on me.

My faith was definitely tested through this situation where the enemy tempted my flesh. When my emotions were going haywire, I kept checking to see if it was getting into my heart. I knew the enemy wanted all that junk to get into my heart, and I'm sure he would have been thrilled if it had caused me to collapse beyond repair. Well, thank God, I got a grip on it and kept it from getting into my heart. I began to look to Love, Who is God. I asked *Love* to kick in.

The joy of the Lord is too precious to be let go of so easily. It didn't leave me. **I let it go**. I stopped fellowshipping with the One Who gives me strength! I went off and did my own thing without Him, which cost me greatly. It was another spiritual growth experience for me. It was another opportunity for me to learn how to walk in love, hope, forgiveness, and thanksgiving and walk right through the dark valley.

I got away from handling this situation through Love, God. The whole of 1 Corinthians 13 tells us what *love* is. Here is a portion:

> Love suffers long *and* is kind; love does not envy; love does not parade itself, is not puffed up; does not behave rudely, does not seek its own, is not provoked, thinks no evil; does not rejoice in iniquity, but rejoices in the truth; bears all things, believes all things, hopes all things, endures all things. Love never fails (1 Corinthians 13:4–8).

So, if there is any failure going on, it will be because we go at it alone, are not casting the care of it on to the Lord, and taking on the responsibility of helping someone without God's help.

Just because someone chooses to stay on their merry-go-round (and possibly even believe it is what God wants for them) doesn't mean you have to also believe that for them. Whether the person created the hardship or someone created it for them is not the issue. It is still theirs, and they can start the process to <u>get off the merry-go-round and on with life</u> whenever they decide they have had enough of it. These things are more in our own control than many have realized.

STOP THE SPIN!

I'm learning more and more that if I truly love myself and people the way God loves me, I will not handle these situations the same way the world handles them. I will not deal with them in carnal—fleshly—emotional love, but I will deal with them through the help of God's love and peace, which is spiritual. That stops the spin and starts the win!

You could spend years of your life thinking that just because they are your friend (spouse, child, family member, etc.), you are supposed to ride the merry-go-rounds of their lives with them. That is wrong thinking. It will take you around and around with them. We can encourage someone we care about and pray for them without carrying what they carry, even if we live in the same house as they do. Compassion and love are musts, but that doesn't mean you put yourself into park, neutral, circling, or reverse on their behalf. This is not selfishness on your part. This is wisdom. What did Jesus have to say when *He* was moved by other people's issues?

> And Jesus, when He came out, saw a great multitude and **was moved with compassion for them**, because they were like sheep not having a shepherd. **So He began to teach them many things** (Mark 6:34; emphasis added).

Just like Jesus demonstrated, the correct way to respond to people around us who are going through hard times is to direct them to the Word of God. It is <u>not</u> to jump into the problem with them, magnifying the emotion of it all. **If we meet them on an emotional level, we will be reinforcing their emotions.**

We all know emotions come and go minute by minute. So, if we really want to help them, we will stay clear of the emotional side and direct them to what will specifically help with answers in God's Word. I learned I must help pull them up and bring them up to the Word's level. *If they don't want to get their answer through God's Word, they really don't want relief from the pain of their situation.* We all need to come to a place within ourselves where we will do what's right no matter how we feel. If someone doesn't want the truth of God's Word, even you can't help them.

For example, suppose someone comes to you for help and prayer because they are in an adulterous relationship and are confused about what they should do. In that case, you can direct the person to what the Word of God says. Suppose they choose to resist the truth about adultery and continue being led by their feelings for this other (outside) person. In that case, you cannot help them any further, so stop trying. They have now teamed up with the enemy of division and destruction and don't care.

Is it possible to remain connected with someone like this yet stay separate from the care of their problem? Yes, but we must stop *talking* about <u>their problem</u> and stop thinking about it. Turn the conversation around to having faith in God and how He can help them as they go through it, constantly directing them in a forward motion TO God. We must never let our emotions out of control, causing us to get sucked into the vacuum that pulls us up onto <u>their</u> merry-go-round. Once on there, the vacuum pressure is harder to pull away from. Just like my story in chapter two about that crazy suction on the Silly Silo at the amusement park!

We can confuse true *love for people* with pity for them—*feeling sorry for them*. If not led by the Spirit of God, we can have a tendency to be drawn toward people *we think* need rescuing, especially if we ourselves are living a life as a victim because of something that happened to us. We are tempted to pity them because we can relate to people going through the same thing we have gone through. This *pity,* which is of the devil, *isn't love* and often enables the person to continue in their problem. It will keep them paralyzed and without hope. Real love for someone will respond to them the way the Bible says and pray for them, staying in faith and expectation that God is working in their life. Instead of being moved on their merry-go-round, you will remain firmly planted on the Word of God for them, and His peace is keeping you still.

> Be anxious for nothing, but in everything, by prayer and supplication with gratitude, make your requests known to God. And the peace of God, which surpasses all understanding, will protect your hearts and minds through Christ Jesus (Philippians 4:6–7 MEV).

What **will help** them is when they are given Biblical answers and can see from our example how they, too, can choose to stop living as a victim and start living as a conqueror. A person with a victim's attitude won't fight at all, or they won't fight *God's way,* to get out of a bad situation. But a conqueror's attitude will **fight the way God instructs them,** so they get out of it. Someone with a victim's attitude can totally change to having a conqueror attitude by *aggressively* declaring in faith God's Word to affect their situation.

If we genuinely LOVE people, we won't allow them to look to us for answers instead of Jesus, hoping we get glory from them. We won't use their situation as a platform for us to practice our preaching. (OUCH!) If we really LOVE people, we will speak the truth to them in LOVE and POINT THEM TO JESUS.

> **Looking unto Jesus**, the author and finisher of our faith (Hebrews 12:2; emphasis added).

I'm training myself to *shake it off* and cast the care of others' problems over on the Lord (1 Peter 5:7). I am also learning to mind my own business while searching my heart to see if the Lord would have me do anything specific for them (1 Thessalonians 4:12). Instead of automatically assuming I'm the person to help them, I usually pray for them. I ask the Lord if I am supposed to do or say anything, and there are times when I am *indeed* the laborer sent for that specific time. It's in those times when the Lord will give us a word of encouragement or some type of help or direction for them, possibly even having us do something for them. **<u>That's how we will stay off someone else's merry-go-round</u>—by only doing what God is leading us to do for them.**

If we are doing things apart from God and His leadings, then it only makes sense that we should not expect to see the real results that only He can give. It doesn't help them one iota if we coddle them, jumping on their *ride* by listening to their situation over and over and over again. God has a better answer for them than that!

> Confess your faults to one another and pray for one another, **that you may be healed**. The effective, fervent prayer of a righteous man accomplishes much (James 5:16 MEV; emphasis added).

There was one specific circumstance when I allowed someone to open up to me and share what was on their heart regarding their marital problems. I listened until I realized it was going *nowhere*. I then gave this person some Biblical advice about how to handle it. To make a long story short, I ended up allowing this person to confide in me more times than I should have. I asked if the Biblical instructions I previously gave them had been applied each time. Each time, there was an excuse as to why they weren't. Each time, I was told, "I am doing my part. They just aren't doing theirs."

Well, I'm sure you can tell just by what I'm saying that this person was not doing their part. They refused to value and take the instruction I gave them. They did not value my time, and they didn't want to obey God's Word given to them. *I recognized* that this person was not open to God's way of doing things, so God could not reveal Himself to them in the situation or help them.

They may be still on that merry-go-round because of their own unwillingness to change.

I got off their merry-go-round.

Most people don't like to go on rides alone, and having someone riding with them is comforting. It allows them to not face the reality of what they are doing if someone else is doing it with them. For this reason, they may always have an open invitation to you. If your flesh is weak and *desires* to feel needed by someone with issues, you will **accept** the invitation. That should be a huge flashing sign reading, "CAUTION!! Merry-Go-Round Ahead!!!"

Someone Else's

Let's examine the components of *Someone Else's Merry-Go-Round*:

- ❖ The Center Post: The unbelief or lie that keeps this merry-go-round spinning is that you believe you are helping them (someone else) by pitying them. In reality, you are actually disabling them from receiving their help from God.

- ❖ The Base: The platform that supports the ride is the pressure you feel or the guilt if you don't take on their burdens (cares).

- ❖ The Decorative Fixtures and Handlebars: Feeling *needed* by them is the appealing fixture and the handlebars that keep you holding on.

❖ <u>The End Result</u>: Although the thrill is that you feel needed, their life is controlling yours, resulting in you missing God's plan for you personally.

Part Two: School Culture Merry-Go-Rounds

God has a personal plan for you, me, and our friends. We are each supposed to be on our own life journey. When we get caught up in the drama life of friends, we will eventually lose focus and get off the path we are personally supposed to be on. If we think about our friends' lives more than our own, we run the risk of completely missing what we were born to do.

> Am I now trying to win the approval of human beings, or of God? Or am I trying to please people? If I were still trying to please people, I would not be a servant of Christ (Galatians 1:10 NIV).

<u>School peer pressure and fear of rejection is a dangerous merry-go-round</u>. It will keep you pleasing people continually your whole life and always going against the conviction in your ***heart***. I've learned how important it is to pick my friends and groups based on nothing except peace in my *heart* and the leading of God's Spirit. Some of the best, faithful friends you'll ever *find* are the ones in the background, not being seen. I found this out when my popular group of friends pretty much abandoned me in high school. My church friends came to my rescue, though! Don't find your worth the same way the world does, based on who they are associated with.

> It is dangerous to be concerned with what others think of you, but if you trust the LORD, you are safe (Proverbs 29:25 GNT).

⟶

100

As I mentioned in chapter four, I was ten years old when my parents separated. My father decided to jump out of his commitment to our little family. My mom was devastated by my dad's rejection, leaving her for another woman. She was forced to raise my two sisters and me on her own. She did the right thing and ran straight to God for help. She got herself and her three daughters into church, and we all got saved—born again. (I remember the day I walked the aisle of our little church and gave my life to Jesus on January 28, 1975.)

Mom gave God an opening into our lives; at the same time, she unintentionally disconnected emotionally from us girls and went into survival mode. She worked long hours to keep bills paid and buy a little bit of food and clothing for us. <u>This was not God's perfect will for my family, but my parents' choices brought this on us</u>. This was **not** God teaching us all something. It happened because of ungodly choices. My mom had a choice to either allow God to help her through it or do things the way the world does and get angry and bitter and lose total control of her life and us girls. If she had not made the right choice, my sisters and I would be living ungodly lives right now and not according to God's will and plan for us. Thank you, Mom!

Let me interject: when parents separate and divorce, it doesn't matter right away if a child is currently connected with a church group or not. Their life has been turned upside down, and they now will begin to look for security in ALL people and things. They need spiritually and emotionally healthy, stable adults with whom they can immediately connect with to help guide them through. Otherwise they will develop a false identity. This false identity will be based on what is happening in their life and not based on how God sees them or what He wants for them. They will most likely find their own people to cling to, even though it wouldn't be God's best plan for them.

They could become the enemy's easy prey to misguide and redirect. The enemy, the adversary, will see that they encounter people and other families who will most definitely let these emotionally hurt and unconnected children into their lives. These people will be on a totally different path than God had planned for the child. They will influence the child to join them on their life journey. The child will most likely be so confused but hungry for emotional comfort. They will attempt to find their security and identity the same way these new people live. This scenario is going on all around us. It's a familiar cycle in most families, as it was in mine.

The enemy made sure the first friends who reached out to me in junior high were kids going through the same thing I was. I was drawn to them because they were very familiar to me. They were hurt, insecure, and basically raising themselves, just like I was. The adults in their lives couldn't even take care of themselves, let alone their own children.

I began to do some illegal things, but at the same time, I hated every minute of it. I craved companionship and acceptance, so I hung around with this group for a couple of years. Because my mother did not give us girls the option of going to church, my eyes finally opened. I would not have admitted it then, but I really did like the breath of fresh air and strength I received each time I went. My eyes opened, and I decided I didn't want to be around these friends anymore.

I asked the Lord for help to break away from them. It wasn't long before the main controlling friend moved away for a short time. I now had a choice to continue doing what I was doing or take the opportunity to choose a different path. I made a choice to get off this merry-go-round of an illegal lifestyle and picked different friends. I was in junior high at this time.

I remember imagining how I really wanted my high school years to be. I watched all the kids involved in school activities and how fun it looked. *In my heart*, I wanted to *achieve something* and not just muddle through and graduate, never accomplishing anything. I was very insecure and socially dysfunctional with adults, but at the same time, I smiled a lot and tried to be friendly to all people. If they spoke to me first, I could smile and say, "Hi," but couldn't really carry on a conversation with them. Sadly, I carried this trait into my adulthood also.

I understand now that being so timid and insecure was actually a result of being *self-centered and self-conscious*. I was always focusing on what *I imagined* people thought of me. Those thoughts are called *vain imaginations. Imagining* is a great ability God gave us and is used to think creatively and on God's things. Oppositely, **_vain imaginations_** are a terrible trap because they are not true.

I forced myself to sit with and talk to _popular girls_ who were active in school and seemed to be from more stable families. Eventually, they let me in. Since I wanted to change bad enough, I knew I had to do something to get involved with them in school. I will leave out most of the details, but I finally decided to become a cheerleader. Ha-ha, _a cheerleader_?! This is a girl who wouldn't even talk to people I didn't know, and now I am supposed to stand up in front of a huge crowd and cheer?! (I had even quit basketball and track because I got so embarrassed anytime someone looked at me!)

I made myself do cheerleading only because our school did not use cheer-leading for competition. I felt I didn't have the talent to compete with others on a sports team, so this seemed like the best option. Besides that, these girls seemed like a lot of fun and maybe wouldn't care so much if I messed up. I tried out, surprisingly made it, and began my journey as a high school cheer-leader. It was awesome to be involved with this new group of friends!

I wasn't the most coordinated girl in the group. So for a long time, I had to make extra effort to do most cheers. Despite that, I was determined; and God helped me stick with it and not quit and run away like my fears wanted me to. I had to take it seriously because I knew this was my only shot at doing something different in high school. I had already decided I didn't want to go back to hanging with my old friends.

My new friends were definitely a better example than the last group. Yet, they were living the life of the typical _popular group_. This became another peer pressure merry-go-round experience for me. I know each friend and their family had their own issues they were dealing with, but I'd say most of them were very _normal_ and active in the community and school in some way. The good thing was that my new friends were all very good students and most of the time gladly helped me with my homework, if you know what I mean.

By my senior year in high school, I had gotten over being _super_ shy, was living the full-blown life of a popular girl, and going steady with the school's star athlete. My friends and this high school lifestyle became my identity. I tried to be friends with everybody. I was prom queen my junior year and head cheerleader for football and wrestling my junior and senior years.

Even with all this going for me, I battled and remained unfulfilled inside my heart. I was torn. I partied with my friends before, during, and after games and then went to church (by force) on Sundays, only to go back to school on Mondays—back into the cycle. ***What a high school merry-go-round!***

At the beginning of this book, I shared a text conversation that took place with one of my daughters. During the conversation, I shared how I decided to get off that merry-go-round and stop playing the wishy-washy Christianity game once and for all. I made this decision on Christmas break my senior year, December 31, 1981.

In the text to my daughter, I shared a tiny bit about the persecution I received for choosing to do that. I came back to school with that decision, and my friends did not understand. They laughed and immediately took it as a joke. Still, later, when they realized I was sticking with it this time, they took it as a personal rejection and stamped me as *"Holier than thou."* I probably would not have *unfriended* them if we had Facebook back then. But I definitely would have stopped *following* them. Well, eventually, they *unfriended* me.

I remember one of the hardest things I had to do to make a statement about my change of direction. Not long into the second semester of my senior year, after that Christmas break, my high school had a secular rock band concert during school hours. I don't recall the group's name or even why the school had them come in. But anyway, I was a little bit nervous about that day because I knew EVERYONE in the whole auditorium would be standing, clapping, and singing to these songs. My heart was screaming, **"DON'T DO IT!"**

My flesh was screaming, "IF YOU DON'T STAND AND CLAP ALONG WITH EVERYONE, YOU WILL BE BLACKBALLED!" (Blackballed means to be excluded socially, ostracized, voted against.[5])

I chose not to stand up one time throughout the whole concert. I sat there feeling very alone, the only one **not** standing up and clapping, except for a couple other people who were deemed *religious*. Surviving that day settled it for me. It strengthened me to humble myself and submit to the leading of the

Holy Spirit. There was no turning back after that event. Now I could never forsake God again because I would totally be seen as a flake! Even though I felt embarrassed, I now cared more for my friends' spiritual salvation instead of caring about what they thought of me, like I used to. I wanted them to know that making a stand for God and what I believed can be done by them, also. Though I really wanted one of them to join me that semester in taking a stand for God, it didn't happen that I know of.

The persecution after that event was hurtful and hard. I even had persecution from teachers. I was still the head cheerleader and involved in school, but I had a new vision and hope for my future. This decision was especially hard on my boyfriend. Now I drove around after work on Friday and Saturday nights, *scooping the loop* all by myself.

People would jump in with me for a couple rounds and then realize I wasn't on the same page as they were anymore. I wasn't laughing at their perverted jokes or stopping at the parties. They soon just got out and got in with someone else. *Hey, I was still a lot of fun!*

One night, someone jumped in the car with me. He had been drinking, so, of course, he was very talkative and emotional. *(People who drink a lot often use intoxication as an opportunity to become open and honest with others. Without it, they don't seem to have the courage to open up and share their heart. Let's just say I might have some experience doing this, ha-ha.)* He started crying. He lived in a Christian home but did the same things I used to do. Like me, he had been partying and living the popular high school life and then going to church on Sunday, acting like a different person.

He said, "Dana, I wish so bad I could do what you are doing, but I'm just not strong enough." I encouraged him and said that if more of us would take a stand, we could make a change around here. He told me he was just not ready yet to take the persecution, and he got out of the car. My heart hurt for him, but I think for myself even more. I decided to stop "scooping the loop" after working at the restaurant each night and just go home. I didn't need to be torturing myself with these tempting situations.

For the next several months, I really delved into God's Word and endeavored to discover His will for my life. I began to only hang out with the friends I had from my little church, even though I felt like I didn't fit in with them, either. I saw these friends as very boring and kind of social nerds. But in truth, they were genuine and safe. The longer I was away from the old crowd, the clearer my vision became regarding the merry-go-round I used to be on. By the time graduation came along, I was so thankful to have made it through. The battle I had just endured of jumping off the merry-go-round *cold-turkey*, and this time *staying off*, had not been easy.

So many times, a young Christian person in school or college begins to get persecuted for being a believer and follower of Jesus, and they flop. They are not grounded. Matthew 13:18–23 talks about the parable of the sower: The one who **received** the Word in the kingdom with joy is also the one who **stumbled** because he had no root. I imagine he was excited and received it as what

READ IT!
Matthew 13:18-23
The Parable of the Sower

he wanted for his life and endured living it for a while. Still, he lost his footing when tribulation and persecution came to him from his friends or other influences. The embarrassment hit, and the pressure was stronger than he was.

Perhaps like I did for years as a young person, many of you have also been to youth rallies, Christian concerts, church camps, and other events. You know, those events were meant to fire up our Christian commitment. But too often, the commitment doesn't last. That is common when the young Christian person mixes with people who have different gods. The god of this world disguises himself as light (2 Corinthians 11:14). If they are not awake and on guard against this, they will not recognize these schemes and detours, taking them away from God, their "first love" (Revelation 2). They will begin to compromise and eventually find themselves living a life opposite of what their *heart* is yearning for—opposite of their *true* identity as a born-again believer in Jesus.

We don't have to be a part of that majority of Christian believers who fall away from their *first love*. We need to think past the little time frame of school, look toward our future, and find God's plan for us as adults, parents, friends, or leaders.

I thank God that I went from spinning to winning in my high school years by getting free from peer pressure! Especially I want to say this to high school and college students: ***If I can get off this merry-go-round, <u>YOU</u> can too!***

School Culture

Let's examine the components of the *School Culture Merry-Go-Round:*

- ❖ <u>The Center Post</u>: The lie that keeps you spinning is believing you will be rejected forever and won't be able to withstand the persecution you might get.

- ❖ <u>The Base</u>: The platform supporting the fearful ride of rejection and persecution is peer pressure to do what everyone else is doing

- ❖ <u>The Decorative Fixtures and Handlebars</u>: The acceptance by friends is the appealing fixture, leaving you holding on tightly, so you don't get a rejection from friends.

❖ <u>The End Result</u>: Holding onto the thrill of acceptance by others will keep you from using this short period of your life to be a witness of God's goodness. By not fully committing to the Lord, you live half in, half out.

Part Three: Work Environment Merry-Go-Rounds

In the work environment, you may have the temptation to ride on several different types of merry-go-rounds. Every person working around you has different life circumstances and drama at home. Most can't wait to get to work to unload everything they are dealing with onto you. The safest and smartest thing for you to do at work is to stay out of other people's drama, or it will become your drama, a seemingly haunting merry-go-round. It will attach itself to you and follow you home every night. It will cause you to come home depleted and drained, so you have to spend your entire evening cleansing yourself from what you have allowed to get **on your mind** and **in your heart** at the workplace. These next verses really bring home what I am talking about:

> Learn to be calm, and to conduct your own business, and to work with your own hands, as we commanded you (1 Thessalonians 4:11 MEV).

> Don't let me hear of your suffering for ... being a busybody and prying into other people's affairs (1 Peter 4:15 TLB).

There is so much junk going around in workplaces, it's crazy! I don't mean everybody is just passing around a cold or virus, either! This is where gossip is exercised, along with griping, complaining, backbiting, jealousy, bullying, and competition, just to name a few. This is where adultery, fornication, and pornography can get started, as well. Greed and "climbing the ladder" at another's expense are most common.

STOP THE SPIN!

It will be tempting to chime into conversations with your opinion and even offer help, but this is when you really need to be led by God as to what you say and do. James 1:13-14 tells us that God does not tempt us, but we are tempted when we are drawn away by our own desires. So, unless you really like the drama, you should avoid getting caught up in it. If you don't, it could cost you your light and witness. You can be comforted by knowing that God's Word says He will make a way of escape for you and won't allow you to be tempted beyond what you are able to bear (1 Corinthians 10:13). For example, He can give you a new job, replace certain people from working around you, or move you to a different department, if needed.

Love your co-workers by staying out of their drama and strife. James 3:16 says, "For where envy and self-seeking exist, confusion and every evil thing are there." Be selective about what conversations you have with them and how much time you spend with them. They may want you to get involved in their issues so badly, but be cautious. This may cause you some persecution but don't fear the persecution.

Fear will keep you riding the merry-go-rounds with them against your heart. Even Jesus was persecuted for how He believed and walked out His life. Don't give in to the pressure of gossip or drama. Those are constants that go around and around and around in the workplace, even Christian workplaces.

Every one of these things requires someone being on a merry-go-round who does not believe in God's goodness and love for them or others. Everyone *exercising* these things also wants someone going through it with them. I can totally relate: I sure don't like to exercise and work out alone because I consider it boring. It is the same with merry-go-rounds.

Caution, though! The more you exercise your flesh with all that *junk,* the more muscular, heavier, and *overweight* it will get! Muscle is heavy. If you exercise your flesh, it will become stronger and overpower your spirit in a minute!! You can go to church every day if you want and read your Bible every day. But if you are joining in with all the corruption at your job, then you might as well forget being able to renew your mind and overcome your flesh. The junk at your job will act as a drain and deplete you from the Word you have put in.

"Do not be deceived: 'Bad company corrupts good morals'" (1 Corinthians 15:33 MEV). If you continue involving yourself, your spirit and *heart's* desires will lose the battle every day. You will be so distracted and not focused on God at all that you could miss the whole reason why He brought you to that job in the first place!

Did you ever think maybe it's not about you? Or maybe there is more to it? Could it be that God sent you, a Christian, to be a light in a dark place for someone else at that job? Could it be that you are there to give someone hope that there really are genuine Christian people out there? *Selah.* ("Selah" means to stop and think about that.)

Staying out of their drama and strife isn't always easy, but it is well worth the peace you will have in your *heart* every day and the faith you will have to pray for them. Our first priority should be to love others the way God loves us.

> A new commandment I give to you, that you love one another; as I have loved you, that you also love one another (John 13:34).

If we get on a co-worker's contagious merry-go-round, we will become critical. And if we begin to criticize them or whoever they are criticizing, then we will never be able to minister God's love to them.

Let no unwholesome word proceed out of your mouth, but only that which is good for building up, that it may give grace to the listeners. And do not grieve the Holy Spirit of God, in whom you are sealed for the day of redemption. Let all bitterness, wrath, anger, outbursts, and blasphemies, with all malice, be taken away from you. And be kind one to another, tenderhearted, forgiving one another, just as God in Christ also forgave you (Ephesians 4:29–32 MEV).

This passage in Ephesians goes on to tell us not to talk filthy or foolish, or joke about crude things, etc. Paul (inspired by God) tells us not to be partakers of these things with other people because we were once darkness, but NOW WE ARE LIGHT in the Lord and walk as children of Light. He states we are *not to have fellowship* with the unfruitful works of darkness. If we love people the way God loves us, we will allow the light of His love to **come out and SHINE! Full SUN! No more partly cloudy days!**

READ IT!
Ephesians 5:1-14
Walk as Children of Light

ON WITH YOUR life

<u>Your workplace is your mission field</u>! Rise to the occasion! One way or another, you will affect the people around you for better or for worse. Consciously be aware of which way you are influencing your co-workers. If you are personally dealing with a situation at home, restrain yourself, and don't bring it to work.

Merry-go-round riders bring their merry-go-round everywhere they go and hope that someone will jump on and ride with them.

Christians: you can avoid these workplace merry-go-rounds. And more than that, *you can change the atmosphere around you—no matter where you are—from one that glorifies darkness to one that is holy, giving honor to our Lord Jesus!*

Let's examine the components of *Work Environment Merry-Go-Rounds:*

Work Environment

❖ <u>The Center Post</u>: The lie that keeps you spinning is that you believe you can have a good Christian testimony *while* participating in the corruption around you.

❖ <u>The Base</u>: The platform supporting this ride is round after round of drama.

❖ <u>The Decorative Fixtures and Handlebars</u>: Recognition from the drama source is the fixture that feeds your desire to be noticed and accepted. The captivating thrill of what's next in that drama strengthens your grip on the handlebars.

❖ <u>The End Result</u>: Giving in to the thrill of drama will cost you the trust of your co-workers. They will not trust your witness nor come to you for prayer and counsel because they don't see you as any different than they are.

Part Four: The Good Samaritan Merry-Go-Round

Have you read the story in the Bible about the *good Samaritan*? The *good Samaritan* came across a hurting man and was immediately moved with compassion. He went well out of his way, spending his time and money to make sure this man was taken care of.

> Jesus answered, "A man went down from Jerusalem to Jericho and fell among thieves, who stripped him of his clothing and wounded him and departed, leaving him half dead. By chance a priest came down that way. And when he saw him, he passed by on the other side. So likewise a Levite, when he came to that place, looked at him and passed by on the other side. But a Samaritan, as he journeyed, came where he was. And when he saw him, he had compassion on him, and went to him and bound up his wounds, pouring in oil and wine. Then he set him on his own donkey and brought him to an inn, and took care of him. The next day when he departed, he took out two denarii and gave them to the innkeeper and said to him, 'Take care of him. I will repay you whatever else you spend when I return'" (Luke 10:30–35 MEV).

Jesus is the ultimate *Good Samaritan*, Whose example in this we all want to follow. But we must be led *by Him* in every situation and with every person. Sometimes we only want to help people because we desire to be a *good Samaritan* and show compassion. Unless we really know God assigned us to help, our *help* could be a mistake. If you know God is telling you to help them, you will also know how long, you will know what your part is, and you will also know when God tells you to go on your way.

113

NOTE: Even the *good Samaritan* didn't stay involved for the entire time it took to heal the man he had found on the side of the road. Instead, he got the man to the help he needed, even financially pitched in, and then went on his way. *He went on his way!*

As we mentioned earlier, helping people who are *really having a hard time* is one of the hardest situations to resist getting involved in. From family members and friends to elderly neighbors, there is always someone around us going through some type of hardship, and we want to help them all. But once you start, it can be super hard to stop. You may feel *pulled or pressured* every time you see them, but it's important to **not let what they are going through drain you.**

Often in these cases, if you look deeper, you will see that it is a merry-go-round they have been riding for years and years. They have become so familiar and comfortable with it they don't think there is any other way to live life. They hate it but feel secure because it's all they know, and it is frightening for them to think of a life without it. Get involved in what they are dealing with only by the leading of the Lord. In and of yourself, you cannot change them or give them the **real help** they need from God anyway.

These hurting ones may never see things the way you see things. Any revelation they receive regarding something they should do differently will come from the Holy Spirit. You could constantly be "casting your pearls before the swine" (Matthew 7:6), wasting precious revelation, time, and resources on people who do not value it.

Let's be like Jesus. Only speak when and what our Heavenly Father tells us to speak, and only do what our Heavenly Father tells us to do—not getting involved unless God leads us to (John 5:19). We can't go wrong by doing that, can we? No, we can't.

I have some experience in what I am telling you. The Lord assigned me to help my dad but gave me clear instructions to do it in a totally different way than what my dad had ever seen from previous people in his life. Because I obeyed God and resisted what seemed like a million urges and opportunities to respond carnally, my dad eventually believed on and received Jesus.

In 2002, David and I talked and prayed about whether we should move my dad in with us to help him. We got the *OK* from the Lord and were willing to do it over the long haul. We agreed that we would do it as long as we knew in our hearts we were supposed to. For the last twelve years of his life, he lived next to our house in a trailer. I took care of him every day in one form or another, along with hundreds of doctor's visits and daily care. His body died just after turning seventy.

He was a recovering alcoholic. Over those twelve years, he was diagnosed with a death sentence for every organ and body part, not to mention his spiritually cold, hard heart. He knew I believed in God and was praying for him. He experienced several healings over these years. Whenever he received a healing from one of his many diagnoses, he would agree with me that God had done that for him, but soon after, he forgot. This went on with almost every diagnosis. God was faithfully showing love to my dad.

Every single day, he unknowingly tried to get me to jump on his merry-go-round of bitterness, anger, regret, strife, and *unbelief of God's goodness.* He was raised **to believe in God, but not His goodness**. He had been poisoned by religious traditions of men and ran away from God and His love into a life filled with hurting people and shame. Every day I had to ask God to help me with my dad, and I had to stir myself up to get quiet before God so I could hear what to do. Regularly, I would pull out my faith confessions and Scriptures and pray for him in faith. The emotional strain was huge sometimes, but grace would come, and it definitely was sufficient for me.

This Scripture passage helped me *sooooo* much when dealing with my dad when he was being contentious:

> But avoid foolish and unlearned debates, knowing that they create strife. The servant of the Lord must not quarrel but must be gentle toward all people, able to teach, patient, in gentleness instructing those in opposition. Perhaps God will grant them repentance to know the truth, and they may escape from the

snare of the devil after being captured by him to do his will (2 Timothy 2:23–26 MEV).

I could have responded to my dad with condemnation and pressure, but it would have only pushed him away permanently. I knew he was stubborn and would not be pressured into trusting Jesus for his Salvation. I had to put my faith in God and stand on Scriptures, but at the same time, my faith could not override what my dad had said, out of his own mouth, several times over the years regarding *getting saved.* He would say in a cocky, squeaky voice, "**Maybe on my death bed**." He was gambling with his time of death, counting on being able to wait until the last minute, receiving Jesus right before he was going to die. (It's not a good idea to see how close to Hell you can get and still make Heaven. This philosophy will keep you living selfishly, not thinking about how your life affects others' lives.)

My dad chose to wait because he was afraid that he would have to become a preacher if he got saved. That may sound funny to you, but he had heard many preachers tell their testimonies about how they used to live a hard life, but when they got saved, they answered the call to preach. The thought of doing that scared him. I don't know if God would have asked him to preach in a pulpit. I know He would have used him to share his journey to accepting God's love with individuals, which would have greatly influenced them. *God is merciful, huh?* He was definitely faithful to me and my family's prayers of mercy for my dad.

This is important to note regarding my situation with my dad: I had to hook my faith with where his faith was. I could not pray against what my dad was honestly believing and wanting. *My dad believed he would wait to get saved on his death bed.* So, as much as I wanted him to accept God's love sooner and really enjoy life, it wasn't going to happen that way. He wanted to die as a Christian but was scared of the Christian life because of all the messed-up religious teaching he'd heard over his lifetime. The diligent prayers of faith and help we gave him (of course, right alongside God's mercy) was what kept my dad on Earth. He stayed in his body long enough for his heart to soften and become open to receiving the love of Father God and Jesus as his Savior.

Before my dad was saved, physical death tried to creep in several times. Often, he would express to me how he experienced **thoughts and fear of dying soon.** Each time I proclaimed, "He's NOT leaving here (Earth) until he's saved!!" My foot was down!! Every day I was standing on God's promises for my household to be saved and many other Scriptures, and I was not going to quit believing!

In the last two years of his life, his heart opened, and I shared God's true nature with him and explained that God was not out to get him. I watched as his heart began to soften. Before he left Earth and went to Heaven, he finally opened his heart to accept God's love and forgiveness for him. He began to consistently recognize it, experience it, and give it out as well. There wasn't a day that went by that he didn't tell my family and me that he loved us. The fear of dying left him, and he received a peace as he'd never had before. Even though he still refused to go into a church building, he did open his heart to God's love, and He received Jesus as his Savior. Now I will get to be with him eternally in Heaven. YAY!! It was a precious thing to watch and be a part of, and I will forever be thankful to God for allowing me to do this difficult assignment.

It took patience and effort from my family and me and a long-term sacrifice of time and energy. God helped me stay off the drama of my dad's merry-go-round and remain stable so he could receive the gift of his Salvation. I could receive the prize at the end of this assignment—the prize of being able to live with my dad in the future in Heaven.

Please understand that this was an assignment my husband and I signed up for *after seeking God about it first.* We had no idea we would have my dad for twelve years. I was not on a merry-go-round just for helping him. I had much peace about helping him and having him live with us.

The temptation, though, was to get on his merry-go-rounds with him. Those merry-go-rounds of strife and frustration kept spinning, yet he was going through the process of being set free from his old way of living. I have to admit, I was not perfect in every way with this assignment. It was hard and taxing on my emotions and flesh many times. But by staying off the merry-go-rounds while I was helping him, I was not worn down and totally depleted when it was over. I was full of joy.

So what is my advice *from experience*? <u>Do not take on this type of *good Samaritan* assignment unless you know you are supposed to.</u> **The only way to help people *without becoming worn out* is to do it through God's grace on you to do it.**

I'll share another experience with helping a family member, but this one didn't turn out quite as good as the one with my dad. This time was also an assignment David and I willingly and gladly accepted from God. We had very specific instructions from the Lord for our part in this family member's situation. Yet, we were still pressured many times to take on more than what God had asked us to do. Someone was expecting us to do more than what we had in our hearts to do and basically shucking their responsibility off onto us.

For a short time, because of the pressure and severity of the situation, we jumped onto their merry-go-round. We tried to help in ways we were not supposed to *and were not graced to*. Thus, we became weary and very heavy and probably did not handle the situation the best.

When we finally jumped off that *good Samaritan* merry-go-round, we truly had so much peace, even though it made no sense at the time. This situation did not end well, and we looked bad in many people's eyes. Still, we had to follow our peace no matter the pressure put on us, no matter what the outcome might end up being. We dealt with the feelings of guilt and condemnation that came with jumping off their merry-go-round. Remembering the peace we had when we did it kept us away from long-term grief and condemnation.

I repeat ... **<u>Do not take on this type of *good Samaritan* assignment unless you know you are supposed to.</u> If God didn't lead you to help ... you're on your own!** (And that is not a good place to be.)

Good Samaritan

Let's examine the components of *The Good Samaritan Merry-Go-Round:*

❖ The Center Post: It is a lie that keeps you spinning when you believe they have no one else to help them.

❖ The Base: The guilt trip is the platform supporting this ride because you are pulled and pressured by them to help you.

❖ The Decorative Fixtures and Handlebars: The good feeling that comes from being the one to rescue them is what appeals to your flesh and keeps you spinning.

❖ The End Result: Trying to be the *good Samaritan* without God's instruction and grace to do it only leaves you drained and worn out.

SIX

MERRY-GO-ROUNDS INVOLVING CHILDREN

Part One: Responses with Children

WHILE RAISING MY children, I have responded in the natural fleshly realm; and I have also responded in the realm of love and faith in God. I can testify that by responding in love and faith in God, I am much more successful at being the Godly example my children need.

Along the way, I have discovered that it's the very first moments of an event, or the report of one, that determine if **we create a merry-go-round for our children or not.** This is especially true in crises or destructive events. Children normally aren't afraid until they see an adult afraid. We have the power, at that moment, to keep the forward march of faith rather than create an out-of-control whirlwind for our children—who are watching us. This is why it is so important that we walk daily according to the foundation of faith in God's Word, which prepares us for the storms to come. We can only teach these little ones what we know through our actions and responses, not just our words.

They notice every response, especially our first response in an emergency, every first word, and every first action, and you can count on them imitating it.

What kind of *Emergency First Responder* are you? Are you prepared and equipped with the *right gear* to be a *first responder*? Are you one who will actually help in a traumatic situation or one who will hinder and cause more havoc during a time of crisis? Are your responses setting a good foundation for how your children will respond in the future?

When our son Luke was little, I had plenty of opportunities to practice responses. He was so active and **always** outside building something, creating something, or climbing something. He would play in the woods and pretend to be a hunter, army man, superhero, etc.! David and I didn't let him just sit around in front of the TV or play video games *all day*, so he learned how to be creative.

Thankfully, David and I weren't the kind of *over-cautious* parents who never let their kids do anything ***for fear they might get hurt***. We were cautious but not fearful. I prayed for him every day, though, and there were many times when I wouldn't let him do something because of the higher accident risk. At age seven, he had a motorcycle. By age ten, he was using power tools—supervised, of course—and was wild about lighting fireworks and having air-soft gun wars.

He still likes to do fun guy things as an adult, and I hope he always will! I included all this so you can imagine the many times we were presented with an opportunity to panic or fear when he had an accident from one of his boyhood adventures.

There were so many times when he would come into the house bleeding, hurt, or covered in mud, ticks, and poison ivy. We never really let him know if we were experiencing fear or panic emotions. He made several different trips to the emergency room for stitches and x-rays on his head, elbow, ankle, and collar bone. He broke off his front tooth a couple of times and crashed his dirt bike several times—once requiring surgery for a broken collar bone.

These are just a few of the events that could have caused us to freak out in fear or yell at him for scaring us, or make him feel bad for all the hospital bills, etc. Even though we felt like it sometimes, we never did that. Although, I did ask him if he wanted to start paying for the hospital bills, hoping to give him a hint that these little accidents aren't free!

I have to say, he is now over twenty-five years old and is a responsible, young but mature husband and father. He is confident and hardworking and doesn't have any fears that I know of. He's cautious but not afraid. He welds, climbs cell phone towers, snowboards the slopes, and jumps off the highest cliff into the river. I believe his lack of fear is partly due to how we never babied him or showed fear during the intense *events* of his youth. We endeavored to immediately pray and then speak to the injury, telling it to heal quickly. This is what he witnessed from us pretty much every time he had an injury.

Before Luke, we raised his three older sisters to be tough as nails and not be afraid to work. *(That's definitely something you don't hear a lot about these days.)* For the most part, they had fun and exciting childhood years, working and playing outside and not spending too much time in front of the TV. Whining and complaining were not options at our house. Coddling their stirred-up **_negative_** emotions didn't happen, and it was definitely *not ok* for them to express those **_negative_** emotions to us, or anybody else, disrespectfully.

As I look back, I realize that there was a big difference in raising our son versus our older three daughters. Luke was born 8 years after our youngest daughter. Thankfully, we were handling our situations and emotions much more positively by then. We had begun to learn how to live out of our born-again spirits and now had a lot more insight on things, as do most people when they get older. We were no longer in the high-stress merry-go-round life we had been living in the earlier years with our girls. So, Luke was exposed to better attitudes and lived in a more Godly atmosphere at home than his sisters knew early on.

By the time he was born, we were just beginning to learn more about the real Bible truths and faith in God and His promises. We were starting to release our faith, resisting temptations in the flesh, and getting back on the path God had for us and back in His plan for our lives. By then, we were also in a church that allowed him to grow up in a children's program and youth group where the kids were taught to go to God's Word for answers to the situations at home and in their lives. **It makes a difference what church we take our children to.**

When our girls were young, we had major stress due to not being in the best place God had for us. During this time, David and I weren't the best examples of managing stress and negative emotions. There were many frustrating events, and our girls saw us *blow it* many times. *Thank the Lord, they also saw us apologize and admit it was not ok.*

Our children certainly didn't sign up to have their parents get out of the perfect will of God, but because we chose to, it affected them in many ways. *They didn't have a choice except to ride the merry-go-round we were on.* I'm thankful that my girls can now see me as a better example for them. They are now seeing that living by the Word of God really works.

You might be in a situation with your child (or someone else's) and face the temptation to cave into fearful and negative emotions. Maybe you have a child or know of a child who has been medically diagnosed with something. Maybe you just found out one of your children was in an accident, has been violated sexually, or was emotionally hurt in some way. Maybe they have problems in school, or maybe your spouse left, and you are raising them yourself.

They definitely didn't ask to be in these situations. The worst thing you can do for your child is to react solely with emotion. They need to see an example of faith in God in the midst of emotion. They need stable and mature adults around them, speaking life into the situation. They do not need to be pampered or felt sorry for during these times. They need to see your faith move forward even when something bad happens.

I am not saying that you should teach them to ignore what's happening or ignore their emotions. I am saying that parents and other close adults should teach children to acknowledge what is going on. And equally important, we should also demonstrate how to take control of feelings of panic, anxiety, and fear and not let these emotions *run the show.*

You should immediately take them to God's Word and show them the victory side of the situation. **Every answer you and I need is in the Word of God!** You should be instilling in your children that emotions come and go, but not God's promises. **God's promises are their strong foundation through this—not what they see or feel**. If they learn this as a child, it will help them from childhood into adulthood. Then, maybe they won't be dysfunctional like many of us were (mostly speaking of myself here).

STOP THE SPIN!

What I'm about to say is so important! It is what my husband and I missed.

We did not have this foundational truth about God and His true nature as revelation knowledge. Therefore, we could not display or teach this to our children when they were young. We must teach them the truth about God's goodness. His unconditional love for them and how He sees them is foundational in helping them stay solid and immovable when the storms of life come.

We must teach them that Jesus came to give us life and life more abundantly. Teach them that anything opposite of the abundant life is from the devil, who the Bible says came to steal, kill, and destroy. (John 10:10)

Teach them God has a good plan and hope for their future a plan to prosper them and not to harm them. (Jeremiah 29:11)

Believe this! **God does not partner with our enemy to teach us something from something bad. But God can,** *if we let Him,* **help us learn something from it and become stronger for the future.** Yes, bad things will happen all around us because of the dying, fallen world we live in right now. Because Jesus went to the Cross, we now have complete authority and victory over the works of the devil and the fleshly temptations. Our children need to see how we can come through any fiery, destructive event and not even smell like smoke. If we will only trust in God's love and promises for us and not trust in what we feel, see, or hear during these times, it will set the tone for how they function. *Isn't that what you honestly want?*

> Many are the afflictions of the righteous, but the Lord delivers him out of them all (Psalm 34:19 MEV).

I heard someone say, "Faith will look at something square in the eye!" We can't boldly do this and command this *something* to stop bothering us if we are filled with fear or don't understand the power of our words and the authority we have here on Earth, ignoring the issue.

We don't shrink back and cower (crouch) down when we get a bad report. We rise up with our Sword, which is God's Word, and go after it, reminding it of everything Jesus did on the Cross. We begin to praise and worship our God, who always causes us to triumph, and thank Him for the victory *before we see it*. We must teach our children this, also! **Teaching them faith *IN GOD* reactions** at the first stages of their understanding is best and will help prevent them from getting on merry-go-rounds. If your child is older, it may take some time to consistently show them your own example of faith responses. The good news is, it's never too late to learn!

Involving Children

Let's examine the components of *Merry-Go-Rounds Involving Children:*

❖ The Center Post: Not truly believing that God can help your child or children is **unbelief** and is the center post of this merry-go-round.

❖ The Base: Your fear that the child will be destroyed or remain that way for the rest of their life is the platform supporting this spin. Because they are children, it pulls on your emotional heartstrings, fueling your spin on the ride of unbelief.

❖ The Decorative Fixtures and Handlebars: The appeal of this faith-less spin is that the child needs you. The child's needs require you to speak on their behalf and represent them. But, not believing God can help your child/children will cause you to grip the handlebars of fear.

❖ The End Result: Children who have been taught to respond in fear and unbelief later repeat these faithless responses.

Part Two: Merry-Go-Rounds with My Children

I can relate to you if you have had a child with major health issues or had a child who was sexually molested and then later went on to live the lifestyle of a drug addict. I have personally gone through these things, and I am still experiencing their effects in some cases. Yet, the Lord has helped me recognize and eventually get off the usual merry-go-rounds created by life's traumatic events.

I'm not saying I was perfect every time, especially when the merry-go-round was going full speed. Still, I can tell you I endeavored to stay victorious and never gave up, even when it looked impossible. *I was always clinging to God in my heart*, even when my flesh wasn't doing so well. *You can cling to Him too.* I'm thankful God is always looking at our hearts!

So many times, in the middle of these traumatic times with my kids, I was very emotional and felt like giving up. I wanted to do nothing more than crumble and roll up into the fetal position. But I knew if that ball started to roll, it wouldn't stop, and my babies would never survive what they were going through. I would make myself turn on praise music or faith teachings to get my mind off the circumstances and symptoms.

It's a lot easier to never allow the fetal-position-ball-of-emotions to form than it is to stop an already formed ball from rolling downhill uncontrollably, knocking down everything around it. I have four children and now also have grandchildren, watching me ... and how I handle every situation speaks something to them.

A Birth Defect

In 1988, our youngest daughter, Cassie Jo, was born three weeks early and sent to Arkansas Children's Hospital for surgery to untwist and resect her small intestine. Just twenty-four hours after going through a very hard and long back labor, David and I had to drive four hours to the hospital to sign papers before they could operate. When we arrived, we were told the situation was not what they thought, but it was so much worse.

After the surgery, the surgeon told us Cassie Jo had only a 5% chance of living until she was five years old because they had to remove 95% of her small intestine. She had eight inches left to digest her food. A central venous line was put into her subclavian vein, and she was hooked up to continuous hyper-alimentation feeds. Eventually, they put a feeding tube into her and tried to drip a few drops per day of formula into her stomach. Her diagnosis was *short-gut syndrome.*

Based on the medical statistics available, the doctors told us she would probably have several infections in her CVL and face several surgeries. There were no transplants for intestines at that time. So, they just basically encouraged us to cross our fingers and hope she made it until they possibly came up with a successful one years down the road.

She had a couple of major resecting surgeries, a few CVL replacements, and some GI tube replacements as she grew. In chapter four, I told you about this part, but it bears repeating. Our pastor and his wife laid hands on her. They anointed her with oil and prayed for her to heal quickly without any infections. We prayed, as well, and asked God to keep her from infections or from ever becoming septic.

Well, we give ALL glory to God! She went all those years and <u>never</u> had one infection in her CVL nor ever became septic like they said she would. She always healed quickly and correctly. *(This still makes me want to run and jump when I think about it!!)*

I will leave out many of the details to keep this chapter shorter, but after she was born, she was in the hospital four months before they allowed her to come home. However, this was *months* sooner than we were told that it could be. I was trained to feed her intravenously and through her stomach tube. She didn't have her first drop of liquid in her mouth until she was over a year old. She was hooked up daily, and I fed her intravenously until she was more than two years old. I designed and made her a special backpack. She learned to walk with feeding bags and tubes strapped on her walker and then onto her back.

Along with the intravenous feeds for over two years, she was tube fed through her stomach until age five. At the age of five, she was still having a lot of symptoms, and her digestive issues weren't going so well. I started hearing teachings about how it is still God's will to heal *everyone,* so I asked the Lord about it!

I began to speak to her body, calling it *completely healed of short-gut syndrome.* Right before she went in to have a red-dye x-ray test study of her intestines, I prayed and had faith in my heart that she was healed. We asked other faith-filled people to join us and agree, laying hands on her before leaving for the hospital, just like I did with our pastor's at the time when she was eight months old.

I listened to what the professionals said but refused to let it in my heart. In my mind, I imagined having a ***shield of faith*** around her and me, resisting fear and anxiety from getting into my *heart*—protecting her from death and the *normal route* of this diagnosis. With God's help, I didn't go into a hole and hide but took charge as a momma bear does with her cub.

I wanted my baby to survive and for things not to turn out how they told me. When I got the bad report after her one-day-old surgery, I was hurting and crying. But I immediately went to the Christian bookstore in Little Rock, AR, and bought some cassettes of children's Bible songs. I know it was *only children's Sunday school songs*, but at that time, I knew any words that spoke about God and Jesus needed to be filling the atmosphere of the room she was in. I bought a little cassette player, and I placed it at the top of her hospital bed. (I'd say that was being off the normal merry-go-round.) The music was uplifting to the whole area: *This Little Light of Mine, Go Tell It on the Mountain*, and *Deep and Wide*. I wasn't playing healing Scripture promises, but it was all I knew to use at the time. Playing them helped create a better atmosphere. One that started everyone toward thinking about God and away from thinking about fear and what all was happening in the NICU.

I wrote a note and taped it up, asking the nurses to continually play the cassettes and to please turn them over regularly. It was extra work for them, but most did it graciously. **I had to be bold and not timid** with them, but at the same time, very thankful for them and never disrespectful. I honestly don't know where I even got the idea to create a faith-filled atmosphere around our baby. I just obeyed the prompting I had inside me.

Not bringing my newborn home from the hospital was on my mental "Never Will Happen" list. Well, it happened; but through God's grace and love, I made it through victoriously. I could have chosen to handle things differently and use worldly coping devices instead of faith in God, but I chose to run to God for help. My mom taught me that.

This was obviously not a merry-go-round opportunity our little newborn daughter chose. We didn't dare create one, either. We were careful to speak positive *faith-filled words, God's Word,* to her and around her. We never allowed a pity party to take place with her or me, even though my emotions were SCREAMING for one.

That day, at age five, the day we prayed and laid hands on her, Cassie Jo was completely healed and has been ever since. With no explanation from medical professionals, the test showed she had a normal small intestine and didn't show she had short-gut any longer. She is beautiful, married, has four children, and eats whatever she wants. *Five percent chance of living until age five?* I don't think so! That is not what I chose to believe. And that was not a merry-

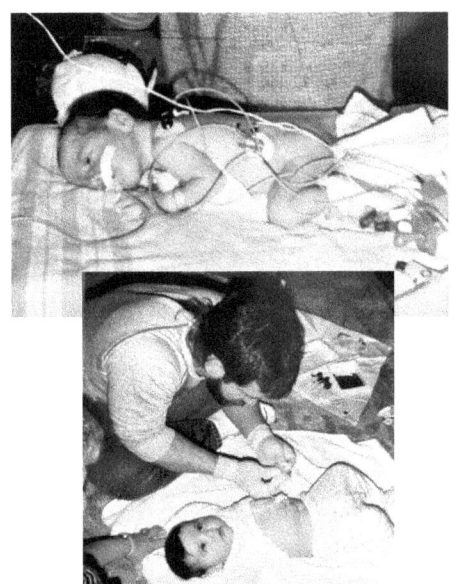

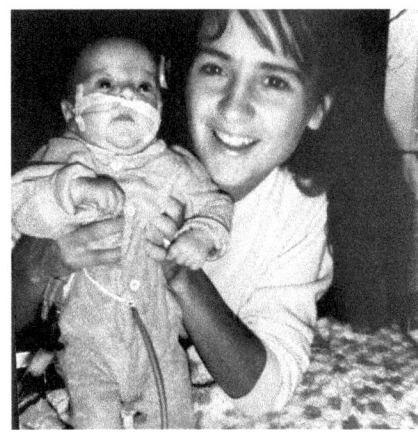

go-round that I wanted to keep riding with the doctors and the other parents in the hospital dealing with the same diagnosis. By God's grace, the totally opposite is what happened! Praise the Lord! *We got off that merry-go-round and on with living life!*

A Sexually Molested Child

When our second daughter was eight years old, she was sexually molested by a teenage boy who was the son of some very close Christian friends. This, again, was **not a merry-go-round any child would want a ticket to ride on.** In one form or another, this went on for two years without us knowing. I remember her beginning to pull away from us during this time—her very close-knit family who loved her. I noticed right away that the family had a weird connection with her, but I didn't know it had to do with him.

We eventually disconnected her (and all of us) from that family. Still, we didn't fully discover all of what she went through and why she desired to be with them until she was an early teenager. By then, she was already very rebellious, getting into trouble, using drugs as a coping device, and beginning to live the lifestyle that goes with all of that. **She had already formed her identity based on** *how she saw herself ... as a bad girl.*

When it was finally brought to light, I rose up against the devil and his destructive works and took a stand for my daughter. I declared she would get through this victoriously, and SHE WILL!! I do have to admit; by the time we found out, she was already snared by the devil big time. (Yes, we should have paid more attention and known better, but we were not walking on the path God had for us when all this was happening to her. We were going to church and, *speaking for myself,* I loved God, but we as a family were not in the place we were supposed to be.)

Please don't tell me this was God's will and plan for us in order to teach us something or that He wanted to use us as an example of how to go through something. If that has been your mindset, let's pull you off that merry-go-round and clear that up right now. <u>*That teaching is absolutely false teaching*</u>*. Any kind of sexual* *seduction is an act of the enemy who wants to destroy all of our lives through his perversion.*

We found out the details long after it happened, so by then, our child had been dealing with the *effects* of this seduction and molestation alone for all those years. This further deepened my anguish over it. I allowed the pain and condemnation **to get inside <u>my heart</u>**, which **affected <u>my prayers of faith</u> regarding her getting freedom from this horrible thing**. I meditated on thoughts of *parental failure* almost constantly. I beat myself up pretty badly for the next several years. This was something on my mental *Perfect Mother List* that I would *never allow* to happen to one of my children … and yet it did.

By the time she was an adult, my husband and I were full-on riding HER merry-go-round. We were held captive and controlled by our *feelings of parental failure.* As we experienced the loss of abundant life, we *felt* that we somehow deserved it because we failed to protect her.

As soon as I learned what my daughter had gone through, I tried to make up for the lost time. I went to the authorities. They were willing to help as much as our daughter would allow them. We realized that exposing her to everything they said would happen through the process would actually harm her worse. ***Our priority was her healing.*** They did what they could regarding confronting and questioning this young man, and we also confronted him. But, bottom line, the damage was already done. We asked him to at least admit it to her so she could have closure, but he refused. The rejection she received from him and his family and the accusations against her as a little girl were probably harder on her than the actual physical molestation. It happened, whether they admitted it or not, and now was the time to face it and let the healing salve of God's Word heal the wound and restore her life … no matter how long it took!

This is a good place to highlight how the religious people in our lives responded to our situation. *It's sad to say, but they didn't know how to respond.* I could see no proof that they had a revelation of grace and God's unconditional love. I've not been perfect in this myself. Still, ***I can just hear my dad say how he would like the religious church people to develop the "heart of the Father" and respond accordingly in these types of situations.*** (My dad is in

Heaven now and knows the heart of the Father more than ever, but even then, he was right.)

At that time, I decided that our church was not the place to go for help regarding our situation with our daughter. I had allowed myself to become vulnerable and share with a few people what was going on with us. Now, I regret doing that with those certain people. Most of the responses I received were judgmental and condemning, which were fear-based. They didn't know how to correctly respond to our daughter or us. They could not help her because they could never get past her *outward* appearance and actions. Her rebellion intimidated people and caused them to react in the flesh.

Later, I realized it wasn't *only* our daughter they didn't know how to love correctly, so I chose not to take it personally. It isn't *only* this particular church group of people responding this way, either. Judgment and condemnation manifest throughout different church groups and denominations everywhere, only they try to call it something else. In my opinion, it runs rampant in the church groups that have no revelation of being *grace-conscious* versus *sin-conscious*.

How could they help her if they themselves had no revelation about Who God (Love) is?

If they hadn't been infected with natural, religious thinking, they would have been able to speak spiritual *truths* to her. **The Truth would have grown roots in her <u>heart</u>, and perhaps she would have run to Jesus instead of away from Him**. Instead, <u>their eyes were fixed on her outward appearance and sinful actions</u>.

If only *we all* would have had the revelation to tell her that God sees her as pure and righteous. If only we all would have never believed and lived our lives with a sin and punishment mentality. But, I thank God for the truth and revelation I have now!

Our church felt uncomfortable and scared. Many could only think of how she needed to be corrected, delivered, and have evil spirits cast out of her. Well, maybe, maybe not. They didn't respond in faith and offered no *real* love or help. This was how I perceived their responses: "She needs to be delivered from that spirit of sexual abuse and repent of the sins she's committed since then!"

I perceived their thoughts and judgments of us to be: "How could her parents *not have known* this was happening to her?" I was made to feel like our little family *secret* should be *kept secret*, and we just needed to get delivered from all of it and move on. One might say this was only vain imaginations coming to me. Still, I differ with that opinion based on the looks and responses we received from many Christians. I am very thankful that I have been freed from the condemnation I once received from them. I shouldn't have accepted it and received it into my heart in the first place.

Drug Addiction, Prison, and Rehab

What we didn't want to happen *did happen*. We went from having a ***young daughter in our home on a merry-go-round*** to having ***an adult daughter on a merry-go-round***, now affecting her two children and the entire family. There were many details I won't take the space to include here. The short version is that she went to many counselors, was in and out of jail and rehab, and then ended up in prison three different times, all before age thirty. The prison was *not a help* to her, and she always ended up back on drugs.

> **Condemnation ultimately comes from our accuser, satan. He uses our own minds, past memories, regrets, and other people, to speak condemnation to us.**

Condemnation became my biggest merry-go-round for several of those years. I would jump off and then jump back on. The emotions ruled me sometimes, and sometimes they didn't. Sometimes when I saw my daughter, I would be in faith and not let her actions move me; other times, I would really get my boat rocked. At that time, that was exactly what she wanted. It was as if she subconsciously wanted to punish us and keep us chained to this merry-go-round. But, thank the Lord for His Word, I kept myself studying God's Word, and my heart became strengthened with the truth of God.

Drug Addiction, Prison, and Rehab: Behind the fence, behind the glass, on holidays and otherwise, we were walking in the love of God for our daughter. But it was my decision to get off her merry-go-round that enabled me to stand strong alongside her and fight for her the right way.

Once I got through the condemnation and began walking in the love of God for her, I was spiritually and emotionally stronger and able to stand strong alongside her. I was able to think more clearly about the situations we were constantly dealing with. I was able to be firm with her and fight for her the right way.

Traumatic Brain Injury

On Tuesday, September 9, 2014, I briefly visited with my daughter. I knew in my spirit that things were getting ready to come to a head with her again, and not in a good way. She was on an out-of-control spin. That night I shared with my husband what I experienced with her that day. David immediately and boldly declared, "She may be going through this, but satan will not take her life!!"

Two days later, on September 11th, she was in a bad car accident just after midnight. I was told by the CICU nurse that our daughter was unconscious,

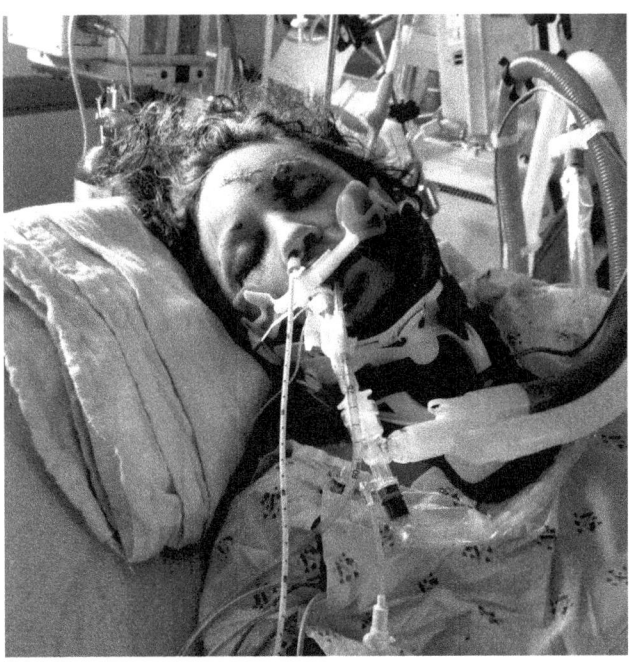

on a breathing machine, and had a traumatic brain injury. The nurse said it could go either way, but because of the length of time before she was rescued and considering all the things wrong with her, it didn't look good, and we should get there. I got off the phone and immediately declared out of my mouth, "She will live and not die, and declare the works of the Lord!"

I knew that once again, our prayers and faith in **God's faithfulness and mercy** would get her through another critical time. This time, though, she was unconscious and unaware of what was happening to her. I also knew we could only take her so far. When she became mentally and spiritually sound, I knew that she would need to start making decisions again for her own life. She would need to decide to **believe and receive** her own total and complete restoration. I mentioned this to the family, and we all agreed.

The doctor met with us as a family. He told us that because of the amount of time she went with almost no oxygen and she was still unconscious with no signs of waking up, it didn't look good. He said it could go either way, if she wakes up. He told us to plan on her never being the same and requiring 24/7 constant care. After he left, we stayed in the conference room and talked and prayed. I was flooded with emotions, but in my heart, I knew she was to live. The *merry-go-round of her life* was weighing heavily on me more than ever, and the temptation to fear and give up on her was enormous. Thoughts were trying to run through my head. I had images of taking care of her in a wheelchair and hospital bed for the rest of her life. I had to capture them and cast them down! BOOM!!

It was a spiritual battle!

> For though we walk in the flesh, we do not war according to the flesh. For the weapons of our warfare are not carnal, but mighty through God to the pulling down of strongholds, casting down imaginations and every high thing that exalts itself against the knowledge of God, bringing every thought into captivity to the obedience of Christ, and being ready to punish

all disobedience when your obedience is complete (2 Corinthians 10:3–6 MEV).

I was not alone, and quickly strength came as I saw our family come together and believe that God would bring her through this. I handed over all the emotions and thoughts to the Lord and cast the care of our twenty-nine-year-old daughter onto God as His powerful grace kicked in. Our oldest daughter's husband, Matthew—as soon as they found out about the report of the wreck—started praying. On their drive to the hospital, the Lord gave him three things that we were supposed to pray and specifically believe for in steps:

Step One: That she would wake up.

Step Two: That she would become fully functional.

Step Three: That she would become self-sustaining.

My husband and I, along with our son, and our two other daughters and their husbands, all asked the Lord for this. We came into agreement that day while sitting in the hospital conference room that this is what would happen. Every person we shared this with came into agreement with us also. We were cautious about who we shared this with to protect ourselves from being bombarded with other people's opinions and experiences, which might bring the temptation to fear and doubt.

We knew we couldn't call *everyone* and ask them to pray because some might be tempted to pray in fear, and what help is that? **(Why should we get others all caught up in it if they are only going to be tormented by the fear of it?)** It's the prayer of <u>faith</u> that gets results, <u>not</u> the prayer of anxiety! **Sometimes you only need to share things with your inner circle of Bible-believing faith buddies.**

The first few days were critical as to how our family would respond to this event. Fear had to be resisted constantly. I heard what all the different doctors said. I heard them say she was not making any ***purposeful movements*** and that it was not a good sign. I saw the atrophy start to set in, and her feet and hands began to curl. I saw firsthand all the other things happening in her body, lungs, and brain. Still, ***I never allowed myself*** to focus or meditate on them. I could not afford to do that. It would cost me my victory! I had to put my eyes

STOP THE SPIN!

There will be times in life when you will need to speak by faith, according to God's Word, to stop the spin in your life. Jesus spoke to wind, waves, bodies, and fevers.

Aren't we supposed to follow after Him? Yes. To follow after Jesus in this, we must only speak as the Father leads us, by the Holy Spirit. We can't expect to speak things in and of ourselves if we want to see changes. Real faith (not wishful thinking) speaks what the Word of God says. When we speak the words of God — what we see in His Word and specific things He gives us to say — we will have a firm foundation to really believe what we are saying and know that it will come to pass.

on something other than what I was seeing! I had to **keep my eyes on God's Word** and not just sit there staring at her in hopelessness.

Just like when our youngest daughter was in Arkansas Children's Hospital off and on all those years, I know I was not the most liked mother the nurses and doctors ever had to deal with. I'm pretty sure I was a conversation piece for all of them, and now again with our second-born daughter. I chose not to shut my mouth. I thought outside the box for other options. I was not robotically only doing what they said without asking God to be involved.

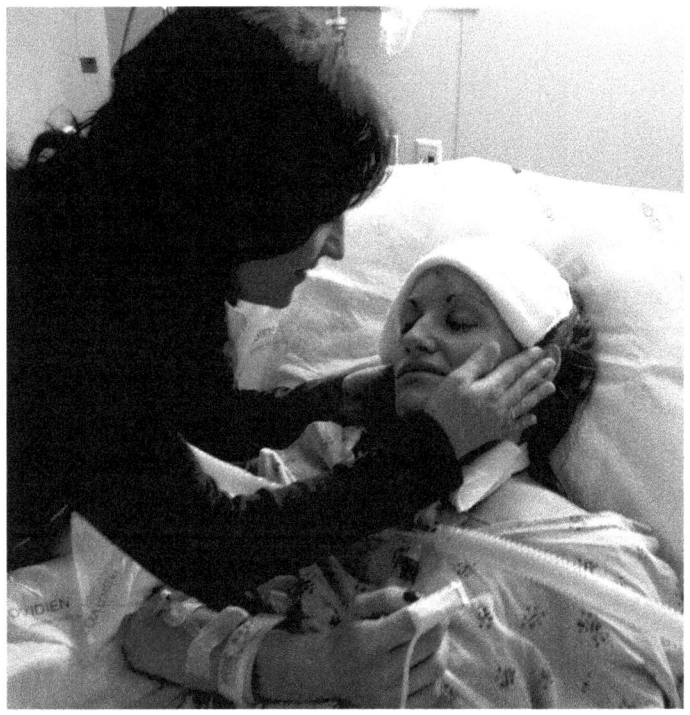

A few days after the accident, the therapist came in with a special boot for one of her feet and a brace for her right arm and hand to help keep them from curling up so badly. When I saw what was happening, I had a prompting inside of me, from the Holy Spirit, to jump on the atrophy IMMEDIATELY and not allow it to go any further. I boldly spoke to her feet and hands and told them to straighten out, and I proclaimed that her feet and hands would NEVER curl up like that again.

The next day I walked in to see the brace off her hand and the boot off her foot. Both items were sitting on the counter next to her bed. The therapist said,

"That was a waste of almost $500 because it ends up that she doesn't actually need them." I said, "That's right! And she never will!" Every day I would massage and speak to her hands and feet, declaring they would function correctly. Our family would speak to her and tell her to wake up and think clearly. We would speak life into every organ and area of her body, ***not believing*** what we were [temporarily] seeing or hearing.

It was definitely ***a trial to keep our faith*** in God for what we prayed. Every day I had to wake up and choose to resist the temptation to just quit. I had to believe that the road to recovery and her final outcome would NOT take place how the professionals were telling me. They told me to start preparing for her to be transferred to Kansas City to a special hospital for invalids. They told me that place would need to train me to take care of her for the rest of her life. When they told me to just accept the facts, I would meditate on Bible promises. As I had many times before in her life, I had to remind myself of Jairus in the Bible ... AGAIN. What happened with Jairus? The messengers came to him and said to give up because his daughter was dead. Then Jesus looked at him and said, **"Fear not! Just believe and your daughter will live"** (Luke 8:49–50). I have meditated on and declared that verse many times throughout our daughter's different life situations.

It was a real battle to stay off the merry-go-round of doing things the way other people do (because they are told they don't have any other options). I chose to believe God *could and would* make a way where there seemed to be no way. As the counselors and medical team were planning and working toward *their goals* for her, our family was working toward *our goals* for her, based on what we believed and had come into agreement on. *WE WON!*

Here's some advice: Once you have received the doctors' professional report, then hear from God. Hear from God FIRST before making any decisions. Then, if you feel led to get a second opinion from another doctor, don't be afraid to do so. We should not robotically follow professionals and their team's instructions/plans without hearing from God each step of the way.

Satan was doing everything he could to get us to buy into what he was selling. Like a salesperson who comes to the door and tries to sell you something, he was hoping we would believe whatever the doctors and nurses and counselors told us and give up on God. *Nope, we didn't buy it.*

The traumatic brain injury required her to re-learn how to breathe, eat, talk, walk, and function all over again. She had to wake up and start making purposeful movements again. I quit my job to be with her in the hospital, then in a rehab hospital for two months, and then drive her to rehab, usually five days a week, one and a half-hour drive *each way*, for the next three months.

Our twenty-nine-year-old daughter had to have 24-hour constant supervision. It was so sad to see her go through this. I loved on her, as did the whole

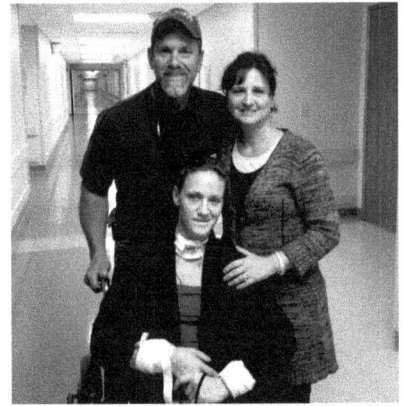

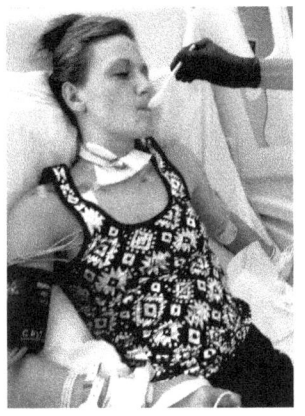

family, but never *pampering* her. My husband kicked in and helped coach her in her therapy. I was thankful he stayed strong because I honestly battled watching her struggle through it. I often wanted to indulge her, especially when *my flesh* was tired, wanting to be coddled, also.

A year later, after refusing to believe and accept what the doctors, nurses, and the social worker kept telling me, she was fully functional. She only had some speech issues and right-side weakness. Now was her time to kick in and take some action toward her total physical restoration, pursue a genuine relationship with God, and receive her total victory from a drug-addiction lifestyle. **I was thankful God helped me do my part**, which was to believe in Him to get her over the hardest initial, physical hurdles.

It was very tempting to get on the merry-go-round of the diagnoses and reports. But even more tempting was to jump on the merry-go-round of emotions. In times like this, we must stay in God's Word and be strong in the Lord and clear-minded so that we do not fail ourselves and the people we love. The world needs to see the victory available to us who are in Christ. None of these things should move us. They are not easy to go through and are almost impossible to survive IF we do not do it God's way.

(Even after going through all of this, it is still time, just like I heard after the accident, for her to seek and receive from God total restoration. It is still time for victory over bad lifestyle choices and habits formed. We continue to believe she sees things clearer every day and wakes up every day with new mercies and strength from her Good Heavenly Father.)

Today, I can humbly say all three things our family asked the Lord and came into agreement on regarding the wreck situation, have taken place:

One: Wake up – Check!

Two: Fully functional – Check!!

Three: Self-sustaining – Check!!!

We give all the glory to God, Who we received our strength and help from! This was one merry-go-round that my family and I did not ride on, even though there was definitely some rotating going on!

Grief & Sorrow

The spirit of grief and sorrow doesn't *only* come to TRY to attach itself to us after a loved one has physically died. I went through a few years, off and on, of pain and regret in my heart and mind because I so badly wanted to go back in time and do a *re-take* of those years when all this started with our second-born daughter. *My heart grieved* for her and us and the years *lost* due to this work of the enemy. I wanted a *re-take* of the times when we were exposed to the judgment and condemnation from religious people.

It amazes me how people would *"let me know"* all the bad things my daughter did to them or the bad decisions **they think** we made that had to do with our daughter's situations. Did they think we were oblivious to it and didn't already know? Just because we didn't shout it out to everyone we saw, did people really think we had our head in the sand?

I don't want to give the devil **any** advertising by telling everyone all the things I knew he was doing through her and how hard it was on everyone involved. We have to stay focused on the victorious end result—the one we haven't seen with our physical eyes YET—and not focus on the negative things we see in the **now**.

I *saw* it as *lost time* and damage that caused our daughter's life events to snowball instead of STOP. If I had just seen what was happening to her as a child and then, if I had later only seen the harmful actions Christians committed toward her and us! Like any *good* parent, I would have done everything I could have to deal with it immediately. And I would have snatched her up and away from the Christians around us.

I wanted to *re-do* the years when we didn't know what we know now. BUT I can't, and I choose NOT TO STAY IN THE PAST ANY LONGER! I choose not to stay crippled from grief and sorrow of past mistakes and failures! Jesus took and got rid of all my grief and sorrows! (Isaiah 53:4) And I choose to believe it and receive it and allow what He did on the Cross to become alive and active in my life! I choose to never again allow the spirit of grief and sorrow to get into my heart and mind, paralyzing and robbing me because of its lies! I got off all the merry-go-rounds of condemnation, regret, grief, sorrow, and fear of going forward.

> Grief is actually a normal reaction to a trauma or loss—physically or spiritually. But, extended grief can become very unhealthy and cause us to be weak and even sick. Being stuck in grief can turn into a self-centered sandpit where you constantly think about everything YOU did or didn't do. This sandpit will keep you focusing on YOUR failure or on how much YOU miss someone and how YOU feel lost and even condemned. I allowed myself to stay stuck in this pit way too long and lost precious time!

No medical doctor, psychiatrist, or counselor can heal a broken heart full of sorrow and regret. Pouring God's Word into me and looking to Jesus is what healed my heart and emotions. Of course, *this worked because* the Bible says **Jesus "has borne our griefs and carried our sorrows"** (Isaiah 53:4). If He already did that for me, why should I ruin my whole life by trying to bear them myself?

I choose to believe these two Scriptures, personally—for myself—and you can too:

> … to comfort all who mourn, to provide for Zion's mourn-
> ers, to give them a crown in place of ashes, oil of joy in place
> of mourning, a mantle of praise in place of discouragement.
> They will be called Oaks of Righteousness, planted by
> the Lord to glorify himself (Isaiah 62:2–3 CEB).

> You changed my mourning into dancing. You took off my
> funeral clothes and dressed me up in joy so that my whole

being might sing praises to you and never stop. Lord, my God, I will give thanks to you forever (Psalm 30:11–12 CEB).

My past failures regarding our daughter were not easy to let go of, but I was determined to stop letting them control me and dictate my future—which, back then, was not looking very positive since I was stuck on the merry-go-round of grief and sorrow. I stopped believing the lie that I didn't deserve to go forward as long as my daughter was still going through this.

I can now honestly say, "I have the memories of those things, but the pain of the memories is GONE!"

Jumping Off the Merry-Go-Round of Grief and Sorrow

One day, my husband came home from work and asked me, "What did you do today?" I replied …

"Oh, I wrote a book!"

Let's flashback to just two and a half weeks before that. I was out to lunch with a couple of family members. They both told how they feel like they are supposed to write a book about their lives. I thought that was great, but I said, "I know I am supposed to write a book, but it won't be about my life." I then told them what I thought my first book would be about. I said, "Don't get me wrong, I have plenty I could write about regarding my life experiences, but I don't think I'm supposed to write a book about them."

HA-HA-HA-HA-HA-HA-HA! (Now that the book is in your hands, you can laugh along with me if you want.)

A life-changing event occurred just one week after that casual conversation with family about writing books. It was *The Text Message* from chapter one! It was the first time I had ever mentioned or even thought about the word *merry-go-round* in this respect. That word would soon mean more in our lives than I ever imagined. A week and a half later (two and a half weeks from the book conversation), I received a phone call stating my daughter was back to repeating some of her past harmful actions.

Right then, I realized I had been caught up on a merry-go-round of her life struggles, and now I had to make a choice. When I got off the phone, I immediately said, "I refuse to get on this merry-go-round!! I will not ride this with her any longer! This situation is not my responsibility!! I cast the care of her and this situation over on the Lord like He tells me to! None of these things move me!! Thank You, Father, for Your help!"

That's when I went to the Scriptures and promises from God's Word. Again, my husband and I began to speak them over her in the face of her destructive life situations that seemed to have just repeated themselves. We haven't stopped believing the best in her or loving on her when we can. We will always be there for her when she decides she really wants to get off the merry-go-round—the same one that, for years, kept our family chained to it. Things like this affect entire families—grandparents, parents, siblings, and children. And this affected ours. We were all grieving and hurt for her. We wanted to take away the pain from her, as well. However, we all agree and will always believe that God is sending laborers to help her (our child) see God's love. We believe that God's promises, which we are standing on, will cause the victory to manifest in her life, once and for all!

The next morning when I woke up, I had thoughts of all the merry-go-rounds I had been on, jumped off of, or even—thankfully—avoided in my life. God helped me to recall memories I had chosen to forget. He led me to look through some of my past journals and diaries, refreshing my memory on everything I had gone through in my life. So many memories I just wanted to pack up in a big trunk and hide in the closet, so I could move on and not have them follow me. I recalled so many times where the enemy had reminded me over the years of the *Perfect Life* list I had made in my mind when I was a young person, how almost none of it had come to pass.

In this time, God touched my heart and ministered His love for me and my life and everything I had gone through. He comforted my heart in knowing that I am who I am because of my life experiences, and I need to be OK with it. I need to be thankful for how God has kept me and sustained me through it all. He reminded me that I ALLOWED HIM to grow me up while going through all these trials. God reminded me how I DID NOT BLAME HIM or turn my back and walk away from Him. He let me know how that blessed and honored Him. I'm not ashamed or embarrassed anymore, but willing to share my experiences.

He has turned my mourning into dancing (literally) and my sorrow into JOY, which is the best medicine ever! He is helping me be in good spiritual shape for His calling on my life. He has helped me to forget those things behind me and reach for those things in front of me! If the things I have gone through—because of other people's decisions or my own self-infliction—can help you, then may God get the glory for your victories too! It was only through His help, mercy, and grace that I was able to survive any of those long merry-go-round rides that He never intended for me to be on!

I promptly sat down at my computer to just write a few notes. Six hours later, still in my PJs, I stopped and realized that it was the beginning of my first book, the opposite of what I had originally thought and said just weeks prior! My husband came home from work and asked what I did all day. I said, "Oh, I wrote a book!" He got a kick out of it!

I want everyone to know that no matter what, and before we see the complete answer to any of our prayers, we MUST keep moving … keep on moving FORWARD, that is! We must keep believing God is faithful and a Good Father God! The dreams God put inside of us must come true! The passions and goals we have in our hearts for God's Kingdom here on Earth must be accomplished! We have work to do and people to show God's love and mercy. Merry-go-rounds can't get in our way!

With God's help and a lot of it, none of these things have moved my husband and me nor kept us from forever missing God's plan for our lives. (We learned that in Acts 20:24.) Serving the Lord is still our first priority in our hearts—never to get on a merry-go-round again. We believe God will help us recognize any that try to come our way. We have moved forward, faster than ever, with an even more clear direction—not just hoping to *someday* live in the Blessing of God, but actually living in it. We enjoy life no matter what's happening around us, what our bank account says, what our children are doing, or how the enemy tries to make us feel. We know that if we as parents are on the right path, it won't be long before our children, their spouses, and grandchildren will also be. **And that, my friends, is what will stop the spinning and bring glory to my God!**

Part Three: Childhood Sexual Perversion & Identity Crisis

Things like this are not fun to talk about, even *very uncomfortable* for most. Still, discussing these uncomfortable issues can help each other. We must be willing to get real, honest, and open, even about things that most of us would like to keep in the dark.

Things kept in the dark corners of your heart—or home—and never brought to light will soon become not only a corner but a whole room, and then a whole home, and then go on to affect other homes. When issues are kept in the dark and never pulled into the light, they never get resolved, dealt with, or truly fixed. I am not afraid of exposing shameful acts of perversion to allow God to wipe away all shame and dirt. I am not afraid of bringing darkness to light so God can cut away all the gross and begin to heal, restore, and renew with the light of His Word.

> He uncovers deep things out of darkness, And brings the shadow of death to light … He dams up the streams from trickling; What is hidden He brings forth to light (Job 12:22, 28:11).

> He will bring me forth to the light; I will see His righteousness (Micah 7:9).

These days, sadly, it would be safe to say that most all children have been exposed to some kind of perversion. Even in my childhood, more children were subjected to it than most people were aware of. As small children, my husband and I were both exposed to sexual perversion, which started us both on the merry-go-round spin to a sexual-identity crisis. I know we are part of a huge majority group with similar stories. I want to personally share our experiences to help people get free from the shame or condemnation because of their own encounter(s) with sexual perversion as a child.

I personally had several *different* forms of exposure to sexual perversion at a very young age, which stole my innocent thoughts and replaced them with perverted ones. I won't go into the nature of them all. But at a young age, I became desensitized to sexual purity. I had very little value for it because I always felt shame. Statistics show that most of you can relate.

This is very sobering to share, but I have decided I will open up about this in hopes of shedding light on some darkness that seems to be at an epidemic stage. Before the age of five, a couple of female teenagers I trusted exposed their *private parts* to me and wanted to *play games*. I played along. By the way, this was in my own house and my parents were in the living room with other adults, not paying any attention to the teenagers in my bedroom.

A few years after this event, I stayed the night at a girlfriend's house. (She was a couple of years older than me.) She wanted to play *touch-tickle games* on our front upper bodies and massage each other's backs in a stimulating way. I played along—again, with parents just in the other room. These two incidences involving females—my same sex—introduced me to body sensations I didn't know existed. It was very stimulating to have someone touch me on those places.

Things accelerated after my older girlfriend and I played this game on a few different occasions. She took me to the bathroom, shut the door, opened the towel closet, and pulled out a stack of Playboy magazines. She said they were her dad's, and he didn't know she looked at them. I was shocked yet very intrigued.

It wasn't long after this when I stayed the night with a different girlfriend, a couple of years *younger than me*. This time, *I introduced her* to the *touch game*. *(See the cycle?)* She played along—parents just in the other room. The next time I stayed with her, I wanted to play again; but this time, she said "No," and that she didn't like it. Suddenly, I felt shame and a sick feeling come over me, and I thought, *What am I? What is wrong with me?* I realized it was not ok to do that anymore, even though I still *desired* to continue. (Just because the desire is

STOP THE SPIN!

Parents! We need to be more spiritually aware of what is going on in our own homes, not to mention our own lives! Don't be fooled by thinking your sexual perversion will not, and hasn't already, leaked out onto your children.

You might wonder why I, at age 5, didn't see anything wrong with playing along with these older girls. When you, as a child, are surrounded by sin and perversion in your own home, it will certainly affect you. Because the majority of my family didn't have a relationship with the Lord, they had become numb to sin and perversion.

Obviously, if parents aren't living their life in a morally pure way, in the good plan God has for them, then the children will be affected. Their children will be vulnerable and exposed to the evil around them, just like I was. If parents have no conviction of sin and sexual perversion, they have opened the door for it to influence and affect their children, as well. As adults, we can stop this spin.

there doesn't mean it's right.) I began to wonder if I was a lesbian—yes, even at that age. Why was I now attracted to my same sex? Go figure!! It's **not** a mystery! But it was to me then.

You see, my older friend, who initially introduced me to this game, had been introduced to this perverted game by someone else. That is how the pattern begins and gets repeated. Ignorantly, she pulled me up on the merry-go-round that she was already riding. Then, ignorantly, I followed the same pattern of introducing the perversion to *my* younger friend. At some point, a person old enough to know better willfully introduced this little game to someone and started the ball rolling.

In truth, it was the reaction of my younger friend that caused me to not want to stay the night anymore with my older friend because I didn't want to play that game anymore. Her reaction brought to light in me that it was actually *wrong*.

This same younger girlfriend had a brother close to my age who would come into her bedroom and want to hang out with us. It wasn't long before we played the kissing game in the closet—yes, parents just in the other room. To me, desiring to kiss her brother *was a good thing*; at least he was male, and it helped me get past the shame of playing the *touch-tickle* game with his sister.

After I was a couple of years older and already attracted to older boys, I began to stay the night with my older friend again. I was then introduced to older boys who, of course, were attracted to young, naïve, and vulnerable girls, open to receiving attention from them. The seductions started coming my way, and I was flattered.

This is how the enemy works to grow his agenda. He finds a vulnerable child, missing HEALTHY emotional affection and hugs from their parents. Through the innocence of small children, he can use them to ignorantly spread his destruction. I could give you more examples of me as a young child being approached by the drunken, perverted men in my life, but you get the picture. And parents, it doesn't just happen to little *girls*.

My husband had a similar experience that I will share briefly with his permission. Around the age of ten, he also was approached by an older male teenager. The boy was old enough to know what he was doing. He did it intentionally, much like the teen boy and our daughter's situation earlier in part two of this same chapter. This teenage boy introduced my husband to sexual arousal, which *desensitized* him to sexual purity. This incident started a young, sexually promiscuous lifestyle for my husband.

By the time he was twelve years old, he was sexually active with an eighteen-year-old girl who was even allowed to move into his bedroom and live with him. (It is hard to believe the adults he was living with at the time approved of this, but they did.) He was on a path of destruction and confusion about his sexual identity at this young age. He believed he was *unable to control* the crazy sex drive, even though he wanted to stop. This crazy out-of-control sex drive totally twisted his view of sex. The incident as a ten-year-old robbed him of his innocent boyhood and darkened how he saw his sexual identity. The spinning of sexual confusion had started. It wasn't that my husband and I didn't know if we were a boy or a girl. We weren't confused about that. But what we were sexually exposed to caused us to be confused about healthy sexual behavior. We had a wrong view of it after these events.

Now, back to my own story: As I got older, I began being introduced to more and more pornography. The initial exposure led me to accept that which followed. The *unintentional* was turned to *intentional*. Eventually, by the time I was thirteen, I was sneaking into XXX-rated movie theaters with older friends—going against the yucky, shameful feelings I had inside me. These magazines and movies caused me to give myself a value as a female: the value of zippo! ZERO! No value!

Thankfully, I did not carry that interest in pornography past junior high school. After changing my group of friends, *I never looked at it again.* It became even more disgusting to me. So, I was free from it, *but the mental residue remained for some time.* The exposure to these influences and experiences left me growing older with a distorted opinion of men. However, because I craved the attention of men, I still allowed myself to be degraded by men. Still so young, I was spinning on emotions and totally confused about sexual things.

> **Childhood sexual-identity crises follow children into adulthood, creating adult sexual-identity crises.**

The sexual-identity crisis started for both my husband and me at a very young age. It started us both on a spin that caused great confusion to hover over us for all the years before we got married. The enjoyable feelings we had encountered and pursued at an early age stayed with us and caused us to *want* to stay on the merry-go-round. On the other hand, the feelings of shame and thinking something was wrong with us made us *want* to get off the merry-go-round. *The confusion was tormenting. We were addicted to these "feelings."*

We kept riding this merry-go-round, even after we were born-again Christians, because we had already developed strong, fleshly habits regarding sex. As teenagers, the churches we attended mostly taught behavior modification and outward appearance changes. We weren't taught that mind renewal on living from our newly created born-again spirits would cause flesh and sin habits to stop. The churches never taught us that we were made new on the inside when we were born again and that now God sees us as clean, holy, and pure. They didn't teach us *why* we needed to read our Bible. It took years before we got completely free from the effects of our childhood sexual seductions.

We rode this merry-go-round right into marriage and carried all our distorted views about a husband-and-wife relationship right on top of it. We had no pre-marital counseling about sexual baggage, so how could we start with a clean slate now as a married couple? We had no one to sit us down and talk straight up regarding healthy thinking toward sexual intimacy in marriage. We ignorantly allowed our tainted views about sex to trespass and to come into our covenant marriage relationship.

I believe most of you can relate to what we went through in some form or another. Like us, you developed your thought patterns about sex from the world and locker room talk. The world says life is all about having fun, and sex is all about pleasure, and whatever form you can get that fun and pleasure is ok and acceptable. The world has portrayed sex as *dirty pleasure* for so long that for them to think of it as *pure* is almost unbelievable. I know married couples who call their intimacy in marriage "doing the dirty." *I hate that!*

The enemy, through man, has perverted what God intended to be beautiful and wholesome. Men now degrade women to the point that most women don't even see themselves as valuable anymore. They have been desensitized to accept the perverted identity of being an object to please men. The men have developed an identity similar to an animal in many ways: very carnal and self-indulgent—acting like they cannot even control themselves.

Sex has been used as a vice in so many ways. For example, "*For my birthday, I want you to give me sex.*" "*For your birthday, I want to give you sex.*" Well, isn't that special?!

It's true that men, living outside the revelation of God's love for them, will treat women special just so they can have sex with them. It's also true that women, living outside the revelation of God's love for them, will have sex in hopes the men will treat them special. Unfortunately, this is how it is even in some Christian marriages. *Boy, is this messed up!!*

If our motives are right and our love for our spouse is genuine, then it is *actually a good thing* that men receive sex after treating their wives special. It's also great if the woman gives her body to her husband to keep him satisfied sexually. Manipulation will not be a factor if our motives and love are pure.

Pure, genuine love is unselfish. For example, married couples should desire to give their spouses a good body massage unselfishly. We can give just because we know it will bless them and actually help their body—rather than as a way of seducing them to give us something in return that makes *us* feel good. ***Check your motives*** and stop visualizing yourself in a *romantic* Hollywood movie that you saw or a romance novel you read. Be genuine.

Listen, these twisted views are exactly what the devil wants. ***Anything good, beautiful, wholesome, and pure comes from God,*** and the devil hates God. His goal is to pervert everything God made for good and use it for evil to keep people, especially Christians, confused about who they really are. ***He wants them totally off track regarding their sexual identity, so their whole life focus revolves around ignorantly perverting what God made for good.***

How It Starts

As I related in the previous sections, the first initial sexual approach was by other teens, which was true for both my husband and me. These events took place in houses with parents just around the corner in another room—not paying attention to what was going on with us. *Parents, don't be so naïve to think these things I've shared can't happen to your children.* I don't want you to be scared, but just aware.

I want to give you some further details about our daughter's situation. I hope it will help you be cautious and aware. We had some friends we trusted, and they had a teenage son. He constantly flirted with our cute little girl, telling her how sweet and cute she was and how much he wanted to have her for a little sister. He got her to trust him and even have a little *crush* on him because he always wanted to play and carry her around.

His first inappropriate physical contact with her was in our own home, while we parents were in the other room. The teenage boy insisted on sitting next to her and then subtly reached over and touched her private areas. She was scared to tell us because she had already developed emotions for this older boy and didn't want him to get into trouble. This turned into two years of him secretly manipulating her to engage in many sexual activities with him. Later, we found out that he tried to "connect" inappropriately with our other two daughters as well.

This teenage boy, who had obviously been introduced to sexual perversion himself, caused our little girl to become totally emotionally and sexually confused. EVEN THOUGH we had previously, more than once, talked to her and our other girls about never ever letting someone touch their private parts, it happened. We now take responsibility for this, understanding that our home was open to strife, confusion, and every evil work. At the time, we were running from the Lord and resisting God's plan for our family. So the enemy was leading us all away from God's ***perfect*** plan and protection for us.

Our children were not protected because we were covered up *in survival mode* and our own problems. We never even let ourselves *imagine* this boy would ever sexually seduce our little girl. Consequently, the healthy sexual value she should have had for herself was robbed from her and never allowed to mature in a wholesome and pure way. Like it would taint any of us, the shame and confusion from the seductions tainted her view of sex and purity. Those views kept the merry-go-round spinning on sexually-driven thoughts and emotions, justifying every kind of sexual perversion.

We should not be cowering down and running scared regarding the sexual perversion and identity crisis attacking our children in this day and age. These things need to be looked at square in the eye and fought against, no matter how uncomfy! Most parents didn't talk about sexual things when my husband and I were kids. If something premature happened to you sexually, then you were pretty much on your own to deal with it. So, people dealt with it by stuffing it down inside of them and pretending like it never happened. THAT is keeping it in the dark. And I don't think it's any different today.

Those of us who had these early, perverted sexual encounters felt like if we didn't tell anyone, then it would never be known. *That's a huge lie!* It eventually comes out through promiscuity, anger, gender confusion, sexual sins, and repeating the offense that was done to us. If we don't value something, we might think nobody else does either. That trains one after another to pull people up onto a *sexually perverse* merry-go-round without a second thought.

Parents: Don't be afraid to talk to your children at a very young age and reinforce **their value** as a BOY or GIRL. Teach them what the Bible says about how the gender we are born with is who we are forever **because it is who God created us, them, to be**. If they ever deal with feelings or thoughts opposite of that truth, teach them how they should cast down those thoughts and feelings and not give place to any of these lies of the enemy. Share with them the truths in the Bible about sexual identity and sexual sins. Speak their gender to them and teach them who they are as a man or woman and their role as that gender.

Teach them to defend their gender, not be embarrassed by their gender. Teach your children not to let other people confuse them by telling them they can decide to change their gender. Definitely let them know that it is ok to say *"No"* to anyone—even someone they trust—who might want to play touch games with their bodies or compare their private areas, etc.

Sadly, too many parents have believed the lies of others. Too many parents have listened to lies that tell them they cannot raise their children according to their Biblical conviction of right and wrong. I was in the store not long ago, and as I went to grab a shopping cart, two ladies and a little boy were also getting one. I wasn't eavesdropping—I couldn't help but overhear what the two lady friends were talking about. The little boy's mother said how afraid she was that her little boy might later decide that he wanted to be gay (homosexual). She said, "I guess I'll just have to wait and see what he decides." SERIOUSLY?!!

Wait and see what they decide is not how to raise emotionally healthy children into healthy adults who are secure in their God-given identities. Does this help explain why we now have a generation of people who are actually *celebrating* sexual perversions? ***Responsible, pro-active, God-honoring parents—where are you?***

It really is ok to talk to your own children about this! Are you going to let the media, public schools, peer pressures, and vain imaginations confuse you and your kids? Are you going to sit back in fear and just let *them* parent your child? *We are the parents*! It is our responsibility to ground our children in truth and help prepare them for what they will be facing.

It was so sad that this young mother thought it was even an option for her son to see himself wanting to be sexually attracted to men. She obviously didn't *see* that she could help her son in these identity-forming younger years. She was *visualizing* this as possibly already happening, and the child was only two or three years old. I envisioned her for the next fifteen years just walking around wringing her hands in fear, not doing anything to help her son reaffirm and get established in the God-given sexual identity he was born with.

We **can** reinforce our sons' and daughters' sexual identity and even turn around the beginnings of a perverted identity and lifestyle. Pray and ask God to help you see if there is confusion starting. If you recognize that your child is beginning to be influenced by lies about his or her identity, then don't panic or freak out. God has a bunch of wisdom. He will give you wisdom regarding how to handle it so that your child will *see* for himself or herself, bringing a personal revelation of who he or she is. **Show them what the Word says about this. The Word is our standard for everything.** If they personally receive the revelation, it will stick.

With God's Word as their foundation, they will never be fooled again, sucked up on the *sexually perverse* merry-go-round! They will realize how God formed them in their mother's womb and how they are fearfully and wonder-fully made:

> For You formed my inward parts; You covered me in my mother's womb. I will praise You, for I am fearfully and wonderfully made (Psalm 139:13–14).

Moving Past the Past!

To move forward into a healthy sexual marriage relationship and stop seeing sex as dirty requires letting go of past perversions. How bad do you want to let it go? The Bible tells us the truth about sexual immorality in multiple places. Now that we are no longer innocent children, we should have our desires changed to line up with His will:

> For this is the will of God, that you be sanctified [separated and set apart from sin]: that you **abstain and back away from sexual immorality**; that each of you know how to **control his own body in holiness and honor** [being available for God's purpose and separated from things profane], not **[to be used] in lustful passion**, like the Gentiles who do not know God and are ignorant of His will; and that **[in this matter of sexual misconduct] no man shall transgress and defraud his brother** because the Lord is the avenger in all these things, just as we have told you before and solemnly warned you.
>
> For **God has not called us to impurity**, but to holiness [to be dedicated, and set apart by behavior that pleases Him, whether in public or in private].
>
> So whoever rejects and disregards this is not [merely] rejecting man but the God who gives His Holy Spirit to you [to dwell

in you and empower you to overcome temptation] (1 Thessalonians 4:3–8 AMP; emphasis added).

(Note: This Scripture is not talking about children who do not yet have their spiritual understanding enlightened.)

READ IT!
Hebrews 12:14; Genesis 2:25; Mark 10:6-9
Godly Marriage Bed

It was a battle for David and me to face this and change our wrong-thinking pattern regarding sex. After all, these patterns had been in place since our childhoods. It took effort for us to renew our minds to the truth about how God actually made sexual intimacy for **husbands and wives** in marriage. **He desires that it be pure, enjoyable, and fulfilling.**

(I could go on and on about this, but that's for another book! So be on the watch for that in the future. However, I will include our freedom story in this chapter about children because I believe it will help many other couples *and* their children!)

How did we get free from the childhood impact of sexual perversion? First, we repented (to change; to turn away from old ways as in Acts 3:19 and Acts 26:20) of our past acceptance of sexual perversion and then flooded our minds with the truth about God's view of us and His love for us. That's what set us free from the stronghold of seeing sex as perverted. This was not a one-and-done thing: Renewing our minds to the truth about these things was a daily process as we became more and more grounded in God's way of thinking.

Being renewed is like the transformation process of a butterfly: the whole purpose of the ugly little worm is to go inside a cocoon and become transformed into a beautiful butterfly, all over a period of time. I absolutely love the illustration of the butterfly's transformation process! As David and I have been transformed by His Word over time (which we learned to do in Romans 12:1–2), the Lord has brought us to a place where these things are no longer issues for us. We are totally free—what the devil twisted is now *un*twisted!

Friends, if you were exposed to early childhood sexual assault and perversion, this is <u>not</u> *who* you are. You can change your thinking and forgive those involved. ***You can change how you see yourself and get off this merry-go-round of sexual perversion and lies.*** The devil wants to keep you there, but *God has a different plan for you.*

Get your Bible out and read it. Meditate on the Word of God—I've given you so many Scriptures in this book and there will be others that God will point out to you. Renew your mind by reading the truth about how God sees you and loves you.

God sees you as PURE.

Let God's Word cleanse and heal you from all the *pain* in those early childhood memories. Allow yourself to live holy and accepted, just as your Good Heavenly Father sees you. You can start today.

My husband and I went from spinning on a sexually perverted merry-go-round to winning in sexual intimacy in our marriage. *You can too! And it will impact all your generations.*

Part Four: Praying God's Word over Our Children

Here are some Scriptures I give voice to when praying for my children:

<u>My Refuge and My Fortress</u>

He who dwells in the shelter of the Most High will abide in the shadow of the Almighty. I will say to the LORD, "My refuge and my fortress, my God, in whom I trust."

For he will deliver you from the snare of the fowler and from the deadly pestilence. He will cover you with his pinions, and under his wings you will find refuge; his faithfulness is a shield and buckler.

You will not fear the terror of the night, nor the arrow that flies by day, nor the pestilence that stalks in darkness, nor the destruction that wastes at noonday.

A thousand may fall at your side, ten thousand at your right hand, but it will not come near you. You will only look with your eyes and see the recompense of the wicked.

Because you have made the LORD your dwelling place —the Most High, who is my refuge—no evil shall be allowed to befall you, no plague come near your tent.

For he will command his angels concerning you to guard you in all your ways. On their hands they will bear you up, lest you strike your foot against a stone. You will tread on the lion and the adder; the young lion and the serpent you will trample underfoot.

Because he holds fast to me in love, I will deliver him; I will protect him, because he knows my name. When he calls to me, I will answer him; I will be with him in trouble; I will rescue him and honor him. With long life, I will satisfy him and show him my salvation (Psalm 91 ESV).

Father, You are my refuge and my fortress. You are delivering my children from any snare of the devil that comes their way. Help me not to fear but to trust You to watch over and protect my children. Thank You for being with my children and me in times of trouble and for showing us Your salvation in this situation.

> The righteous man who walks in integrity and lives life in accord with his [godly] beliefs—How blessed [happy and spiritually secure] are his children after him [who have his example to follow] (Proverbs 20:7 AMP).

Lord, help my life be an example of walking in integrity.

> All your children shall be taught by the Lord, and great shall be the peace of your children (Isaiah 54:13).

Help me, Lord, to let You teach my children without my interference. Thank You for causing great peace to be on them.

> So pray to the Lord of the harvest to send out workers into His harvest (Matthew 9:38 AMP).

I ask You, Lord, to send laborers to help bring light and revelation to my children when they will not receive it from me.

> Assuredly, the evil man will not go unpunished, But the descendants of the righteous will be freed (Proverbs 11:21 AMP).

Thank You, Lord, for delivering my children from all the works of the evil one.

> Praise the Lord! Blessed is the man who fears the Lord. Who delights greatly in His commandments. His descendants will be mighty on earth; the generation of the upright will be blessed (Psalm 112:1–2).

Lord, help me to delight myself in You and Your ways. Thank You, Lord, for blessing my children on Earth.

> Thus says the LORD, "Restrain your voice from weeping and your eyes from tears, For your work will be rewarded," says the LORD; "And your children will return from the enemy's land. There is [confident] hope for your future," says the LORD; "Your children will come back to their own country" (Jeremiah 31:16–17).

Thank You, Lord, for helping me follow Your plan for my life of service to You and cast the care of my children on You. Thank You for bringing my children back to what they know in their heart is right.

> I will contend with him who contends with you, and I will save your children (Isaiah 49:25).

Thank You, Lord, for contending with those who contend with me through misleading or harming my children. Thank You for saving my children from the works of the enemy.

> So will My word be which goes out of My mouth; It will not return to Me void (useless, without result), Without accomplishing what I desire, And without succeeding in the matter for which I sent it (Isaiah 55:11 AMP).

Thank You, Lord, for helping me believe that Your spoken Word is going forth and accomplishing what pleases You, causing it to prosper in what You sent it to do.

> Now this is the confidence that we have in Him, that if we ask anything according to His will, He hears us (1 John 5:14).

Lord, I know You have a good plan for my children, and it is Your will to save them, deliver them, and bless their life here on Earth, so I ask that it be done, and I thank You for it in advance!

> The Lord has remembered us; he will bless us; he will bless the house of Israel; he will bless the house of Aaron; he will bless those who fear the LORD, both the small and the great. May the Lord give you increase, you and your children (Psalm 115:12–14).

Lord, thank You for blessing me. I believe You are increasing me and my children more and more all the time because You are mindful of me and my love for You.

I call my children blessed, righteous, and in God's plan for them!

I call them living according to who they are because of Christ in them!

Thank You, Lord, that Your mercies are new every day for my children and me!

STOP THE SPIN!

Here's something that I learned regarding interceding in prayer for our children. I hope it helps you:

When the Lord wakes you during the night, and you have a leading to pray, do it right then. Don't think you can do it in the morning after your alarm goes off. There is a reason He wants you to pray and intercede right then. I have been awakened many times during the night to pray for our daughter and later found out it saved her life from destruction.

When you sense a prompting inside you to stop and get alone and get quiet, do it. God wants you to hear the answers He has regarding the situations. He wants you to stay focused, strong IN HIM, and not moved and driven by your raging emotions.

When the Lord gives you a prompting to get your Bible out and study a specific subject, He is trying to help you. He wants you to get bold in faith regarding something that is coming up. If you ignore or procrastinate in heeding (paying attention to or taking notice of) these leadings, you are procrastinating and forfeiting the help He is trying to give you. We should value and honor these promptings from our Lord. This is part of being proactive and a team player with God.

SEVEN

SPOUSE AND MARRIAGE MERRY-GO-ROUNDS

Part One: Your Spouse's Merry-Go-Round

THIS IS PROBABLY one of the hardest merry-go-rounds to *avoid*. You love them, live with them, and have a spiritual and physical bond with them through the covenant of marriage. However, thankfully, **you are not responsible for your spouse's relationship with God.** Because you are only responsible for *your* relationship with God, you can obey God's Word regarding your part as husband or wife. The key is to not let what they are doing detour you from that. Keep your heart and mind stayed on God and His Word, NOT on the emotion of the relationship. You can't do that, though, if you are just sitting around meditating on your spouse's failures.

Don't get on their merry-go-round.

For many years in times past, my husband and I had different views on spiritual and natural things. *(You might not have thought so if you met us because we were very active in church most of the time.)* I won't get into the specifics, but it seemed we were on two different paths most of the time. I think many married couples can relate to this.

It takes extra effort to make it through hard times because of differences. It is never impossible to be victorious. But suppose you are going one direction and your spouse is going another (even if they think they aren't). In that case, it definitely can hinder good, fast results. Yes, you might say that isn't fair; but you did marry them. [*Smiles.*] Most likely, your vows included a promise (by you) before God to stay with them for better or worse. *Mine did.*

Romans 15:5–6 is one of the prayers I prayed over my husband and me, even in the face of differences, and I still pray it over us:

> Now may the God of perseverance and encouragement grant you to <u>live in harmony with one another</u> in accordance with Christ Jesus, so that together you may with <u>one voice glorify the God and Father of our Lord Jesus Christ</u> (MEV; emphasis added).

Before you start changing the rules of your marriage covenant, be sure to stop and ask the Lord first. He might have something very specific He wants you and your spouse to do **together** to further His Kingdom on Earth, and you could mess the whole thing up! He needs you to be mature and unoffended, believing in His promises to get the job done. If we do not, you and I are the ones who will stand before God and be accountable for what we knew to do and didn't do because we used our spouse as an excuse.

<u>**We do have the ability to win our spouse over to the Lord**</u>. Still, it definitely won't be accomplished through pulling on them, nagging at them, or being contentious until you get your way. By the way, *contentious* is not just mentioned in the Bible regarding women, even though there was a time when I got pretty good at it. [*Wink.*]

What is important is … God is our source—not our spouse—so we aren't supposed to be looking to them to meet our needs. ***<u>God meets our needs,</u>*** and <u>we shouldn't be trying to figure out how He will do it or whom He should use.</u>

There are a lot of Scriptures we can stand on when praying for our spouses. But if we ourselves are not obeying what God has *told us to do,* then we might as well forget about getting good results with our spouse. You can still move forward in your life and have great things happen for you, even if your spouse isn't on the same page. Change yourself, not them. By doing it the right way, we have the ability to win our spouse over to the Lord, even if they are *already* a Christian! (Think about that!)

Speaking for myself, as a wife, I made many mistakes regarding this, ignoring the things God told me to do even when I knew *His direction* was the answer. It actually opened the door to what I call *marriage cancer*. It was foolish, and I believe it cost us years of healthy living in marriage unity and victory. It was destroying our children and us in every way. Cancer in anything equals kill, steal, and destroy.

> *Side note:* I remember the day when I got the huge revelation that I should actually be practicing the *Love Chapter* (1 Corinthians 13) on my husband! Then, I realized I should be with my kids too! Ha-ha! Who'd have thought?! Knowing I should practice it on other people was a no-brainer. But, for some reason, I didn't want to bring it in the house with me. I know, you have never been like that, right? Don't judge me!! [Smiles.]

Now, my husband and I have a victorious marriage testimony. He is allowing me to share with you some of the things he went through and overcame, along with my own side, in hopes it will help you. *I eventually* decided to obey God and **consistently** do what He told me to do to get new results—free from disease. *The merry-go-round was getting real exhausting!*

We had a marriage cancer, and *we both* were using the world's way to fight it, but it was only getting worse. God is the only One who can truly heal any sickness and disease. Our family and marriage had a disease, and the *medicine* I was using was not working. (Doctors and therapists can only *help* and direct us with healing—**the life of Jesus living in us and through us is the Source for**

our healing.) I lived with a negative, hateful attitude regarding my husband and expected positive, healthy, life-giving results. That's stupid!

This reminds me a lot of what Albert Einstein said, which I'm sure we've all heard at least once, *"The definition of insanity is doing the same thing over and over again and expecting different results."*

For years, I did it all wrong. I jumped off and on the emotional marriage merry-go-round instead of consistently treating my husband the way God's Word says to do. I was never *Dana Downer* to *other* people, but I often was to my spouse. The breakthrough came when I recognized that I was sabotaging our victories by getting frustrated and talking wrongly to him. I then began to make **purposeful** movements that would cause change to come. I began simply practicing the unconditional love of God toward him, which is shown in the *Love Chapter,* 1 Corinthians 13. Finally, I got off the merry-go-round!

I began to pray for him and prefer him. (You might think, "Well, Yea-ah! Everyone should know that!" I can testify that it's not so easy if you don't *feel* like it at first and you are right in the middle of all the chaos.)

I honestly have always strived to be his helpmeet, endeavoring to help him get into his place within the Lord's perfect will. Even when we went through rocky times, this remained my heart's desire and priority, except I tried to make it happen *my way*. I mainly married him in the first place because we talked about living our lives together for the Lord's purpose—full-time. I'm no dummy! Ha-ha. I also knew if he was doing what he was supposed to do, it would go well with our children and us, and I could get into my perfect place with the Lord. I knew that God is faithful to His promises.

So, honestly, my motives were to get our whole family into God's plan for our lives.

I just did it the wrong way.

I will share more details about our marriage later in this chapter, but the bottom line with any marriage is that *it takes work.* Every day, it takes making an effort to let the Christ-like attributes inside us flow out of us if we are born again. If we are, then the Spirit of Christ lives in us, and the old, dead spirit is now a reborn, alive, and new spirit. But once that happens, if we don't read and study God's Word, renewing our corrupt natural mind, we won't think differ-ently. So, we will just keep acting like our *old self*, going 'round and 'round.

> Therefore, if any man is in Christ, <u>he is a new creature</u>. Old things have passed away. Look, <u>all things have become new</u> (2 Corinthians 5:17 MEV; emphasis added).

> Do not be conformed to this world, but be <u>transformed by the renewing of your mind</u>, that you may prove what is the good and acceptable and perfect will of God (Romans 12:2 MEV; emphasis added).

The devil is thrilled when new Christians never get their mind renewed. He knows that his best chance to keep them from moving forward in their new life is for them to <u>never</u> become transformed by getting into God's Word to *reprogram* their mind. He wants them to <u>never</u> fellowship with other believers, make new friends, and <u>never</u> start serving the Lord in the local church body. He will work overtime to cause them to detour from any spiritual growth at all. He wants them to be weak and useless in God's kingdom and keep them living the same life they have been. He knows they will be frustrated, and his goal is that they become **so** frustrated that they just give up and decide the Christian life isn't for them.

I know what you must be thinking. No, I didn't get off track regarding the spouse merry-go-round. Not at all. Christian marriages have the same disease, death rate, and failures as the world! This is happening because they are not us-ing God and His Word to change them and their situation, so they are getting the same results as the world gets! It's like ***they are resisting God instead of resisting the devil***. James 4:7 says, "Therefore submit to God. Resist the devil, and he will flee from you." But instead of the devil fleeing, ***<u>it's their spouse fleeing from them!</u>***

The devil has blinded the eyes of so many Christians regarding this. We are supposed to submit ourselves to one another, to God, and His way of doing things! We should be drawing near to God, Who is where our help comes from, and humbling ourselves so we can get more of His grace to stay in the marriage instead of running off and quitting!

> But He gives more grace. Therefore He says: "God resists the proud, But gives grace to the humble." Therefore submit to God. Resist the devil and he will flee from you. Draw near to God and He will draw near to you. Cleanse your hands, you sinners; and purify your hearts, you double-minded (James 4:6–8).

Ok, I guess you know my soapbox now! It's the one where I am passionate about people actually putting time and prayer into changing themselves *first*. It's the one where *people stop quitting on their marriages so fast* without really even *giving God's Word a chance to work*.

My husband and I stayed together, but working through marriage difficulties happened *against all odds*. I am thankful that we have one of the very few marriages in our immediate families that have not ended in divorce. This didn't happen by accident. I have to say that by both of us employing God's strength, and BY HIS GRACE ONLY, we kept from separating, over and over. Often, I could not *fully* understand or explain his actions. Still, I knew I truly wanted a happy, fulfilling relationship with him. It was worth the effort and the time it took for the change to come.

When you look at our marriage path, all the baggage we brought into it, and later, at what came against us, God is by far the ONLY reason we are still together. Two selfish, hurt, wounded, and stubborn people with their own agenda? Are you kidding? We had to choose to repent, forgive, and cooperate with God's Word!

Yes—it takes forgiveness. But even if you have forgiven each other and no *repentance* came, then reconciliation will not happen. After *choosing to forgive*, ask God to help bring *repentance* to both your hearts and actions, so it doesn't keep repeating itself over and over. (2 Timothy 2:25) When *repentance* comes, you can be reconciled back together and on course.

I hope you can see things differently now and decide to obey what God has told **_you to change_** regarding the merry-go-rounds of your marriage. Remember, focus on and do ONLY your part. You are not held accountable for your spouse's spiritual walk or growth. You are only held accountable for yours.

Nowadays, many married couples are quitting, wimping out, and throwing in the towel too soon. *They are missing a miracle in their marriage by quitting before giving themselves and God a chance to change it.* Their emotions are being led by pride and the father of all lies, the devil. Let's humble ourselves and help change those statistics and show the world we are truly different! Because we are.

Spouse & Marriage

Let's examine the components of *Spouse and Marriage Merry-Go-Rounds:*

- ❖ The Center Post: You keep spinning because you believe that God can't use you as an individual, even while married. This lie is causing you to constantly try to change your spouse in your own ways.

- ❖ The Base: Your spouse's *issues* affect your home and the people in your home, causing you to deal with their choices and attitudes daily.

❖ The Decorative Fixtures and Handlebars: The blame game is the appealing fixture on this ride! You believe you get to blame your spouse for what is happening or not happening in your life.

❖ The End Result: Blaming each other (or trying to change the other) results in neither of you moving forward on God's path for your lives—not together as a married couple nor as individuals. You are BOTH stuck.

Part Two: My Marriage Corrections

I'm sure every Christian can relate to how they have been detoured from doing something for God, something that was in their heart to do, by giving in to the lies, fears, tactics, and schemes of the devil. *The enemy was all too successful in keeping my marriage on a merry-go-round, using everything in his arsenal to divide my husband and me. He tried to keep us beaten down and powerless from ever living our married lives for the Lord or ministering God's Word to people.*

My husband and I would like to open up our lives and share our story with you about how, when first married, we were not on our toes, so to speak, regarding the devil's lies, fears, schemes, and distractions. The Bible says in 1 Peter 5:8, *"Be sober, be vigilant; because your adversary the devil walks about like a roaring lion, seeking whom he may devour."*

The enemy is a spiritual outlaw and thief—a rip-off artist! He was looking to find an opening to come in and be able to steal, kill, and destroy us in one form or another. The enemy looks for a weak spot that he can dig at and eventually break through and begin using his evil works of destruction on us. He was able to interfere with God's plan for us for many reasons.

Mainly, we were vulnerable at the time because we did not understand who we were IN CHRIST. *And,* we were not fully believing nor faithfully committed to what God told each of us in our hearts before we were even married. The enemy's goal was to totally divide us and detour us from living our lives for God and doing His Kingdom business.

Because we, as a husband and wife team, didn't fully value our covenant with God and each other, we had problems. Because we didn't protect the calling from the Lord we knew we had together as husband and wife, **we were not prepared for the attacks against us**. We should not have been so ignorant and unaware to think we could *never be detoured* from off our path.

When we got married, we were Christians and had the vision to serve the Lord full-time *together* for our whole life. We both desired to go to Bible school and get our foundation for ministry. Right away, though, we never took the time to invest in our marriage bond and truly become *one*. We didn't understand and value the marriage covenant and our vision to serve the Lord as we should have. We were young and continued to do whatever our family told us to do **instead of *leaving & cleaving***. We didn't boldly set our face like flint and run after God's plan for us.

> Therefore shall a man leave his father and his mother, and shall cleave unto his wife: and they shall be one flesh (Genesis 2:24 KJV).

My husband says at that time, he feared what his family and friends thought of him more than he feared not doing God's will. *He was deceived into believing he could please both them and God.* The enemy used every lie, scheme, and distraction he could to try and get us off course.

It wasn't long before we allowed our family and the world to begin to distract us from our vision. Eventually, we recognized it and started seeking God **again** about moving away from family and going to Bible school. By this time, we had our first daughter, and I was pregnant with our second daughter, so we focused on my husband going somewhere to get *his* Bible degree. After much seeking, we found one that we had peace about. It was in a state far away and between both sides of our families. God worked out every detail needed to pack up and move there and for my husband to start classes.

He went to Bible school and graduated. After graduation, he applied for a job, but he didn't get the job. Immediately, his family offered him a job starting a business with them. By this time, we were really off track because of the cares of the world and disobedience to God, so we didn't even see this as a huge detour to our calling. We always justified whatever we did by saying we would do ministry along with it. Ministry was still in our hearts and kept coming to us. We even called part of the business name "*Solid Rock*," knowing that Jesus is our Solid Rock. Because of the confusion that **_we allowed_** into our minds, we compromised and went into a business that my husband actually hated doing. Crazy, huh? Was God leading us to do this? No!

This business with family ended up being the biggest mistake of our marriage. It cost us so much in so many ways with our precious family, children, finances, and marriage. There was so much strife and division resulting from being out of God's will. Friends and family members were always (yes, I mean *always*) allowed to come between us.

There was no initial *leaving & cleaving* at the beginning of our marriage. So, standing up to family or friends was something my husband did not do at that time. My getting *thrown under the bus* by him was normal when family or his friends were around. Yes, I accumulated a lot of emotional scrapes and bruises that needed to be healed.

Acceptance had such a control hold, and pleasing them was such a stronghold in him. He recognized this later. After a disastrous ending with this family business, my husband separated himself from his family. He began to *try* to cleave to me. (Thankfully, our prayers were answered, and later we were reconciled with them. We have developed a closeness with them that is *so precious*. God is good!)

Off and on through the years, I would *try* praying Bible promises over my husband and our marriage. It never lasted long. I would become frustrated and overwhelmed and want to quit. I would weigh out leaving him versus staying with him. *I was torn between my flesh wanting to run and the thoughts of my children being raised in a divorced family with a step-parent who might not love them like I do.*

Also, one of the biggest things that kept me going was the thought of me leaving him and him crumbling into pieces, NEVER becoming the man of

178

God that I had in my heart for him to become. I knew that if I gave up on him and stopped fighting for him to get into God's plan for his life, he would most likely fall apart and get even further from God and his purpose here on Earth. I would hold myself responsible, and my children probably would, also. I knew God would not be pleased with me. That sad thought and vision of a possible horrible ending for my husband's life was heavy on my heart and outweighed the hard times. It was God's grace that kept me going.

This merry-go-round circled for years and years and years. I had quite the collection of prayer books containing "Bible promises for your marriage and husband." I would get excited and pray using these promises for a few weeks. I would immediately see results and then slack off, believing the devil's lie that everything was fixed now so I could back off. Then BOOM! It wouldn't take long, and we would be right back to the strife and division, causing me to want to pack up and leave.

I craved to live in God's will and effectively minister to people with my husband. But, most of the time, we were a wreck and in no shape to speak life and freedom to anyone. Anytime we tried to minister to people together, it was difficult for me because I knew we still had so much to work on ourselves. I hated it.

I don't want to portray the wrong picture—my husband wasn't out carousing around like one might think, or doing illegal things. He was in church regularly, but **he had hard-heart issues just like everybody who runs from the Lord's plan for them.** He was not genuinely yielding to what was in his heart on a day-to-day basis, so he had no peace or joy most of the time. This, of course, affected everyone in our home and every relationship he had.

My husband says he was afraid to live—afraid to let God have his **whole life**. He had so much fear because he didn't understand the full aspect of the Good News of Jesus Christ. He lived feeling afraid and condemned for every single thing he did. That fear kept him from believing things could change. Condemnation and disappointments kept him from having any vision at all. We both longed for help and relief from this repetitive cycle. We both talked about wanting to find a church that could give us real answers and help with receiving our victory, even if it meant moving hours away.

In August 2005, after being broken again, we changed churches. It was *then* that our breakthrough came. We found what we saw as our "*Braveheart.*" We found a pastor and church family that would help save our marriage, even our lives, and lead us into true victory. We began to hear Biblical faith being preached. And, we could actually **see** a whole, different, **new way of living** a Christian life (and *doing church*, so to speak).

Change did not happen overnight for us; but, for the first time in our marriage, we finally had true hope of having full victory. To me, this was the last try. I had made up my mind. I would walk away and start my life over as a single woman if this didn't work for us.

I allowed the Lord to work on me too. Immediately, I had promptings to control my mouth and thoughts and to begin to consistently speak differently about our situation. I began to really **believe** that change could and would come to my husband and our marriage. In July 2006, I made a three-page list of positive things to say and pray for my husband. The more I believed and said them, the more I could see glimpses of hope for him.

It seemed like all I was doing for the next several years was getting HARD, HARD correction from the preaching of the Word of God. (Correction still comes regularly *from God's Word* as I read it—praise the Lord.) God helped me not run but receive correction and change things in myself. My husband and I were still having ups and downs in our relationship, but I kept the hope in the frustrating times, and that hope kept me going.

In 2011, our oldest daughter, Jessica, gave me her printout of New Testament Prayers in Scripture that she was praying. I grabbed ahold of them and started praying them ... but ONLY for my husband, and not over me too.

Again, it didn't last long because *my motives* were wrong. (Can you say, *Merry-go-round?* Ha-ha!) The truth is, I was still so mad at him for not surrendering his life to God and keeping to our marriage plan. (Maybe *you* are still mad at your spouse for something? I hope sharing my story with transparent honesty will help you get off that merry-go-round.)

My (wrong) intentions were to change my husband and go *forward* with **my** life—once HE was *fixed*. WOW! I was always, all these years, waiting on my husband to get *fixed*. I had no vision outside of us ministering together as a couple, so I knew he had to change some things and get on track before that could ever happen for us. This thinking hindered me from going forward.

I could have let go of him and cast the care of him onto the Lord sooner, but in all honesty, I was hurting so much that, off and on, I found that I wanted to punish him. I believed the lie that it was not fair my husband didn't keep his commitment to me and that *he* was hindering me. At the time, this ended up actually punishing and tormenting *me* more than him. *Pretty dumb, huh?* God gave me the directions to get out of the mess, and I didn't follow them.

The true, lasting victory came when I finally got to a place where I chose to completely **stop focusing on my husband's shortcomings.** (Which, as I saw them, were half-heartedness and unwillingness to submit his life to God's good plan for us.) I told the Lord I wanted to change and would go forward and obey Him *with or without my husband* in whatever way God would allow me to. I meant this even if it meant me living my whole life staying married to him, going to Heaven never having fulfilled my husband's and my calling together as a married couple. I let go of that dream in my heart, and **I stopped doing things *my way*.** Things were then able to change. **I was getting off the merry-go-round, finally and permanently!!** YES!!!

I picked up the printout of New Testament Prayers in Scripture **again**, and this time, I prayed them—not only for him, but for *me first*, and then us together. (I added these in chapter fourteen for you.) **This time it wasn't robotic reading and speaking. I pointed them like a machete in my hand, and I chopped away the heavy brush around us, clearing a path to the highway!! I believed in the power behind the Word that I was praying.**

I also meditated on all the Scriptures from Proverbs about contentious women and foolish people and many other passages of Scripture that would help me. *I asked the Lord to help me change everything I needed to become a better wife and helpmeet for my man.*

It is amazing how God's Word works! Within two days of me putting forth the effort to resist my old pattern of doing things and begin praying and speaking all these Scriptures **over myself FIRST, <u>I began to change.</u>**

Then my husband began to see a difference in me and my attitude. He stopped being as defensive and distant as he had been. Next, I soon had the ok from the Lord to pray these Scriptures over my spouse and me <u>together as one</u>: never again praying them JUST for him while thinking he was the only one who needed change.

Gradually, I started seeing a major change in both of us, and we were bonding as we never had before. We have been making purposeful movements toward God's plan for our lives and marriage, especially in the past few years. We started warming up to and preferring each other, and the whirlwinds and aimless spinning had stopped.

We started doing what was needed to get off the enemy's merry-go-round of traps and distractions. I have enjoyed watching the Word of God open the eyes of our understanding (from the Ephesians 1 prayer). I have watched God wake us both up to see a clear direction for His plan for us as individuals *and together* as husband and wife.

I have been so blessed to see my husband's desires change. He now allows joy and excitement to come up and out of his heart. I have watched him stop burying himself in work and the TV. I have witnessed him humble himself and repent of everything that hurt his relationship with God, me, our children, and others. I have seen his heart soften and his prayer time with the Lord take off like it never has before. His heart is now so tender for God and people. Talk about "over and above what I could ever ask or think!" WOW!! God is sooooo faithful!!

> Now to Him who is able to do exceedingly abundantly above all that we ask or think, according to the power that works in us, to Him be glory in the church by Christ Jesus to all generations, forever and ever. Amen (Ephesians 3:20–21).

And, *God helped me to change my heart and my actions*. I asked Him to convict *my heart*. I asked God to cause a *yucky* feeling to rise up in me whenever I started to nag at David, make pointed jabs at him, or be contentious in any way. Yep—and God did! I went around with a lot of *yucky* in my gut for a while until I practiced correcting immediately the things that caused it. I began to HATE not walking in love with my husband. I hated it more than I liked the bad-attitude-toward-him *punishment* I gave him. Listening to me, you might be feeling sorry for my husband and what he had to put up with, ha-ha! Honestly, we had a lot of good and fun times together. Still, for years the undercurrent of dissatisfaction and discontent was lurking in the background. We are so glad we got off that merry-go-round and on with a new way of living!

He and I have changed from being marriage partners to friends, even best friends—having fun together more than we ever have since first married thirty-nine years ago: going on dates and getaways (without children), dancing

and laughing alone together at home (yes, without our kids around), and finally connecting and becoming ONE—not only physically, but as one in our hearts.

Over these past seventeen years, we flooded ourselves with teachings about love, honor, obedience, and getting on the path of God's will for our lives. We began to act on the words spoken to us and then watched the layers of lies and false teachings begin to fall off. It was finally getting through to us. **God's will and plan for us both together as one slowly became clear again.** I'm so thankful I didn't quit and hit the road!

It has been over twelve years now of me **faithfully** using God's Word to bush-whack through the jungle of junk. My husband now uses God's Word the same way, and together we cleared a path, not just to the highway but also to the interstate! We are now rolling with clear direction and unity and using

God's Word daily as a road map to see which way to go next. **This is the most fun together we have ever had. We have gone from spinning to winning in our relationship!**

My husband finally lets me be his helpmeet and does not resist it. He has gone back to where we first got off the path. In 2017, we packed up and moved to attend Charis Bible College for three years *together* as husband and wife. He is obeying God in other things he knows to do, also. *My husband is no longer paralyzed with fear and rebellion*. And *I am no longer motivated by fear and rebellion* against my husband.

We are no longer unaware and ignorant of the enemy's tactics against our marriage calling. By God's grace and help, we'll never again get off the path of what we are supposed to do for the Lord here on Earth. We would probably say, if you asked, that we are finally living the dream that has always been in our hearts—and that you can too!!

Yes, we missed almost thirty years of pure peace and joy because of not following God's good plan for us. We missed years and years of not loving and helping people the way God planned because we were so self-centered and caught up in our own issues. We hindered our children and caused some destruction to come to them. (It's definitely humbling myself to share all this.)

BUT!! God loved us through it and has had mercy on us.

All of our children are increasing and allowing God's love to motivate them more and more. Now, my husband and I every day read and study God's Word TOGETHER and talk about it and pray—preaching back and forth together. We encourage each other and prefer each other. My husband has taken the lead, and **I HAVE LET GO TRYING TO *MAKE IT HAPPEN*.** God is growing us up fast (per my husband's prayer) and is helping us make up for the lost time.

God helped me cling to hope and the *first* word He gave us when we were married. God helped me not to quit and run away. God helped me STAY FULL OF FAITH, AND FAITHFUL TO HIM AND THE CALL I HEARD. God helped me **believe His Word and use it to change my circumstances and get off the merry-go-round.** I regret not sticking to it and using the Word of

God faithfully years ago, but God has been merciful and faithful to me and my steadfast *heart* for Him and His plan for us.

I'm so thankful to God for His patience and mercy toward us—for sending people to us to be bold and honest with us, and at the same time, our biggest cheerleaders. If we hadn't accepted His healing plan for us, I would be an emotionally (and probably physically) sick and divorced single woman now. I most likely would STILL be unfulfilled from not doing God's plan with my spouse. *Instead, we are on track*. God is helping our children, also. The *marriage cancer* was identified and put to a stop from growing. Healing and divine health will continue in our marriage relationship more and more every day as we yield to God's ways of doing things—**LOVE!**

I encourage all husbands and wives not to give up on their marriages and **only** use God's Word to change things, not their own agenda, as I did for years. **Using God's Word is what got us off our nightmare merry-go-round.**

It is never God's will for marriages to be sick and die. It is His will for them to go forward and be alive and thriving, getting stronger and healthier every year. So, if we want His will for our marriages, both husband and wife must do their part to make the change happen. **Don't wait for the other, but be the first one to jump off the merry-go-round of the enemy's plan to destroy your marriage.** Do what it takes to get off and cause a change to come. Just think, my husband and I would not have the awesome things happening in our life right now, as a married couple, if one of us had quit.

God's Word is working mightily in us, and He is helping me and my husband fulfill His plan for our lives. I'm so thankful!

We stopped spinning and began winning in our marriage relationship!

EIGHT

COMPULSIVE BEHAVIOR AND ADDICTION MERRY-GO-ROUNDS

Part One: Under the Influence

B Y THE AGE of sixteen, I was already beginning to use alcohol as a coping device. I was a Christian, but I did the same things most new Christians do—I looked to myself for help instead of looking to Jesus. **This is the BIG-GEST temptation for any Christian—the temptation to put our eyes on ourselves and take them off of Jesus**.

So there I was in high school, living a *lukewarm*, hypocritical Christian life. I began drinking alcohol with my friends. I didn't like the taste or smell of beer, so it was never my choice of drink. I preferred hard liquor, with some different sweeter flavors added to it. Soon, I was drinking alcoholic beverages any chance it was made available to me, at parties and with the people I ran with. You could say *I was always under the influence*—always under the influence of peer pressure and my weak flesh, of course!

Because I had no foundation as a young Christian teen, I went against my heart and jumped on this partying merry-go-round. I was emotionally hurt, wounded, and confused. This seemed like a good way to help me fit in and cope. I didn't have a real connection with church friends because I felt like I couldn't relate to them, and I didn't think they could in any way relate to me! So, I just went with the flow with my school friends. I felt they were my best *fit*.

I didn't consider any consequences or that drinking could totally ruin my life if it went too far and turned into an addiction. My friends and I thought we had many good excuses—reasons we needed something to help us *cope*—none of them were worth the risks we took to drink underage and party so hard.

If one of my friends or I had any boyfriend drama, we would drink. If my friends and I were trying to fit in with the older partiers, we would drink. If we wanted to be flirtier with the guys, we would drink. If we were away for an overnight ski trip or cheering for a state wrestling tournament out of town, we would drink. I was part of the *self-help* group, HA! I started to notice I was craving it when I didn't have it. I began to think a lot about it, looking forward to the next time I could get it, even though I would end up sick and throwing up almost every time I had it. Morning hangovers were normal for me after a previous night of drinking. I was getting pretty good at covering up my puking in the bathroom by telling my mom it was just the flu or some other lie.

Before long, I began to have disturbing thoughts. I would see myself as a *powerless, supposed-to-be Christian woman* later on in life. That woman was still drinking socially with friends, laughing, partying, and acting obnoxious, still showing no regard for what she put in her body. She had no regard for the direction of her life. It began to scare me.

I started thinking about how alcohol had a hold on some of my family members and all the destruction it did to them and their lives. **These were alarming thoughts as I saw myself doing these same things after high school, then during college, and later as a wife and mother. They motivated me to resist the *urges*, tastes, and use of alcoholic beverages.** About to start my final semester in high school, and hearing all the plans my friends already had in the works for after graduation, plus talking to the school counselor, got me thinking more realistically about my future. Did I honestly want to continue being a hypocritical Christian and secretly go back and forth between two totally different sets of friends and lives? Because I didn't have any realistic plans for my life, the temptation to continue doing the same thing through the end of the year was actually a real option. But, I couldn't ignore the tugging I felt in my heart to stop *going with the flow* and come off Christmas break ready and determined to start over fresh my last semester in high school.

Even though it was *the thing to do* in my group of friends, I had honestly begun to get to where I really didn't enjoy drinking *that much*, so I stopped. I shared my testimony earlier about how I decided to stop being a *lukewarm* Christian during my senior year Christmas break. I invited Jesus to lead me, and I changed my mindset about hanging out with *only* friends who were better influences.

I committed to following God's lead, knowing the persecution that would follow. What I figured would happen happened. After becoming *sold out* and *on fire* for God, I wasn't very popular. Still, it was a price I was willing to pay to not wind up living the life of an alcoholic. Alcohol was a big part of my family's everyday lifestyle. And, because of how much my flesh could have continued liking it, I realized that there was a big chance I would become an alcoholic. Most teens will go ahead and finish out high school without changing, and then after high school, when not around their friends any longer, will secretly make the change. I knew I was not supposed to wait. It was a *"this is your last chance"* feeling I had inside me.

Not long after getting married, especially during high-stress times, I would have **HUGE URGES** to drink an alcoholic beverage—to buy some liquor and have it in the cabinet, *just in case*. I had thoughts of seeing myself getting up during the night and getting a yummy alcoholic drink while the kids were sleeping and through the day drinking and trying to hide it. I imagined myself beginning to fit in with some of my other family members who were heavy drinkers and having them accept me a little bit better. If I drank with them, then maybe I wouldn't appear to be such a boring *party killer*. I held to my commitment, though, and I have never given in to those craving urges again with God's help (not my own *self-help*). I made Jesus my Lord, and now I am using Him and God's Word as my coping device. This way of coping is the best high I have ever had, and there are NO next-morning-throbbing-head-hangover side effects!

MY ADDICTION TENDENCIES STOPPED when I started looking to Jesus for help and using God's Word as my coping device. I was being *Spirit-led* and didn't even know it.

> For as many as are led by the Spirit of God, these are sons of God (Romans 8:14).

> I say then: Walk in the Spirit, and you shall not fulfill the lust of the flesh (Galatians 5:16).

Walking in the Spirit and the Word of God go hand in hand. As I read God's Word more and allowed it to influence me, I was actually walking in the Spirit. Even though I didn't understand it, the principle worked anyway. As I was walking in the Spirit, according to God's Word, I wasn't desiring to do the works of the flesh. Using God's Word was like getting powerwashed from the inside out. I started feeling cleaner, and so I started acting cleaner.

Has Your Flesh Become Your God?

> And God spoke all these words, saying: "I am the LORD your God, who brought you out of the land of Egypt, out of the house of bondage. You shall have no other gods before Me. You shall not make for yourself a carved image—any likeness of anything that is in heaven above, or that is in the earth beneath, or that is in the water under the earth; you shall not bow down to them nor serve them. For I, the LORD your God, am a jealous God, visiting the iniquity of the fathers upon the children to the third and fourth generations of those who hate Me, but showing mercy to thousands, to those who love Me and keep My commandments" (Exodus 20:1–6; emphasis added).

> And Jesus answered and said to him, "Get behind Me, satan! For it is written, '<u>You shall worship the Lord your God, and Him only you shall serve</u>'" (Luke 4:8; emphasis added).

> <u>You shall love the Lord your God with all your heart</u>, with all your soul, and with all your strength (Deuteronomy 6:5; emphasis added).

No other God besides Him?!?! This is huge! It can be easy to read over these verses and think, "I don't have any gods before God …"

Let's think about it, though. What kinds of things could be *gods* put before the One True God?

See, most Christians wouldn't dream of having a carved image as their god and bowing down before it. But many Christians have other things as their god, other than God. The list is endless: career, family, emotions, fashion, desires, food, your FLESH—all of these and much more can become any Christian's god if they serve it over and above Jesus.

Society has made alcohol and drug usage a way of everyday living for people. People *serve* it, even to the point of addiction. It is a social act, and if you want to fit in socially with the world, you must be an alcohol drinker or drug user. **When I gave my life to live for Jesus, my God, I gave up fitting in socially with the world and *serving* liquor!** You can too!

And what about all other compulsive behaviors?

Compulsive <u>behaviors</u> can be just as life-altering and paralyzing as *harmful <u>addictions</u>*. There are many harmful ***habits and behaviors*** the enemy uses through our flesh to control and destroy people's lives: manipulation, self-centeredness, anxiety, criticizing, strife, being dishonest, arguing, gossiping, judging, pride, jealousy, fear, paranoia, pornography, procrastination, laziness, complacency, offenses, self-pity, excessive talking, feelings of insecurity, etc. You can be *under the influence of* any of these behaviors and serve them daily if you choose.

Whose influence are *YOU* under? Are you like I was in high school? Are you under the influence of your old, dead nature (which is now considered your flesh), or are you under the influence of your new, born-again nature in your spirit? Consider these probing questions: Do you serve your flesh by giving all your attention and all your thoughts and time to what *it* wants? Does your flesh rule you? Does your flesh motivate you to do something or not do something? Does it tell you when to get up, when to go to bed, what to eat, what to watch, etc.? Do you obey your fleshly desires *over* your heart's desires?

If you do any of these things consistently, you must honestly consider that **your flesh is your god,** and the Lord Jesus Christ is not! If your God is the One and only Lord God (who created us and the heavens and earth), then you will serve Him and not your flesh. One of the biggest areas where the fleshly, carnal nature can become someone's god is addictions, specifically drugs and alcohol. While under the influence of drugs, alcohol, or any addiction, that person is not in control. *It* controls them and influences them to take on the characteristics of *its* nature and purpose.

Any addiction and compulsive behavior we have is a merry-go-round for our flesh to ride and have a great time on, just getting more powerful and influential! On this type of merry-go-round, you just fit into the world's way of living. Just *Que Sera, Sera*—what will be, will be: we just take it as it comes and don't have anything to do with what direction we are going in life. That type of reasoning, *what will be, will be,* is just an excuse for us to live in the pleasures of our flesh *without* taking any responsibility for our direction or outcomes. It is an excuse to be lazy about spiritual growth and enlightenment. If we insist on yielding and living according to our flesh, we aren't even *letting* God help us!

The key to getting off this merry-go-round is not about modifying your behavior to change your life. It's about **changing your mindset, getting your focus off yourself and what *you* can do,** and **walking in the light of God's love and truth**—His Spirit—and what He has already done IN you.

> It is the Spirit who gives life. The flesh profits nothing. The words that I speak to you are spirit and are life (John 6:63 MEV).

Who's Got Your Focus?

Have you ever heard of the *law of focus*? The law of focus reveals exactly what we are being influenced by. If we have **microscopic** focus, we will always look downward and magnify small things, causing them to appear bigger. However, suppose our focus is like a **telescope.** We will always look upward with telescopic focus, looking at something big that appears far away and bringing it closer to us into true focus.

As born-again Christians, there are two focuses we must have to live victoriously over all fleshly behaviors. The first is *upward focus*—UP unto Jesus. The second is *inward focus*—IN who we are IN HIM and what we have as we remain IN HIM. Jesus-focused is comparable to the telescope—which is always pointing upward. We look UP to Jesus and magnify Him as greater than the problems we are dealing with down here. Looking upward to Jesus and inward to who we are IN HIM, in our spirit, causes us to be influenced by His strength and His love. The new life HE gave us will appear bigger and be brought into true focus. Let's be like the telescope—look UP, and magnify UPWARDS, bringing things into true focus.

In contrast, being sin-focused is comparable to focusing through a microscope, constantly looking DOWN through a magnifying glass, making what we see appear bigger. God isn't sin-focused, just staring at our fleshly actions hoping we don't fall off the bandwagon or go off a cliff. And, since my Bible college experience almost forty years ago, I've learned I don't have to live that way, either!

Your life goes in the direction of your focus. The fear of doing something wrong *is no longer* my focus. But neither is my focus like it was *before* going to that college. I no longer have to live focused on my fleshly self, always trying to fit in and party like the best of them, just to cope with emotions. If our focus is being led by our physical cravings and desires, we'll undoubtedly be led in the wrong direction. I can personally testify to this Biblical principle. Living your life led by the *cravings* of your emotions WILL LEAD YOU away from Jesus and straight to heartache and destruction!

Then, when desire has conceived, it gives birth to sin; and sin, when it is full-grown, brings forth death (James 1:15).

Personal freedom side note: Now, I can have a glass of wine if I *want to* (notice I didn't say *crave to*), and it isn't because I want to fit in. If I don't drink, it's not because I'm afraid someone will see me; and if I do have a drink, it's not because of social pressures or because I'm addicted or hoping to get drunk! I can totally be around friends and not care if they have a drink or not. It makes no impression on me either way. I'm not feeling pressure to join them, and almost always, I don't. I have wine at my house, and I'll have a glass here and there. My husband drinks a beer with a meal, here and there. We don't focus on it the way we used to. It doesn't use us and control us the way it used to.

You could be thinking, *Why would you even want to have a drink of any kind of alcohol with your background?* You see, there was a time in my life when I would not have been able to, and I knew I couldn't touch it. And if you have had weaknesses in an area in your life, you may be in a time when you need to stay far away from it, as well. It wasn't until I got stronger in the revelation of who I am IN CHRIST and no longer focused on messing up that I was able to be free to have a drink of wine if I wanted. I am no longer drawn away *by the lust* for alcohol like I used to be, so now, for me, it's like having a soda. I don't drink eight cans of soda in a row, so why would I do that with alcohol? See, I'm free from the hold of alcohol, and it is no temptation to me anymore.

For freedom Christ freed us. Stand fast therefore and do not be entangled again with the yoke of bondage (Galatians 5:1 MEV).

NOTE—*David and I spent years away from drinking any type of alcohol before we got to this point.* We don't use alcohol to fit in socially nor as a way to cope any longer. We don't *get hammered* or even close. We also aren't *afraid* to have even one drink because of religious lies trying to influence us, like years ago! Wow, has my thinking been made free in this area!

__WE__ *have control of our behavior*. The more we yield to the *flesh*, the more carnal we become. We can say "NO!" to our flesh. We can say "YES!" to God's Spirit. And so can you. The more we yield to the influence of God's Spirit inside of us, the more of Him will manifest through us. ___Walking in the Spirit is supposed to be a lifestyle for born-again children of God___. Our new, born-again spirit is supposed to be what influences us. The choice is ours, though. If we don't choose to walk in the Spirit, we will have a lifestyle of living in the flesh and all the CORRUPTION it leads to. The flesh represents the old way of life, which died when we were born again. Living according to the flesh is living like we are still in bondage to sin. *Walk in the Spirit, and you won't have to worry about the lusts of the flesh creeping in there.*

Walking in the Spirit doesn't have to make us look and sound weird—even to our old party friends. It makes us in control, awake, and aware. When Christians start to look and sound weird, they stick out like an ugly *sore thumb* and become ineffective in their witness to the world.

What does it look like to walk in the Spirit? How do you walk in the Spirit when your flesh wants, craves, or desires something every day? You *follow the instructions* given to us in God's Word, and it will *change your mindset*:

> For those who live according to the flesh <u>set their minds on</u> the things of the flesh, but those who live according to the Spirit, the <u>things of the Spirit</u> (Romans 5:8; emphasis added).

If then you were raised with Christ, <u>seek those things which are above</u>, where Christ is, sitting at the right hand of God (Colossians 3:1; emphasis added).

<u>Set your mind on things above</u>, not on things on the earth (Colossians 3:2; emphasis added).

… and be <u>continually renewed in the spirit of your mind</u> [having a fresh, untarnished mental and spiritual attitude] (Ephesians 4:23 AMP; emphasis added).

And <u>do not be conformed to this world</u>, but be <u>transformed by the renewing of your mind</u>, that you may prove what is that good and acceptable and perfect will of God (Romans 12:2; emphasis added).

God is so awesome!! Before the foundation of the world, He picked all of us to be IN HIM (Ephesians 1:4). God equipped us, through Jesus, to be victorious! He shows us the difference in what will keep us in bondage versus what will keep us walking in the liberty Jesus gave us! He gives us a head's up on how all this failure and victory stuff works—AND, He gives us the CHOICE!! How awesome is all that?!! Wow! I totally love Him!

What about in the face of tragedy? A tragic event <u>will ALWAYS</u> **TRIGGER** some type of emotion in us—positive or negative—and we will respond by looking for a way to release or cope with that emotion. At the initial moment of the traumatic event, we have the opportunity to walk **in the Spirit** (*if we are a Christian*) OR yield to *fleshly, carnal ways* to cope.

Here's the scriptural answer to how we are to respond to difficult situations THAT WILL ARISE in our lives:

Likewise, you also consider yourselves to be dead to sin, but alive to God through Jesus Christ our Lord (Romans 6:11 MEV; emphasis added).

CONSIDER. If we *consider* ourselves dead to sin, we basically think of ourselves as dead to sin—we look at ourselves as dead to sin instead of being sin-focused. Being dead to someone or something means you don't give it attention or put any focus or thought toward it. You are dead to them and dead to it! When you focus on Jesus, the Spirit of life in Christ Jesus flows from you through your spirit into your soul, which is your mind, will, emotions. This focusing on Jesus and His Word, coming from your spirit, will do the work. This will act as a **superpower** that puts the deeds of the flesh to death. It does not happen by your *willpower*.

> For if you live according to the flesh you will die; but if by the Spirit you put to death the deeds of the body, you will live (Romans 8:13).

Look back to Romans 6:11. Dead to sin—alive to God. It doesn't say to ignore sin. It clearly says to consider yourself dead to sin but alive to God. Any carnal actions can be REPLACED with spiritual actions. Any carnal thoughts can be REPLACED with spiritual thoughts. Sin has no influence over us as we focus on our new life in the Spirit—alive unto God. ***Changing what we allow to influence us will change our life's direction and outcome.***

Let me give you some examples to connect with:

> ➢ If you ***feel <u>hurt</u> in your heart and emotions***, you might turn to a type of substance *pain killer* that relieves that pain. The alternative is to turn to LOVE, Who is God, and meditate on how Jesus bore your griefs and sorrows, so you don't have to.

➤ If you *feel critical, angry, disappointed, and judgmental in your heart and emotions,* you might want to lash out, gossip, and vent on someone, usually the people closest to you. Remember: hurting people hurt people. The alternative is to forgive and trust LOVE, Who is God. Choose to obey the love commandment for people, loving them how Christ loves us: *A new commandment I give to you, that you love one another; as I have loved you, that you also love one another. By this, all will know that you are My disciples if you have love for one another (John 13:34–35).*

➤ If you *feel you are in a <u>hopeless situation,</u>* you might want to give up trying and let yourself get depressed. The alternative is to have faith in LOVE, Who <u>is</u> God, and start **meditating on who you are in Christ**—if you are a Christian. If you aren't a Christian, you can become one now—just turn to and pray the Prayer of Salvation at the end of this book.

➤ If you were *<u>aroused sexually</u> at an early age*, through being molested or exposed to pornography, you have a whole bucket load of ways you might release the *emotions you are feeling*. The alternative is to first choose to leave the past behind and be healed by LOVE, Who is God. Meditate on how God sees you and who you are with Him living inside of you. Know that it <u>wasn't</u> God who exposed you to that or caused that to happen to you for a reason—those are lies. **God sees you whole and pure in Christ.**

➤ If you *feel like a <u>loser</u> after playing a lottery ticket* and didn't win, you might want to keep playing until you feel like a winner. The alternative is to replace the feelings of being a loser by believing you have already been made victorious. Believe that you are already a winner through LOVE, Who is God. Then, you can *stop* looking to *win the lotto* (or other similar efforts) as evidence that you are a winner. **Believing on the promises of God for your life always makes you a winner!**

➤ If you *feel <u>unsatisfied</u>, <u>bored</u>, and <u>unfulfilled</u>*, you might try to find satisfaction through eating good, tasty treats and foods more than you should. The alternative is to believe you will find your path of purpose through LOVE, Who is God, and feed on God's Word to gain spiritual growth, nourishment, and purpose for your life. **Hunger and thirst for HIM as an alternative!** (Matthew 4:4)

➤ If you *feel <u>afraid</u> to follow a dream* in your heart because of the fear of failure harassing you, you might become a workaholic, so you can say you don't have time to follow your dream. The alternative is to get into God's Word and **cast out fear through the revelation of LOVE,** Who is God, and then go for it.

➤ If you feel *<u>stressed</u> or under severe emotional <u>pressure</u>*, you might want to use something or do something that calms down your feelings, like *veg out* in front of the TV every night. The alternative is

STOP THE SPIN!

Negative responses and coping alternatives all turn into addictions if they are repeated over and over. Stop the spinning, and learn a new way of living.

to believe **you can be delivered from all your troubles through LOVE**, Who <u>is</u> God, and make yourself get up and do something different.

Need help? Don't we all? Thankfully, we are not left helpless! As we make the Word of God our coping device, allowing Him to powerwash our minds, we are sure to overcome compulsive addictions! Rather than repeating problems over and over, we will come over and over our problems by the power and help from Holy Spirit.

> My help comes from the LORD, Who made heaven and earth (Psalm 1:21).

> And I will pray the Father, and He will give you another Helper, that He may abide with you forever—the Spirit of truth, whom the world cannot receive, because it neither sees Him nor knows Him; but you know Him, for He dwells with you and will be in you. I will not leave you orphans; I will come to you (John 14:16–18).

Part Two: Why Don't They Just Stop It?

I have had lots of experience dealing with individuals living with addictions or those who had already been in jail, prison, and/or rehab. Many of these are my own family members. I volunteered for thirty-five Sundays at an outside homeless church. Almost all of the 100 people we served and ministered to each week were addicts of one sort or another. I also trained as a chaplain for a county jail, which involved Bible studies with incarcerated women. I've spoken to all of them to some degree regarding their different addictions, circumstances, and heartaches.

Some of these individuals have shared why they believe an addict goes back to their addiction after stopping it for some time. Their answers were usually dependent upon their current state of addiction, whether they were active or not. If they were <u>active</u> at the time, the most common answer was that they just couldn't help it, and most believed it was just part of their lot in life. They admitted the addiction has control over them but don't know why. *(It indeed has control over them, but what's the honest root as to why?)*

For those who had <u>not been active</u> in the addiction for a while, their mind will be more out of the loop of doing it over and over again. These people usually admit that an addict will return to the drug (or whatever it is) because they want to and are not completely ready to give it up yet.

Suppose an addict tells me they believe they have no self-control regarding the addiction. In that case, I have a certain picture that flashes before my eyes. I see the addiction with arms, *physically grabbing them* without their consent and abducting them. I see it FORCING THEM to look at something, FORCING THEM to drink something, FORCING THEM to steal something, FORCING THEM to say something, hit something, feel depressed, and so forth. It's like they're saying the addiction has a gun pointed to their head or threatening to hurt someone they love and says, "YOU MUST DO IT, or else!" Seriously, if this is what they are trying to make people believe, I don't believe it!

The truth is, it's in their control to <u>at least</u> make a decision to stop, ask for help, and submit to the help. But, addiction will always have control over the addict ***until they take back the control they have given the addiction.*** <u>It always starts or ends with their choice.</u> **These addictions are real; there's no doubt about that.** We don't ignore the fact that someone has constantly been repeating a harmful act. If we know the root of their reasons, we can better help.

After my own research and learning from my personal experiences, I gathered some reasons I think some quit and some don't. I'm not a professional, but these are things I see: (1) They don't KNOW God, and how He can give them a new heart that's not broken, (2) they are in punishment and unforgiveness mode, (3) they blame their behavior and addiction on family and upbringing, (4) rehabs aren't using God's Word to permanently heal and deliver them, and (5) they believe the addiction adds *more thrill* to life, and life would be boring without it.

Let's look at each of these possibilities and challenges more closely:

1) They don't KNOW God and how He can give them a new heart that's not broken.

Every person I've ever met living with an addiction has a *broken-heart* condition. Their heart has been hurt, wounded, offended, abused, forgotten, neglected, used, and treated with what I call *love with conditions attached*. God's kind of love—no strings attached—is something they've never experienced and most likely don't believe even exists, not for them, anyway.

My heart would like to tell them this Good News (and, perhaps it might be that you are someone who needs to hear this too):

God has a new heart for you. He wants to remove your heart that has turned to stone and give you a heart of flesh, a heart that has lifeblood flowing through it. He wants to put His Spirit in you and give you a new spirit and a new life—eternal life that starts right here on Earth, right now.

> Then I will sprinkle clean water upon you, and you shall be clean. From all your filthiness and from all your idols, I will cleanse you. Also, I will give you a new heart and a new spirit I will put within you. And I will take away the stony heart out of your flesh, and I will give you a heart of flesh. I will put My Spirit within you and cause you to walk in My statutes, and you will keep My judgments and do them (Ezekiel 36:25–27 MEV; emphasis added).

Why wouldn't they want this if they knew about it? Because ...

2) **They are in punishment and unforgiveness mode.**

Often, people on addiction merry-go-rounds aren't willing to forgive themselves. They are punishing themselves—mentally and emotionally beating themselves and physically abusing themselves. Some may feel like I felt regarding the sexual molestation of my daughter. For a long time, I didn't forgive myself or allow myself to move forward. In a sense, I held onto those merry-go-round bars because I felt like if she was still suffering, maybe I should be too. The "center post" that stabilized that lie was that if she suffered the effects of her pure and innocent body and thoughts being stolen, then I still needed to be punished for not seeing what was going on at the time. I didn't want to believe I could (or should) go forward and enjoy life if I felt like she couldn't live her own life, free from shame. I had to forgive to move forward, and that included forgiving myself.

Forgiveness of the person who wronged them, violated them, and stole from them is very important. Just as important is for the person stuck in addiction *to forgive themselves*. They will need to forgive themselves for any crimes and injustices they have committed. And, going even further, they will have to completely forgive the whole of their past experiences in life: Forgive the fact that something bad happened to them; Forgive the fact that their life hasn't been what they wanted or thought it would be; Forgive themselves for times they themselves may not have done what was necessary or the times that they couldn't or didn't stop the bad things from happening to them.

The grief and sorrow from these actions and the results are attached to them and will not release them if they won't first release themselves. In reality, they give the memory permission to continue violating and stealing from them when they don't forgive. It's like the crime committed is still being committed if they won't forgive themselves.

When people finally receive the gift of forgiveness that Jesus gave all of us over 2,000 years ago, they (we) come to understand ***undeserved forgiveness***. The result? They (we) can then forgive others—even those they (we) feel do not deserve it—because Jesus did it for us. We *received* forgiveness from Jesus so we are fully able *to use* His forgiveness (which, having received it, we now have inside of us) to forgive others. It's supposed to be easier than we make it.

Step one is to stop mistreating themselves (ourselves) as Ephesians 4:31 (MEV) says:

> Let all bitterness, wrath, anger, outbursts, and blasphemies, with all malice, be taken away from you.

And then, step two, keep the forgiveness chain reaction going, like Ephesians 4:32 (MEV) says, beginning with themselves (ourselves):

> And be kind one to another, tenderhearted, <u>forgiving one another, just as God in Christ also forgave you</u> (emphasis added).

Forgiveness removes the sin, the shame, *and the blame*, which is the next reason people on the addiction merry-go-round keep spinning.

3) They blame their behavior and addiction on their family and their upbringing.

I've heard some addicts say they believe they were just born with an addictive personality. Like, if it's not one thing, it's another thing they repeat over and over. The truth is, because of the sin-fallen nature of all mankind, we all have the ability in the natural to have addictions. But if you are *born again* with Jesus as your Lord, you've been given a new nature, one free from addiction, free from *any* fleshly hold. There comes a time for all of us when we need to live from our born-again nature and exchange those sin traits for our new Christlike personality.

It is true that some people are born with addictions because of what their mother did while they were in her womb. It is true that whatever the mother was into during her pregnancy can naturally affect the baby, especially if it is substance abuse. I've been to Arkansas Children's Hospital NICU and seen the newborn babies going through withdrawal. It is extremely real and extremely sad. I realize that if these babies born to parents with addiction issues **_are left in the home with those same parents_**, they have a big chance of repeating what their parents do. Because they will learn to THINK how their parents think regarding life. Some people call this a *generational curse*. But, it is actually a *generational thinking pattern*. It's all they have known. The way they think and see things needs to be changed before they will stop.

In certain situations, a person may have been born addicted to a substance and then, even as an adult, are still addicted to the substance. BUT! That doesn't mean God made them that way *in the womb!* This can apply to many situations in people's lives. God is not a mean, confused God. He didn't want some babies to have addictions or birth defects due to a mother's lifestyle! **God is good, and the plans He has for you are good plans!**

STOP THE SPIN!

Don't believe the lies. People cannot be in their RIGHT MIND to believe that God wanted to single them out and give them some kind of physical, mental, or emotional difficulty (like they won the prize or something). They act as if He wanted them to be born that way. That is a lie. (I actually had people tell me this garbage regarding our youngest daughter being born with Short-Gut Syndrome.) Decide today to get OFF that merry-go-round and ON with your new way of living!

God is good, and the plans He has for you are good plans!

I realize whatever family we come from and how we were raised *will have a stronghold* on our thinking and perceptions *until that way of thinking is replaced.* Just because we were raised a certain way does not mean God **wants** us to think that way or perceive ourselves that way! It just means that we were exposed to it while growing up, and it had a major influence on our *thinking.*

I think of a *stronghold* as something we *strongly believe.* It's like our thinking is being confined to only one box. The cool thing is that if we decide to believe something different, that particular *stronghold* leaves us. It loses our permission to stay! That's why it is so important to change who and what we are listening to, who and what we are watching, and who we hang around with. It affects what we believe, and what we believe in our *hearts* is how we will live.

Let me offer an example. Suppose we believe depression controls us because we have a history of family members controlled by depression. In that case, we will never stop agreeing that we have it. We will never **start saying**, "I'm getting through this! God has set me free from this! I am not depressed like my family says we *all* are!" Or, suppose we like the drama and attention from our family by submitting to the depression. Why would we want to say something different and give it up? We have to get to the place where we hate repeating our negative family patterns bad enough to want to make the change!

David and I used to be on the altar care team at a previous church where we prayed with many hurting people. Before serving on that team, we prayed for people even outside the church building. Sometimes people who wanted prayer would tell us they were depressed because their mom and almost everyone in their family struggles with depression. They said it just runs in their family.

People who believe this are *almost* impossible to help. It would rock the whole family boat if just one person found out the truth that it only runs in their family *because* they just keep accepting it. And because family members keep repeating how they see their family behave, respond, and live life. Just think … what if they *stopped* believing it and eventually didn't need meds anymore and got off disability? What if they proved they could actually begin to function without depression? They might get a lot of persecution from the family, but now they would be setting a new pattern for the family to follow!

Believing God's Word over everything else is the key to end the spinning and embrace a new way of living.

4) Rehabs aren't using God's Word to permanently heal and deliver.

I've been exposed to the secular AA (Alcoholics Anonymous) meetings and many other groups' twelve-step programs. I've also been in a CHRISTIAN twelve-step program. These programs teach the addict to *accept it* because it is *their disease,* and *they can't help it.* They even make the person dealing with the addiction to confess at every meeting, *"Hi, my name is _____ and I am a_____."* This is **ludicrous**—which means foolish, unreasonable, or out of place, as to be … ridiculous[6].

At the suggestion of a friend, I went to an AL-Anon meeting once, over thirty years ago. Growing up, I was exposed to many family members who were either alcoholics or real close. Either way, their drinking affected me and everyone they were around. At the meeting, I had to say, "Hi, my name is Dana, and I am the victim of an alcoholic." We all spent the evening sharing our sob stories, wishing those things never happened to us, and giving ourselves an excuse to act messed up! There was no focusing on resisting that false identity of *believing* we were and always would be *victims of alcoholics.*

How depressing it must be for people to **be made** to attend those meetings every week and repeat that same thing over and over! And, then, to have everyone sit around talking and comparing their personal experiences with addiction—like it is a *Big Fish Story.* Like, who will win the trophy this week for having the biggest and baddest addiction?! How about writing a *different* story? It could be called: How the Big Bad Addiction Fish *Got Away*!

People's situations are magnified and glamorized in these mostly secular group settings. They are often made out to be helpless victims of their addiction, now forced to live their entire lives with the *burden* of their addiction. Along with the burden of their addiction, they also feel they are victims of the legal system somehow—through incarceration or community service. Because of this philosophy, they can always find some reason why they can't move forward. They have been taught to believe things will never change. They *believe* that they are and always will be helplessly stuck in the same situation. *These programs are not helping people to truly move forward!* They are teaching people to live with and coddle their problems.

Put yourself in their shoes for a minute. If you are told *and believe* that you are an addict and always will be, how would you ever be able to dream or set goals? You would <u>never</u> have hope to achieve your goal and have a dream outside of your addiction. Supposedly, that is your lot in life, according to some people's *beliefs*.

I know people who have been forced to go to these group meetings and said they were a joke. It was not a secret in our family that every time my dad was sentenced to attend AA group meetings, he just *snowed* them. My dad actually used to laugh and brag about how he had them so deceived. He said he would get them to believe he was all cleaned up from alcohol to the point they even had him leading the class! (Funny, but not funny!) He told me he would walk out the door and go straight to the store and pick up a twelve-pack on the way home, get drunk, and pass out again and again. Wow! But I know he isn't the only one like this. I have other family members who've said similar things.

Some *Christian* help groups don't give much hope or help either. Whatever happened to Christians using the LIVING WORD of God and the LIVING FELLOWSHIP with GOD and the whole armor of God to once and for all resist the addiction? What happened to Christians **changing their thinking** by renewing their minds, so they think of God differently, think of themselves differently, and think about the addiction differently? **People who learn to do this receive a different result called *permanent freedom*!**

Why should they sit around and confess their sins over and over and over again? Why not sit around and confess their right standing with God through Jesus, over and over and over again?!

The freedom is possessed by repeatedly hearing, receiving, and earnestly confessing righteousness in Jesus instead of repeatedly confessing, "I'm

an addict." If they are a Christian, they are free from sin and addictions—NOT an addict!

The problem is that many groups are led by people, even Christian people, who don't believe in the ***complete and finished work of the Cross.*** So, they are limited to what they can teach and impart into the addict's freedom. Suppose leaders have a limited, distorted, and watered-down version of Scripture. In that case, they can only offer a limited view to the group. If they only believe their sins are forgiven but *now whatever happens in their life is <u>God's will</u>,* they will filter all their teachings through that idea. They will teach the group to take NO RESPONSIBILITY—from the point of Salvation on—for their own faith, beliefs, obedience, actions, and victory.

On the contrary, God's will, based on how Jesus taught us to pray (often called *The Lord's Prayer)* in Matthew 6:9–13, is that we live on Earth as it is in Heaven. ***Free! Victorious! Whole in every way,*** not living in acceptance and survival mode!

<u>The rehab missing link</u> is the link that connects them to permanent freedom. That link screams, *"DON'T ACCEPT IT!"* The common teaching is acceptance and tolerance of the addiction or whatever their issue is. To be effective, they should be teaching them not to tolerate and accept anything that is robbing them of a good, healthy, and prosperous life. Since they aren't, the people in the group are not seeing how they or their situations could ever be any different!

Changing how we think and see ourselves—changes how we act! Just think if these group leaders would use genuine Biblical materials that teach about righteousness in Jesus instead of teaching about man's natural tendencies. Wow! We would begin to see people who have been caught in addictions turning away from their destruction! They would be turning to Jesus!

The answer to them *wanting* to let go of it is found in their *hearing the truth* about Jesus and *believing what God's love did for them.* Inviting Jesus into their situation and using HIS strength to overcome addiction empowers them in a measure they've never yet experienced. Then, the next step is tapping into their purpose in life and the heart desire (calling) that God put in them. When they find this out, they will <u>want</u> to replace that fleshly habit with the spiritual identity and purpose God gave them.

If I had my way, I would take all the people in these groups and begin to repeatedly *tell them the truth* about who they are IN CHRIST, as a saved person! I would constantly pour truth into them and teach them how REAL LOVE *is not an emotion*, but it is God Himself. I would do this until they finally <u>decided to receive the truth</u> and let their mind begin to get renewed. I know it would work because … LOVE never fails. Then, after they got the revelation of their new identity and how God sees them, I would gradually let them loose to go and practice living the truth. Doesn't this sound a lot like *discipleship*?

I would love to protect all the addicts in these groups from those who will only bring them back into the bondage of condemnation by focusing on their sins and past actions. What a difference it would make in their heart and lives if they were discipled and taught correctly by the truth about God's grace and love for them and about who they really are! I've already mentioned Psalm 107, but it bears repeating:

> Then they cried out to the LORD in their trouble, And **He saved them** from their distresses. <u>He sent His word and healed them,</u> And <u>rescued them from their destruction</u> (Psalm 107:19–20 AMP; emphasis added).

If God said He sent HIS WORD and healed and rescued them, then why isn't HIS WORD being used? *His Word* is the true Gospel of Jesus Christ. Jesus said He <u>is</u> the Word, didn't He?

> In the beginning [before all time] was the Word (Christ), and the Word was with God, and the Word was God Himself (John 1:1 AMP; emphasis added).

Some rehabs and help groups are still using all kinds of made-up, man-made ideas, hoping they help. Personality profiles supposedly help the addict settle with a personality trait and find productive activities that appeal to them based on their current personality trait. These personality profiles, even so-called *Christian* ones, imply that one is born with a certain personality *and even negative desires.* These basically teach that this is who one is and <u>always will be</u>. They don't leave room for the working of Holy Spirit inside to change one's personality at all.

I can tell you that as a little girl, I was very strong-willed and, at times, a very mean and angry child. But I have since allowed the Holy Spirit to sweeten me up [smiles]. I don't even relate to that personality any longer. *Personalities and tendencies can change.* You can be transformed by renewing your mind to the Word of God. It's an ongoing transformation process that continues over our entire lives. This Biblical truth stands opposite of those who believe, "You are who you are."

I know of a couple churches that have a really good recovery program. I also know of some that have a pretty good program. Still, they implement some of the secular rehab and recovery teachings into it. The world's way of doing things should not be all mixed in with God's perfect plan and design for recovery. *Wouldn't it be great if every church offered a discipleship program for their people that was based on and structured according to the Bible?*

And finally, discipleship would help teach how fun and amazing the life of freedom in Christ really is!

5) They believe the addiction adds more thrill to life, and it would be boring without it.

This is a lie from the enemy, which he wants people to be stuck believing. This is one of the stumbling blocks that lead to the recurrence of addictions. The truth is that they just need something to do that they absolutely *love doing*—something they can't wait to wake up in the morning to go do. Doing something healthy and productive birthed from the passions and giftings inside their heart will light them up! I have observed that nearly every person spinning in addiction typically likes to help people. So, helping other people will thrill their hearts and keep them from being bored.

Because this is not often taught, there's a good chance they don't have a clue what pushes their passion and gifting button, though. It's going to take some digging. They will need to spend *quiet* one-on-one time with God, hearing from Him, and learning what it is that **He wants to bring out of them for their enjoyment in this life**. He knows them better than we or anyone else does. So when they go to the Source, He Who created them, it is easy to discover purpose, what they are uniquely created to do here in this earthly life. But this will only happen IF they truly want to stop serving their flesh and start following Holy Spirit's leadings.

How will we and others know if they truly want to stop serving their flesh? They will stop serving their flesh! They will put action to their talk. They will start to focus on getting results by keeping busy doing something they really enjoy. This will be easy for them because it is something they already like to do, such as a hobby or ongoing art project, sewing, physically working out, hiking, or doing yard work. They might take up photography or a computer course, volunteer somewhere like a nursing home or animal shelter, help in a community project, or join a service team at church. Perhaps they might help an elderly neighbor clean their yard or just sit and listen to them tell stories about when they were younger.

If we sincerely look, we all can find *something* that *stirs us up on the inside* and focuses our thoughts and productivity toward someone else. <u>*Giving* can be very satisfying if we let it be</u>. We each must find that something and establish these new patterns. My daughter is one of the most giving people I know. She volunteered at a retirement center for a while. All she did was help with the activity of BINGO. They loved her! This kept her mind on being a blessing to the elderly and replaced her thoughts and actions of doing something *unproductive* for herself. She has also used her creative ability to sew fun quilts and give them away to a lot of people. Giving—it's so fulfilling because giving is the heart of our Heavenly Father.

These are all really good suggestions that are very productive and doable. But, if those holding on to addictions aren't active and doing the things God dropped in their heart to do, they won't last long in staying off the old merry-go-rounds. They will be right back in the old place, bored and dissatisfied, with too much unproductive time on their hands. *There is something that God has placed inside each person's heart that fits them just perfectly and will fulfill them so much that they will never want to go back to being flesh-led*. So, the goal is that they let themselves use the giftings they know they already have and discover just how thrilling that life can really be!

Staying Off Their Merry-Go-Round

Here's my encouragement to you: Really focus on staying out of the drama, emotions, and lifestyle the addict is living. <u>**People living in harmful habits and addictions need to see the example of someone being stable, strong, and unafraid. They need to see the pattern from someone coping with their life events in a mature and scriptural way.**</u> Let your gentleness be known to them. Love them, but do not get involved in such a way that you get yourself uprooted and off your own good course, pulled up from the suction of their *silly-silo* merry-go-round vacuum.

You have to let go and keep your distance for this to happen. Give them the space they need to make their own decision to stop. They might need some support and help to stop, but the first step is that *they decide* TO STOP ONCE AND FOR ALL and then stop repeating it over and over!

If we could *make them* decide to stop this repeated non-sense, it would be great! If we could *make them* decide to stop hurting themselves and others and *make them* stop running from God's way of doing things and *make them* believe in who they are IN CHRIST JESUS, it would be great! But, since we can't, we must stay strong, level-headed, and focused on Jesus, patiently waiting for them to come to their senses, <u>**even while they are in *destructive mode***</u>.

We have to treat them like God the Father treats us. Does He *make us* do anything? Does He *make us* stop hurting ourselves and others? No, He doesn't. He loves us enough to allow us to make our own choice to come to Him. So, stop wasting your time, energy, and thoughts on being all caught up in trying to *make someone* change.

They have to make their mind up! *They* have to put THEIR OWN FOOT DOWN! Only then will they see that having a <u>Biblical victory plan</u> (one that involves mind-renewal) and executing that plan *through their own free choice* will bring freedom to them. Once they honestly **DECIDE** to stop, they will have to choose to do what it takes to stay on their *victory plan of action* and do it every day. They will have plenty of opportunities to choose whether to stay off the merry-go-round and keep moving forward or not. It's exactly how I get to choose every day if I start getting drunk on hard liquor again … *or not.*

Even if someone is in a mandated recovery program, they don't have to agree with what the program is wrongly teaching them about being stuck on this addiction merry-go-round—just waiting for it to pop up its ugly head years down the road. Intstead, they can take God's steps to their recovery.

The key is *for them* to consistently read God's powerful Word to get their thinking renewed. They will need to change from only being a **convert** to becoming a **<u>disciple</u>** of Jesus Christ.

Are you willing to back off and stay out of the way so God can love on them and work to soften their heart and change their desires? I am. It hurts my pride and emotions to stay out of it … but I am. The reality is that lives depend on us doing that.

Part Three: Stop Running Interference!

Our fleshly responses, motivated by fear, <u>will hurt the addict</u>. Our spiritually mature responses, motivated by faith and wisdom, <u>will help them</u>.

In my and my husband's experience with our second-born daughter, we eventually, **after SEVERAL FAILS, stopped the merry-go-round we had created. We started doing something different, moving forward; we got off the merry-go-round and on with life.** Had we stayed out of God's way, her merry-go-round lifestyle would have already ended. We have learned a few things along the way … the hard way, though!

We learned that when **addicts** (of any kind) are continuously told everything they need to do, all they need to change, it causes them to run harder to get another fix. This is a trigger. They become even more overwhelmed. They

214

begin to think it's just more stuff they CAN'T DO! *(Our hope is that you can learn from our mistakes with this and save yourself, a friend, or a family member the hurt and condemnation it causes.)*

For instance, telling them that they *need* to stop doing what they are doing. They *need* to go to church. They *need* to read their Bible. They *need* to hang out with new friends. They *need* to stop listening to that junk. They *need* to stop watching that garbage. They *need* to change how they dress. They *need* to get a job. They *need* to grow up. They *need* to stop thinking of themselves. They *need* to be more responsible. They *need* to get an education. They *need* to wake up earlier. They *need* to go to bed earlier. They *need* to eat better. They *need* to stop being lazy and unproductive. They *need* to stop being confused. ARE YOU EXHAUSTED YET?!

If YOU are, I guarantee that now you know how *they* feel when hearing this stuff constantly. It just about makes you want to bang your head against the wall, doesn't it?!

When we say things like this to teenagers or adults, it shows that we require them to focus on performing <u>our</u> list of dos and don'ts. It says we won't accept them unless they do *or* don't. God doesn't want us to perform for *Him*. We shouldn't require people to perform for *us*. It's like saying to them, "You are never doing enough!" or "I won't fully accept you until you do everything I think you should do."

The pressure caused by telling them everything they need to do or not do can be almost unbearable, but if you love them, you will not pressure them! Using pressure is not love. God has taken away all pressure and given us His Love. Use God's love as a tool working FOR them, not against them.

Relieve some pressure on them. **Don't give them more pressure** by wanting them to perform OUTWARDLY. They will only turn into actors and actresses—really *good performers who get you to believe they are someone when they really aren't.* When they consistently start to hear that <u>**God loves you no matter what you do,**</u> it will cause them to believe it. Their heart will soften and change, and they will WANT to love God back. Out of their love-filled/God-filled heart will begin to flow the other fruit of God's Spirit. Our focus will be backward—failing to bring any real fruit—as long as we focus on change from the outside in instead of the inside out.

> Of course, we know that God is not *approving* of the sin and bondage they are living in (and we shouldn't either) because He sent Jesus ONCE and FOR ALL to set us free from all that. BUT, that doesn't mean He stops loving them. They just haven't received the revelation of that love and freedom yet.

The biggest help you can give an addict is to tell them you love them, even as they do what they are doing. Tell them God loves them, anyway. DO NOT TELL THEM GOD IS MAD AT THEM!! Where in the New Testament does it say that?! If they are Christians, remind them they have *been made righteous* through what Jesus ALREADY did. They don't have to try through their own good works to get Jesus to do something more than what He's already done. Again, it is not based on what they do or don't do.

Because the devil can <u>only lie</u>, he tries to convince people that addicts don't really know what they are doing wrong, so they *need to be told what is wrong. The lie is that they need <u>you</u> to tell them what to <u>do</u> to get free, to change.* <u>Most of the time, the changes suggested are also lies. Those lies from the enemy will keep them bound up.</u> **The only thing they really need to do is turn their eyes to Jesus**—to turn their eyes away and off of focusing on what they are doing—and believe what Jesus has done, what He has done for them already, and <u>Who</u> He is.

> Or do you despise the riches of His goodness, forbearance, and longsuffering, not knowing that <u>the goodness of God leads you to repentance</u>? (Romans 2:4; emphasis added.)

Our daughter kept her distance from us. I can't really blame her because we were figuring this out as we went and most of the time figured wrong. It is normal for people to push away and stay clear of someone who is mad at them.

If they view you (or God) as being mad at them, it only makes sense **to them** to stay away from you or Him. But that's not how God wants it to go down.

The enemy uses fear to motivate family members, like us, to say these things. There was a time when my husband and I were caught in the deception that if we could just SEE our daughter doing the things we told her to do, she must be ok. If we could just SEE her act ok, we weren't afraid. At that point, we would let down our guard and slack off being aware of her other symptoms. We were deceived through fear. The enemy knows keeping your focus on religious, legalistic actions will distract from getting to the root of the addiction problem and keep them bound up. We so badly wanted her to just change that we forgot how we truly wanted the change to come from her heart. We were trying to force a change, and it pushed her away.

We played right into the hand of the enemy out of ignorance. As I said, we were learning as we were going through this. We didn't have Christian friends who we could talk to about this. How could we rightly help her when even we were expected to *perform*—in church, at the store, at gatherings, you name it!

As a parent, I admit I made many mistakes early on and caused more damage to the situation with our daughter. Take it firsthand from someone who was taught wrongly and got **tough love confused with condemnation**. This is a tool the enemy uses. *Many Christians use this tool and don't realize it.* It is hurtful to constantly remind them of everything they are doing wrong and ask them why they keep doing it or haven't changed yet. What a hurtful mistake. These are useless acts and questions that definitely cause the situation to keep spinning on the *pedestal of unbelief.* **Condemnation is devilish work and gives people NO hope or belief that they can even change. Condemnation is a sign someone is still living under the Law of sin and death, which brought condemnation.** (That is in Romans 8.)

If an addict is a Christian, Christ lives inside them. In their spirit, they have taken on His mind and nature. If we insist on keeping them bound to *dos* and *don'ts*—before we act like we love and accept them—it's a major confusion. They are thinking, "God loves me the way I am, but my parents don't." We need to separate the actions they do or don't do from the relationship of love we have for them. God loves *us all* unconditionally, *right?* Apart from our actions. So why is it so hard *for us* to separate actions from our love and acceptance of the person? We are a work in progress, learning how to love God's way, aren't we?

If they hear from you how much you love them, no matter what they do, they will want to love you back! It's kinda how it works! God even says so in 1 John 4:19 (emphasis added): **We love Him because He first loved us.**

The enemy knows if he can keep them from hearing about how Christ already set them free, and if he can keep them from having a spiritual heart change, they will never have a life change. God's Love and ours can help them to see that Jesus has already dealt with the sin and bondage issues. When they begin to see themselves as God sees them, through the work Jesus did on the Cross and His resurrection, they will begin to believe there is hope. Their heart will start to desire to do whatever it takes to stay free from the very thing that is *condemning their heart* and keeping them running from God and the people who love them.

You may want to help them so badly. You may even wish you could go through it instead of them. ***You can't go through it for them***, but you *can* choose to *think* of them the way God *thinks* of them. You can tell them how God sees them through Jesus. You can love them and give them hope by encouraging them in what God's Word says. You can pray for them and pray that God deals with the root issue in their heart. Pray for them instead of just focusing on the kind of fruit they are trying so hard to produce for you, God, and themselves.

I'd like to share with you a powerful and life-changing entry from my personal journaling while writing this book. After hearing the words I recorded in the journal entry (included on the next two pages), I knew I had the *"OK"* from God to stop *waiting* for my daughter to change and go forward in His plan for me. Along with a little video vision revelation, He said to me, *"Go about your life and only focus on what I'm telling you to do."* With God's help, these words are something that I will never forget. These words He told me can help you to also stop interfering and move forward.

My Personal Journal

Today, spring of 2017,

As I am writing this, my second-born daughter has chosen to get back into the drug lifestyle. Again, I have gotten back out my Scriptures and am praying and speaking them over her. Speaking life over her.

I resist fear. I resist doubt and unbelief in God's Word. I resist the temptation to crumble and not move forward with my own dreams. I declare that she is our seed, and the seed of the righteous will be delivered (Proverbs 11:21). I believe it!! I have cast the care of our precious daughter on to my Lord (1 Peter 5:7). He is where my help comes from.

I also pray the New Testament prayers over my husband and me so we will stay strong together and walk in the love God has placed inside our hearts for her, each other, and everyone involved in this difficult situation. It's not easy, but staying in faith and love is the key to our victory.

Page 1

219

Page 2

The Lord is good to me and gave me a little video vision revelation that is helping me. I saw our daughter walk through our kitchen door, looking like she was obviously on drugs. I saw myself say, "Hey Honey, come on in."

We just sat around and talked. I offered her food. I saw myself treating her normal instead of acting shocked or fearful about how thin and worn out she looked or how spastic she was acting. I gave no attention to it. I just loved her and treated her like she was totally clean and healthy.

Inside my spirit, I heard the Lord tell me this. He said, "This is what it means to not jump on her merry-go-round. Go about your life and only focus on what I'm telling you to do. Believe My Word and confess it over her. Do not let what she is doing interfere with what I am telling you to do. That is what satan wants.

You honor me (by believing My Word, confessing it over her, and following my instructions); I will (always) honor My Word over this situation." (Meaning, His Word will be able to be activated and work in this situation because I believe it and speak His Word.)

STOP THE SPIN!

You should never give up believing the best for them, but at the same time, get to the place where you can say (probably while crying), "No matter what they do. No matter if they lose their life. No matter if they never ever choose Jesus to be their Savior and even die and go to Hell, I will continue to live my life for the Lord my God."

This sounds harsh to some people, but when I said this and got off my second-born daughter's merry-go-round, God was able to help her in ways that I couldn't.

Part Four: Addiction Red Cross Workers

If I could write two open letters to those in these addiction cycles, they'd read something like this:

Dear One living with an addiction,

I want to bring to your attention something you may not yet be aware of: *Addiction Red Cross workers.* These are people who like knowing THEY are the ones coming to your rescue. They have a hero complex. They want you to think you need them. **They want to feel *needed* by you.**

People who call themselves your friends and truly believe they are your friends, but supply you with the substance of your addiction, <u>do not love you</u>. They don't see it, but they don't truly care if you ever get delivered from the addiction. If they are honest, they will admit how they need you to stay on their merry-go-round and in their group with them to feed their own need.

Unknowingly, this group of people is who I have termed ***The Addiction Red Cross***. They feel like they are coming to your aid because you are a victim of a storm, a victim of a catastrophe, disaster, calamity. They attach who you are to some devastating event that has happened to you in your life. If you stay a victim and never become the victor, you will continue needing them, and that's what they thrive on. It's one of their own addictions.

These workers might tiptoe around you so they don't upset you and cause you to go off the deep end. They are willing to do whatever it takes to keep you settled down and away from the edge. Mostly they do this because they don't want to look bad by appearing like they aren't helping you.

However, if they truly cared about you, they wouldn't give you the deceptive, outward, and temporary fix. They would point you to the ***real*** RED CROSS, Jesus, Who can give you the genuine and forever fix that will cause you to jump off the merry-go-round of addictions. So, that is why I am writing this letter to you.

Yes, you went through a catastrophic event. Yes, you were injured and still need help and healing. It's your heart that needs healing, though. It's your mind, will, and emotions that need renewed so that you think about and see yourself differently. It's your sin-consciousness that needs to be changed. One of the keys here is to live this victory over sin and death this side of the Cross of Jesus and not focus on a sin-filled life any longer—sin-focused. Focus on what Jesus dying on the Cross did for you. I have a whole bunch of Scriptures in chapter fourteen to help you with this focus. They have served me well, and I know they will help you in your journey too.

Your Cheerleader to Victory, alongside Jesus,
Dana Marie Ecklund

My second letter would be to those who are or might be the Addiction Red Cross workers. So first, **ask yourself this question:** *Am I an Addiction Red Cross worker?*

Addiction Red Cross workers supply addicts in their family (or others, people they call friends) with their drug of choice. Note: Often, the person receiving the substance abuse *medication* is also handing it out to others. But it isn't necessarily always drugs they are supplying. They supply emotionally dependent people with an emotional *fix*. They supply obese people with comfort food and drink. They are the *supplier* for whatever people want to use as a medication to stop the pain or give them something to help them cope temporarily. *Is that you? If so, this next letter is for you.*

Dear Addiction Red Cross Worker,

If *you* are the Addiction Red Cross worker, please think about what you are doing! Supplying the addict with whatever they are using to medicate themselves is like a bad doctor who prescribes and supplies the wrong medicine. The *medicine* you are giving them is poison and causes their symptoms to worsen. The *medicine* you are supplying them is killing them. It's making them dependent on *YOU* as their source for coping instead of getting real help. It's keeping them caught up in the lie that God can't even help them.

You might try to comfort them by making them think that nobody else cares … except you. You lead them to yourself because you need *your fix*. Wake up to your *proud self* and stop trying to play Jesus, the one and only true Deliverer!

If you are an Addiction Red Cross worker … again, think about what you are doing. You can't truly love these people whom you call friends and family if you are aiding in their suicide and self-destruction! You are deceived into believing you are helping them. In reality, you are killing them in several ways because you are hooking with the devil and his mission, to kill, steal, and destroy these life-storm victims.

Do you *want* to be an Addiction Red Cross worker? Do you *want to be needed* and come to the aid of victims? Ok, I get it! Then do it right! Become an advocate for Jesus Christ and His "IT IS FINISHED!" *work* He's already done on His Cross. Getting a revelation of what the finished work of the Cross did to finish addiction is the only way to permanently help those you say you desire to help. Getting a revelation that Jesus loves them so much that He BE-CAME THE ADDICTED ONE FOR THEM is what will set every person permanently free from addiction. (Reading the Scriptures in chapter fourteen will help them and *you* too.)

I ask you to honestly answer these questions: Do you want to be NEEDED by these life-storm and life-earthquake victims? Are you working for the god of this world—the one who can only imitate God? Would you rather have them look to you instead of the One True God? *Selah (stop and think about that).*

Does it sound like I'm being pretty harsh toward you, Addiction Red Cross workers? In all honesty, I love you and want you to get the help *you* need, also. I'm passionate about this because I have witnessed the actions and devastating results of the Addiction Red Cross for too many years.

I have seen firsthand, through prison ministry and through my own daughter's experiences, what goes on in prisons and rehabs, as well as when someone is released from prisons and rehabs. Had my daughter truly received the real, lasting help she needed, Addiction Red Cross workers would have been out of a job. I learned ... every one has a twisted addiction of their own.

It always goes down something like this (so often that I could bet on it): Someone would immediately contact my daughter, or she would contact them whenever she was released. I believe they all knew that *simply* being locked up behind bars hadn't actually helped any of them. It only kept them off the streets long enough to hopefully get clean and start thinking clearly. So, everyone who gets released knows they come out still needing help in one form or another.

Enter the *rescuers*.

These contacts were usually former addicts, if not current ones. They called to *offer help* for anything she needed. *It became obvious to me that the first one to her rescue was usually the one who still needed help themselves.*

It was frustrating to watch as a family member because I so badly wanted *everyone involved* to just get off that swirling ride! I wanted them to get off that spinning merry-go-round and move forward into living out the awesome life God has waiting for them.

So, *if I'm talking to you* as an Addiction Red Cross worker, I hope you receive my encouragement to let go and resign from this line of *work* and allow God to do *His work* in your life. (And theirs!)

Your Cheerleader to Victory, alongside Jesus,

Dana Marie Ecklund

Compulsive Behavior & Addiction

Let's examine the components of the *Compulsive Behavior and Addiction Merry-Go-Rounds*:

- ❖ The Center Post: You are not yet putting your trust in God and using His guidance, wisdom, TRUTH, and power to be made free.

- ❖ The Base: This lie is supported by the fear of change never coming and the lost hope for a different life. The lie says it is easier to give in to fleshly cravings than resist them.

- ❖ The Decorative Fixtures and Handlebars: You are clinging to the thrill of doing it. What you are doing is an immediate satisfaction to your flesh every time you do it.

- ❖ The End Result: While you are clinging to the thrill of doing it, the enemy destroys your life and tells the world that not even God can help people like that.

NINE

STUCK ON THE LEGAL-SYSTEM MERRY-GO-ROUND

A s CHRISTIAN PARENTS, we know the thing that will help our daughter the most is her receiving a revelation of how God's love extends to her personally, no matter what she has done. Ultimately, we know that the revelation of God's personal love is what will help each of us, including her inmate friends. **To us**, it was not the right choice to keep our daughter in programs and correctional facilities that only reminded her of her faults. We have learned by experience that it is not productive or helpful to spend her days with other people dealing with the same *hard-heart* issues. What she needed, and what every recovering one needs, is help in receiving that revelation so they can get off the merry-go-round of false identity. If you feel stuck in the legal system, *God has a way.* His Way is *always the best way* to get unstuck—off the merry-go-round, stop the spinning, and on with living. You just need to ask Him and follow His leading.

I share, with permission, my husband's story in hopes to help you see what I mean:

When David was fifteen years old, living in Iowa with his mother and stepfather, he got into a lot of trouble with the law. The judge gave him two options after committing a crime that was *the straw that broke the camel's back.* The judge told him and his mother that if David didn't move to California to live with his dad, he would be sentenced to a boy's reform school. It was a gamble as to which one to pick. There was no guarantee that doing either would actually reform David. They didn't know it at the time, but God had His own good plan to reform David. They did not know God's plan, so they went with their *gut feeling* and chose California because what they did know was that David needed to be plucked up out of his situation. He needed to live around a different culture and group of people who saw things differently. If they hadn't picked California, David would have missed an open door waiting for him to walk through at this time. Let me explain …

He was given two high school options when he arrived in California at his dad and stepmom's house. His stepmom took him to visit both schools. David went by his gut feeling. He thankfully ended up attending the high school where God had already set up his reform help, a different group of people. He started school there in the middle of his sophomore year, and soon, one day at lunch, a group of guys on the football team befriended him. They encouraged him to try out for the football team. He did try out, and he made the team! He immediately became close friends with this group of guys.

During tryouts, he caught the attention of the head football coach and the other coaches, as well. David quickly found out that this football team was led by coaches who were ALL Christians. He had never experienced love in his whole life as they showed him. They were all more than just his coaches and teammates. They were his new people—his reform team. The head coach loved David and paid his way to the church's summer Bible camp, where David was introduced to Jesus!

A couple of years prior, standing on the edge of the Iowa Riverbank, David said to the Lord, "God, if you are real, then I need to know." At the Hume Lake Summer Bible Camp, with all his macho football buddies right there with him, God answered the question in David's heart, "God are you real?" That week,

God showed David that He is real, and He has a new life for him. God just needed him to get to the right place to get the right kind of help.

Choosing to move to California and leave most of his family was a hard choice—but the right choice. God needed David and his parents to make that choice so that David could meet this football team and group of coaches. Just a couple weeks after that summer camp, David was riding his motorcycle down Escondido Blvd. He heard the Lord speak to him in his heart and say, "I want you to *preach My Gospel*." With tears streaming down his face out of his now tender heart, David said, "Yes!" And his new life began! New opportunities for making the right decisions came with it, and new opportunities to follow God's leadings.

> I was only twelve years old when David permanently left living in Iowa. However, I still remember when he was sent off to California. He came by my house to give me a necklace and say goodbye. He also told me he would marry me one day. Yes, it was coming from a sweet-talker, but I believed it.
>
> Heart-broken, I said good-bye, not knowing it was the best thing for him to do at the time; and later, I would receive him back as my born-again husband.

Let's resume our visit about the legal system ...

There really are some good Spirit-led programs and facilities that would be a better option than what most encounter now. In the least, it would get many hurting and addicted lives off of the streets with hopes of giving them more time to change how they see things. For the most part, living together in lock-down with other people in similar situations is hardly ever the right answer.

My husband proved this out. I'm so thankful David chose to move to California and live with his dad. Had he gone to a reform school in Iowa, he would have lived with a group of men who were on the same destructive path he was on. While living together, whether in a reform school or as an inmate, the residents of these facilities typically share their experiences, feel sorry for each other, and believe they are *victims*. They are taught they are *born* with addictive behavior and a personality that is so different from others that they just can't help it. The narrative of false identity is reinforced.

This wrong perspective and teaching will not give anyone a different perspective or hope for a different life. They make bonds while they live together and go through the programs together. They have "someone who understands what I am going through" to later hook up with whenever they are released. Usually, they will end up repeating what they just came out of. Experience and statistics show that this <u>almost always</u> happens, and it repeatedly occurs because of what they *believe*.

Over the years, we learned that you will be taught to believe you now have an outlaw identity stamped on you forever because you have been in the legal system. You are constantly told this in one form or another. People stuck in the legal system are taught that punishment for their outlaw behavior is the only thing available to them. Punishment and condemnation are how *the system* hopes it will cause them to change.

They are given all kinds of not-so-wonderful advice and survival instructions during *intake*. "Gotta be tough to make it in here! Change your attitude! Submit to all the rules, and you'll get out of here sooner! Do what you're told when you're told to do it!" These *words of advice* are not bad, but if they aren't coming from a submitted heart grounded in God's love and truth for them, it is just *performance*. They just want to please the guards and warden and get through their time there. *(Doesn't this sound like the attitude of some teenagers, just "doing their time" at home until they turn eighteen and can be released? That is a warning sign of this merry-go-round.)*

The newly incarcerated person is given an ID number. This ID number is stamped on their clothes and paperwork and attached to their photos. They are called out from their cells by their ID number or their LAST name. Not even called by their first name. Most don't even know their inmate buddies' first names. This begins to wear on inmates and causes them to accept and take on a false identity, which zaps their hope! Some inmates have accepted it to the point they keep their prison clothes after being released, and brag about their *rap sheet* as if it is a medal to be proud of receiving. They tend to accept the lifestyle and ID given them and turn loose of all hope. It hurts my heart. Sadly, most people who ever spend any time incarcerated will spend the rest of their lives just living with this lie of false identity.

We should not forget the ones in prison and in the legal systems. Pray for them and send them encouraging notes if you are led by God in your heart to do so. God is after their heart. Pray for laborers to come across their path, even while incarcerated, and show them God's unconditional love for them. *That doesn't mean they get a free pass.* When they finally hear and believe the true Gospel of Grace and Jesus Christ, it just means that they will want their heart changed and get off the legal-system merry-go-round forever.

The remainder of this chapter is coming from my heart to you. I write this to you with a mother's heart, you who are currently incarcerated, out on bail, on probation, or parole. I write this to those who are currently being overseen and restricted by the legal or rehabilitation system. I am reaching out to you, the ones feeling stuck with no hope for life outside of it.

I'm not oblivious to the state of the facilities out there. I understand the conditions of the system you are assigned to due to your legal situation. Through my daughter's experiences and my time in training to be a prison ministry chaplain, I've navigated the legal system, parole system, and rehabilitation systems. I know how it has its own culture and way of doing things and how you are forced to live by it. The whole legal system can be frustrating, especially *if you do not believe* you will ever get out of it. **I know those with felonies and other people with misdemeanor charges who *feel* caught, trapped in these systems.** My daughter, and everyone else I've met within the system, has (at some point) thought it impossible to ever get out of the *unhelpful* cycle they feel caught in.

The system does not make sense to me, but there aren't any other options at this point. As a parent of a child who was caught in the legal system, I have heard the same stories every time our daughter was incarcerated or assigned to classes or rehab. Being in *the system*, you know that the people indulge each other, take on the care of each other, offer help, and make plans together for when they get released. They talk about how no one understands what they are dealing with and they should *stick together*. Some of it is not entirely bad, but honestly, it still keeps everyone in there playing *'ring around the rosie'*, and eventually, *they all fall down* again because it is NOT REAL HELP. If you've been there or are there, **I know you relate to this.**

I am aware that **corruption** keeps the merry-go-round going round and round. Corruption denies hope for change. And, yes, the portion of corrupt employees in every system feeds the problem. They are often officers or other people whom you are supposed to be able to trust. Even within the system, there are those employees who are part of the drug cartel, sex rings, money laundering, etc. The reality is, they don't care about the people they filter their business through, and they don't care if those people ever get out of the system or not. Many would actually prefer they didn't.

<u>This is a merry-go-round that has been spinning since the fall of man and has grown to have a huge stronghold in every society.</u> I know from our own experiences that there are people in the community with immense influence and power over those in *the system.* This influence is *only* because of their money. These controlling people use these trapped individuals to increase their wealth or meet their own physical cravings. (*Me—cringing inside.*) They have no REAL care whatsoever if you ever get free. Because of fear and unbelief, you might feel like you have nowhere else to go except back to the same corrupt people for help. I have seen this happen firsthand.

> Know this: These few corrupt officers and influential people in the community are no match to the power of God working on your behalf if you will only look to HIM for the help and favor you need.

I say that it's time to break away from these controlling and manipulating people! Put your trust in God, as your SOURCE, Who <u>*genuinely* loves you and Who will meet all your needs according to HIS RICHES in glory by Christ Jesus!</u> (Philippians 4:19) It's your choice. Do you believe this?

Once in a legal system, I understand you no longer have control. The court basically takes away all your rights and decision-making power. Most of the time, the family isn't allowed to give positive suggestions or influence the court. You might be given the option to play "Let's Make a Deal." Still, you have the constant temptation of losing hope and just giving up because you know *the system* usually gets its way. Yes. The system and lawyers decide the best *punishment* for your illegal action—the best reform techniques. They will, maybe, *every so often,* offer you a plan of action to help you start over in life. Still, it's always based on <u>their limited guidelines and protocol</u>.

We know that God's system—The Good Gospel News—is based on mercy and grace, but the world's legal systems are not. So, once you are in their system, you have to do things their way. The heart of the judge can be changed, and I have seen it happen, but it is not the *character* of the legal system to change and do something different in your favor. Most don't offer any *outside-of-the-box* solutions. By that, I mean solutions and help based on God's Word. This worldly system focuses on your *punishment* and so-called *correction.* They send you to *rehabilitation centers* hoping you get *rehabilitated.* Still, they know the chances of you repeating the cycle, again and again, are enormous. Yet, they don't really have any other plan of action to offer you. It's one of the most obvious merry-go-rounds I've ever seen and been involved with.

Suppose you decide to keep breaking the law. In that case, the legal system has the power to keep you on its merry-go-round. You can find yourself repeatedly appearing in front of the judge, again and again being sentenced to these programs. It is likely that many wouldn't accept an *outside-of-the-box* option, anyway. Too many would rather stay running from God's plan and refuse to do things His way instead of having a different life.

If you *believe* you are stuck in the legal systems, ask yourself and honestly consider these questions: ***Is this really a legal-system merry-go-round that I'm stuck on? Or, is this a rebellion merry-go-round I'm deciding to stay on because I refuse to obey the laws intended to keep me safe?***

Like Jonah, are you rebelling against God and running from doing what God leads you to do? It's possible that Jonah was afraid and ran from God because he thought he would only be God's *puppet* and viewed God as wanting to *control* him. Do you recognize yourself being at all like this? Do you recognize yourself as running from God because you don't believe He really has a good plan for you? Do you believe His plan would require you to surrender your power to make your own choices?

Side note: To some people—Christians are viewed as weak and only puppets who do God's work for Him. This rumor and false information are being spread about God and the love relationship He has with us.

Do you have the same philosophy as most law-breakers? "I'm not going to be anyone's puppet. I'm not going to let anyone *control me*! I am my own person, and I don't want to live my life fenced in with rules and boundaries." Funny! If you *believe* this philosophy and despise authority and submission to law and order, **the enemy** is actually **CONTROLLING YOU. YOU ARE HIS PUPPET!** You are already OUT OF CONTROL and on the enemy's merry-go-round if you believe this. He has you so deceived that you actually think *you* are in control of your life. ***Please hear my heart for you.*** I hope that reading this helps you see the truth about what's really going on.

If you say you are in control of your life and still make decisions that hurt yourself, your children, and other people, which land you behind bars, I question your *sound mind*. If this is how you believe, then, honestly, you should not be allowed to run free outside of the legal system restraining your <u>harmful and illegal actions</u>.

Don't get offended. Just hear me out. It would appear that the enemy is *using you* to hurt yourself, your children, your family, and other people. You are nowhere near being *in control* of your life and living free! You know this inside.

The truth is, your real enemy has you bound up in stubborn rebellion and self-pity. To serve the devil, you have even been willing to sacrifice your body, life, children, family, and all of God's gifts in you. All the while, you falsely believe that it's *you* who is in control.

I'm cheering for you, though! I truly believe deep down in your heart (even while you are hoping you don't notice it) is a desire to let go of being in control and give the steering wheel to Jesus.

You _can_ stop being the enemy's puppet! You can stop despising the laws and authority meant to protect you and stop using coping devices outside God's way of doing things. You can change your bad attitude of fear and unbelief in God's love for you and take the steering wheel of your own life _away from the enemy!_

You are not supposed to be a _slave to sin_ and the enemy's works. If you set boundaries for yourself based on God's love for you, your new identity IN CHRIST, and God's way of doing things, you would not be _bound_ like a slave to these laws and systems. Your heart boundaries would keep you out of illegal and immoral activities that repeatedly thrust you into these spinning systems.

I'm talking tough to you because I know you can handle it. If you are caught in the legal system, you most likely got there because you _are_ tough. You most likely have developed a hard exterior tough-guy/girl appearance and living with a hard-interior protective shell around your heart. You have trained your emotions to feel tough, your mind to think tough thoughts, and live the _bad to the bone_ life by your own strong will and self-power. Am I telling the truth? This reminds me of the song _"Bad, Bad Leroy Brown[8],"_ he was meaner than a junkyard dog!

Again—I'm being very frank with you because I love you and believe in _the you_ that God wants to come out and really enjoy living _the free life._ He has that new way of living ready and waiting for you to step into. I'm sure you've played hide and seek before. Do you remember saying, _"Come out, come out, wherever you are"_? That's what I'm saying to you—the **you** whom God knew before you were in your mother's womb and whom He chose before the foundations of the earth. _Stop hiding out!_ Stop covering yourself up in shame! Stop running and hiding from your past and your closet of secrets. Face them head-on, get off that merry-go-round, and on with your new way of living!

You can move forward onto the path God has for you. This is the path where your life's purpose and heart's desires will be identified and activated BY HIM. Your part is to get rid of that bad-and-tough guy protective outerwear and put on God's even more powerful protection of His Love.

STOP THE SPIN!

You are well-equipped and well-able to change how you perceive your life up to this point. You are able to stop viewing yourself as a victim and stop living like one. How? You have the Greater One living inside you if you are born again!

(If you are reading this and are not born-again, settle that right now – turn to the back of the book, find and pray that one simple Salvation Prayer, in faith!)

In Christ, you can do everything you need to get out of any mess that came as a result of how you have responded to your life circumstances. I believe in the new you that God re-created. The new you can now overcome the power of sin in your life and go forward into God's amazing plan for you. God doesn't see the old you who you were before you were saved. I don't look at that old you. You shouldn't either!

Remember this:
"You are of God, little children, and have overcome them, because He who is in you is greater than he who is in the world" (1 John 4:4).

Suppose you *are* a Christian, caught in an illegal lifestyle, and stuck in legal systems. In that case, you can start **believing** who you are IN CHRIST, put your faith and trust in God's love and good plan for you into action, *and get out.*

God will bless any effort you are honestly giving toward letting Him live through you. **Living your life for HIM is where the REAL FREEDOM is!** Christ HAS MADE YOU RIGHTEOUS AND FREE—**FREE** to believe in Him and His Word, *or not.* **FREE** to choose His plan for you, *or not.* **FREE** to love Him, follow Him, and build His Kingdom, OR love the world, follow the world, and build the enemy's kingdom. *No strings attached!* (He doesn't want you as His puppet!)

Even if you are currently incarcerated, you can live in Christ's freedom and bring others into that freedom with you. You have to serve the time anyway, so why not practice living a Spirit-led life, even behind bars? Spend your time getting to know Him. Learn how Jesus can live through you and lead people to Himself through you while you're in there. Turn what was meant to destroy into that which brings life.

The bottom line is that you do not have to make their way your merry-go-round even if you are caught up in these systems, going through everything you have been sentenced to do.

You can go through the court system and any other situation with a positive, faith-filled attitude. Looking to God for your strength and wisdom to stay off the merry-go-round of emotions, strife, and repetition *is possible.* You can show other people the REAL way to stop repeating the same thing over and over and get out of the legal system. You can make the best of it, and come through it better and stronger, with a greater plan of action, making it possible for you to never return to it again. With men, this might be impossible, but with God, all things are possible—**to him who believes!**

Remember: If you want different results, you must be willing to do something different. **Do the opposite** of what *merry-go-round riders* do. Do something different—the right *something.* Even if you are going through something out of your control (or someone you love is), have faith in God! *Make His* *promises personal.* Accept His Word as the truth and light. His Word **_will_** lead you out of the darkness you live in.

READ IT!
Mark 9:23, Mark 10:27, & Mark 11:22-24
It's not impossible!

Again, start doing the opposite of what merry-go-round riders do. Merry-go-round riders don't pay attention to what choices they make. *You* have to train yourself to pay attention to the choices you make. On purpose, make a movement that gives you *purposeful movement* (a deliberate, planned, and consciously directed movement) and not only repeated movement but an intentional movement in the right direction.

If you *never decide* to get off this merry-go-round and have a change of heart and attitude, **you really don't give *the system* much choice.** You say you desire to change and even know what you need to do to make things change. But if you still choose not to take action toward getting change, then perhaps you are enjoying the **spin and drama** of the merry-go-round more than you want to make an effort to get off. Laziness may be working harder *on you* than you are working on getting off the merry-go-round.

You can't be lazy and procrastinate if you *genuinely want to get off.* Don't think you are fooling people, either. Your actions will reveal how badly you really do want off. If you *really want to get off the merry-go-round* <u>and stay off permanently</u>, you will look to God and do whatever God leads you to do to make that happen—and people will know it.

It's also possible you aren't doing what it takes to get off yet because you still believe the lie. What lie is that? The lie of the devil (and the system) that, "This is your *lot in life* and the only plan God has for you, so why should you try to do something different?" If you still believe that, you haven't settled it, once and for all, that God is **ONLY** good, and He **ONLY** wants good for you.

Settle that. Let this book help point you to the truth in Scripture that will settle that!

If the opposite of good is happening to you, don't blame God! God is the only One Who truly loves you unconditionally. *An evaluation needs to be made.* **Evaluate yourself. Do any of the choices *you* made have something to do with where you are right now in your life? When bad things have happened in your life, have any of your responses led to where you are right now? Think about that.**

Have you ever heard of *jailhouse religion*? I'm sure you've seen it and possibly experienced it a few times personally. It's when someone gets caught breaking the law and gets sent to jail or prison or lockdown confinement. While in there, they *get religion*. Most people are truly sorry for what they did wrong. They are more than just sorry that they got caught. They truly do want to try and change. But once they are released, it seems to slip away.

Jailhouse religion is much like what I had as a teenager, my every summer experience with *summertime religion*. Going to church camp every summer was awesome. I went away for a solid week of Bible teaching, worship, fun games, and good talks with other teens my age who wanted to live a Christian life. BUT THEN, school and peer pressure started again, and my *summertime religion* went away until the next summer.

Does that sound familiar to your situation or ones you have seen? *The best thing I ever did was stop that ride and get off the merry-go-round!* Like I spoke about in chapter one, I intentionally decided to be ALL IN.

Once you are released from being incarcerated, I know it's tempting to go back to what you are familiar with and hang with the same familiar people. It can be scary to find new friends and groups of people to hang with. I can relate, but the scariness doesn't last forever. If you are honestly sincere about changing your people group, ***ask God to help***. He would love to help you get established with different groups and friends who better influence you. He's just waiting for you to want it and ask Him. The key here is how badly do you really *want* it?

Don't just *say* you want to change, but actually DO something about it! There is a deception going around that makes people believe that **just because they want something** means it will happen *automatically*. This is a lie. It's a merry-go-round of deception: believing that you can keep doing what you are doing and still go forward just because you *say* you want it. You are *not seeing* that your movement *isn't forward movement*. It is actually just going in circles. You are spinning, not winning.

This seems simple, but it is a scheme the devil has used over and over on Christians. It goes something like this: People get all excited at church or get a revelation in the Word of God about something. We might hear someone else's testimony—like my daughter through my text or you through reading this book. Then, immediately the enemy comes to steal it through petty little cares, emotional hurts, offenses, and distractions of this world—worth nothing at all compared to eternity. IF it wasn't *valued* and received as *a word from the Lord to help in a time of need,* it will not be thought of much longer after hearing it.

Remember the text message from chapter one with my daughter? In chapter one we left off with great promise:

> (COURTNEY) … We keep letting life and temptations pull us back in. **But I'm ready to live the real life!**

You can read my response in chapter one just before she stepped out to the grocery store. I am going to pick up now on the rest of that story, *after she returned from the grocery store,* because it fits so well in this chapter.

> (COURTNEY) Your text is very encouraging. I definitely want and need to get to that point in my life.

> (ME) You're on your way!

> (COURTNEY) Yes I am!!!

I included the rest of the text here because the reality of the spin is … less than two weeks after this text she was binging on drugs again and soon after ended up back in prison. Even though she had another relapse, this conversation with her to this day *still brings me hope.* What she shared came from her heart and the *God-given* desires she really does have, but by her own confession to me, has regularly and regretfully ignored over and over. Her battle has been to make the effort and do what it takes to get a different result. It will require her and anyone dealing with the same thing to go through a period of time where she consistently resists her fleshly desires and allows her God-given heart's desires to have the greater influence in leading her.

To this day, I still believe she can and will at some point start following her heart into a new forward moving way of living. I'm going through my everyday life anyway, so I'm choosing to believe the best and stay in agreement with what she said in her text to me in December 2016. I think we all have someone in our lives who needs us to stick with them and not quit on them, don't you?

If people know what they should do to make things change and still choose not to take action toward getting it, then it is obvious they are enjoying the spin of the merry-go-round more than they want to make the effort to get off. In other words, it's not painful enough or costing them too much *yet.* It's like this … people do things that give them pleasure. If the pleasure is one that ends up causing destruction, they will need to get to a point where the pleasure of doing it turns to pain when doing it. We all eventually arrive at that day where the discomfort of staying on the ride going nowhere is greater than the effort and fear of changing for something better.

Consider this: Incarceration is defined as *being confined.* I'm not speaking of facilities such as the county jail or the state prison. Whatever *caused* you to be in these legal systems is what you are a prisoner of. It's your *state of mind.* **It's what you are thinking in your mind that is keeping you captive to this merry-go-round lifestyle.** Again, what's keeping you confined are the lies you are believing.

If you want off the merry-go-round, you MUST be willing and do something hard but different. Do you remember the story of my husband David earlier in the chapter? You must take action if you want a change. You must choose to get off the merry-go-round! ARE YOU HEARING ME? He and his parents went with their gut feelings. Most of the time, you just gotta go with your gut feeling—no matter how hard it is! Especially if you aren't familiar with hearing the voice of Holy Spirit on the inside of you.

God is always trying to lead you and help you any way He can get it across to you. When David chose California and the high school he went to, he didn't have the Spirit of God inside him yet to lead him, but God could still give him a *gut feeling* to heed to. After he received Jesus into his heart at Bible camp that summer, David could then recognize God's Spirit speaking to him. God can do the same for you! God is not a respecter of persons, but He is a respecter of faith and obedience to His leadings.

SO, **there is GOOD NEWS FOR YOU!!** Today is the first day of the rest of your life! Today, you have been given the gift of breath. Today, you have another opportunity to choose life or death. You have this moment right now, but you don't know whether you will still have the gift of breath one hour from now.

Don't wait until your death bed and hope you have time to choose Life.

You are precious to God, your Creator. He's the One Who knew you before you were in your mother's womb. He's the One Who has the RIGHT PLAN of reform for you. He's the One Who deposited an assignment in you to complete here on Earth. He's the only One Who can empower you to discover that assignment and do it.

God is waiting on you to open your heart and life to Him and let Him guide you out of the mess you got yourself into. God is waiting for you to allow Him to guide you into a life more abundant, provided to you through Jesus—a different life than you are familiar with. It's a wonderful, peaceful place of rest and fulfillment. Rest—now doesn't that sound nice? No more running and hiding and trying to figure things out! No more repeating the same destructive behavior. No more tormenting thoughts and fears.

OK—I wish I could just hold each one of you right now and personally lead you through all of this. I'm a mom. What can I say? But it is true! YOUR life as-

signment from God is available *only to you*. No one else can live it out for you. No one else can accept it but you. ***Will you accept it?***

> Then Jesus cried out and said, "He who believes in Me, believes not in Me, but in Him who sent Me. And he who sees Me sees Him who sent Me.
>
> I have come as a light into the world, that whoever BELIEVES in Me should not abide in darkness" (John 12:44–46; emphasis added).

Legal System

Let's examine the components of the *Legal-System Merry-Go-Round*:

- ❖ <u>The Center Post</u>: You keep spinning on the ***Legal-System Merry-Go-Round*** because you believe the lie that you are permanently stuck.

- ❖ <u>The Base</u>: The lie is supported by rebellion because of the victim mentality. The platform supporting you is the fear that this is your lot in life, that it will never be different for you.

- ❖ <u>The Decorative Fixtures and Handlebars</u>: You may be holding onto the idea that being in the system is easier than actually putting effort into becoming a productive member of society. Being in the legal system makes you think you don't have to take responsibility for yourself or anyone else.

- ❖ <u>The End Result</u>: These lies result in repeated offenses, recurring correction sentences, and multiple incarcerations.

TEN

OUR OWN MERRY-GO-ROUND

W E ALL HAVE our own merry-go-round stories. I share mine in hopes
they will help give you hope and let you know that you are not alone
or the only one who has life merry-go-rounds you want to get off.

In the summer of 1983, David came from California to my small town in
Iowa to propose to me. I had recently finished the one year of Bible college I
told you about in chapter four. I was totally sold out to living my life for God
and wanted to marry a man who would be in the ministry. He testified to me,
and everyone else, that he knew he was supposed to become a preacher. So, I
accepted his proposal, believing that we would immediately attend a different Bible college in Los Angeles, CA, together as husband and wife. Then,
we would start our life together as ordained and full-time ministers for Jesus
Christ. I had my perfect marriage and life of ministry all planned out!

We married that August and even announced in the local paper our marriage and future plans to attend Bible college together in California. Together,
we wrote a vision list with all we dreamed of doing. How exciting life would
be! Right?

245

After getting married and moving to California, we came crashing down to Earth. We realized we had missed all deadlines to start school in the Fall. We also woke up to the fact that financially, we could not do it right then, or anytime in the near future, for that matter. Our family helped us get on our feet, but we were still forced to kick into *survival mode*. I got pregnant four months into our marriage. David was working full time, and between work hours and traffic, I hardly ever saw him. This was the beginning of our marriage—spinning right into the rat race on the *survival-mode merry-go-round*. It was not exactly the life we had first pictured.

Part One: Big Dreams Going Nowhere

When I was a child in elementary school, I remember organizing, designing things, and leading several little events and clubs in our neighborhood. One of those summers, living in my little town of three hundred people, I put on a carnival! My family really didn't have any money, so I collected pop bottles and sold lemonade to raise money for anything small I wanted. I heard about the Jerry Lewis muscular dystrophy fundraising kit—and the kit was free! So I mailed in a request to receive a carnival kit to help Jerry raise money for the kids. When it arrived, I put on a carnival for the neighborhood! I made a whopping $15 that day. I was able to help Jerry's kids and provide a fun event for the neighborhood at the same time. *I loved it!* Another time, a couple of years later, I put on a haunted house in the basement of our house and made some more money—I got that idea from our Methodist church down the road. I was always dreaming up something!

I consider mine a great childhood in so many ways. (Although, indeed, the real and long-term effects of basically living in poverty and my dad's absence did show up in me later.) As a child, I would play along the river banks in the summer and ice skate on the town slough in the winter. I would make flower baskets for the elderly for *May Day* and leave them on their doorsteps and help our elderly neighbors rake leaves and clean their houses. I was pretty imaginative and could make a clubhouse out of anything. I can remember being very creative and having BIG DREAMS. Then after I got saved at age ten, I remember imagining all of the ways I could use those BIG DREAMS for the Kingdom of God. I dreamed of helping people in so many different ministry avenues. I have always been a very giving person, and then at age ten, I discovered a deeper purpose for my giving.

I brought those dreams and my deeper purpose excitedly into my marriage. My husband David and I both had BIG DREAMS. But, somehow, life seemed to have interfered; we had gotten off the *path of purpose* and onto *the life path filled with merry-go-rounds*. We now had more important things to do in life, like … being in survival mode!

Regretfully, that is what I said for years: *"I'm in survival mode!"* (I was definitely living according to what I was saying.) My BIG DREAMS became only memories in the back of my mind. And, my husband's story is much the same. He, too, had BIG DREAMS—David dreamed of preaching the Gospel and teaching God's way of doing government—dreams which sat on the back burner for many years.

We went years in survival mode. This caused frustration in both our personal lives and marriage. (It affected our children also until we finally got off the merry-go-round of *dreams not moving forward,* but I will pick back up on that later.)

Unfortunately, as I grew older, I got knocked down a few times and began taking on all the *cares* of happenings in my life; I stopped creating things for the Lord's Kingdom. I didn't realize it then, but I **started creating *emotional merry-go-rounds*** for myself! I stopped believing in those dreams (that were going nowhere) and stopped seeing myself ever being able to do them.

Part Two: Our Frustrated Self

There are many areas in my life where I rode *small merry-go-rounds* for years. The problem is that the little spin cycles became *very big merry-go-rounds* the longer I stayed on them. My spinning rides were mostly self-made, caused by *frustration*.

I believe this is very common—nearly everyone can strongly relate to the frustration of having BIG DREAMS going nowhere. I figure if I can expose my own rides, it might help you recognize some of your own frustrating spin cycles. I shared earlier how, as a child, I had a lot of imagination and drive. In many ways, that is a good trait. But, although I have always been very self-motivated, I could also easily become bored if things weren't rolling forward fast enough for me. Because I was always *go-go-go*, I thought everyone should be *go-go-go*. If they weren't, I had a tendency to get frustrated.

My happiness, peace, confidence, and outlook on life were all based on what others were doing or not doing. If they weren't doing what I expected of them, I would get frustrated. Can I just define *being frustrated* as not believing something can change? Because my happiness depended on *someone else* changing, I would stay in the vicious cycle of anger and frustration, just trying to cope with it. It helped *me* change when I stopped being so self-centered and having ultra-high expectations of other people.

I realized that what I expected of other people was unrealistic and not based on anything except the high-pressure expectations I had on myself. I'm pretty sure I lived this way as a cover-up for my own heart issues and insecurities. I was constantly looking for the real me to come out of these high expectations. But the *current* (or then current) real me only frustrated myself, and most definitely others, along my way. Talk about a frustrated, dysfunctional person! That was me! It was like living always looking for the next *amusement ride*.

This first particular amusement ride I'm about to share with you resulted from using a false coping mechanism that never helped me. It was more like a bandage covering my issue and giving me an emotional release; it had no positive result. I allowed this quick fix to keep me in darkness in this area of my life.

When there was strife between my husband and me, I would often run away from the problem instead of walking in the light I had of God's Word. I would jump in my vehicle and drive just to get out of the house and away from everything. I wouldn't even tell my husband I was leaving most of the time. Sometimes I would just go flea market shopping or take a scenic drive so I wouldn't have to think about what was going on. I would drive and drive and drive for miles, never wanting to turn around and go back home. I would be crying and crying and telling God everything He already knew was going on the whole time. I was being weird and immature, feeling sorry for myself and hoping somebody would notice I was gone.

This did not really help me, even though I thought it would every time. It never helped us get past anything. It only made my husband shut down more. *Running away* was a cover-up and a false emotional release that was unproductive. It was a temporary fix that never brought any lasting help. Running away from what we know to do is not walking in the light of God's Word that we have heard. Every time, I still had to come back home to the same feelings and thoughts I had run away from. To be honest, this is something I did when I was a kid.

STOP THE SPIN!

Feeling sorry for ourselves keeps us in darkness and will not get us through something victoriously. When we are dealing with something, we shouldn't run to things that are quick fixes or emotional cover-ups (things that cause someone to ignore what's really going on).

These unhelpful coping methods won't allow us to face any of the giants in our lives, let alone defeat them. But with the Lord's help, we can take control of our self and confront these obstacles right away, putting the brakes on any fear and confusion before it starts.

When I would be upset as a child, I'd jump on my ten-speed bike and just ride. I would ride five to ten miles at a time—thinking I was leaving everything bad behind me and hoping it would all be different when I got back. There were times I would stay gone all day and hope someone would miss me when I was gone. I would get home most of the time, and nobody even knew I was gone all day. More than once, I would hide in my neighbor's shed almost all day until I was so hungry I decided to come out. I figured I would hear my family calling my name, asking where I was or something, but I never did.

As a grown, adult mother and wife, I found myself trying to use the same coping mechanism I used as a little child. *And it still didn't work.* I spun and spun and got nowhere fast. And, that, my friends, is the sure sign of a *merry-go-round.*

Eventually, these issues were addressed in my life *as I dismantled the pieces and the supports that were holding them in place.* I was spinning around the need to prove my frustration was justified. As an adult, I ignored the understanding and revelation knowledge I had that told me otherwise. I supported the lie by relying on doing what I'd always done—run away and hope they missed me! I held on to self-centeredness because I believed the lie that I was an unwanted child, rejected, and forgotten—partially rooted in experiencing my dad leaving our family.

I'm sure I'm not the only one who has used coping devices such as this one, so I hope this honesty helps you dismantle your spin cycles too! Thankfully, the Lord helped me heal, grow up emotionally, and stop requiring this negative attention. I stopped jumping into the vehicle and leaving and stopped abandoning my children and husband for a couple hours at a time, and I decided to deal with my emotions. I no longer run off all emotionally upset, even though it is sometimes tempting.

There was nothing wrong with me taking a walk or a drive to clear my head, but I needed to do something besides only thinking about my problem when I was gone. I needed to *clear my head and look into my heart* to see the correct picture. That is where the understanding *clicks*—within our hearts. I needed to deal with my own part of the cause of stress and strife. By praying and asking the Lord what I should do and then acting on what He said, He helped me recognize **self-centeredness** as my <u>major</u> problem. And that helped me see that my husband was <u>*not*</u> my major problem.

STOP THE SPIN!

Having a self-pity party, and being more concerned about our own self-image is us living our lives according to the flesh.

Self-centeredness is doing things ourself (apart from the strength and wisdom we get from God). Self-centeredness is not living by the Spirit.

We get strength and wisdom by living by the Spirit, out of our new image, made in the image of God.

So, yes, years and years ago, I used to try to get my husband's attention in negative ways. It sounds funny to me now. I'm glad I finally got bored trying little attention-seeking acts, which never really worked for me as I wanted anyway. Ha-ha! I am also thankful that my husband didn't *baby* me during these immature moments of *manipulation*. His response seemed insensitive to me at the time, but it helped me learn to *put on my big girl pants* and grow up! God knew I needed a strong man! My husband also needed a strong wife. Thank God, that is what I finally became: emotionally and spiritually stronger and stronger every day!

Now, instead of running away or using attention-seeking acts to manipulate, I get alone with God and begin meditating on how much He loves me. I encourage myself in how the Lord thinks of me and how I'm <u>wanted, accepted</u>, and <u>NOT forgotten by Him</u>. This is where I get genuine peace and joy and not just a quick fix. Changing my childish self-image to match God's image of me is key to changing how I see myself now.

Usually, at the first sign of those old patterns tempting me, I start confessing Scriptures over my situation and turn on praise music. I begin thanking God for everything He is doing behind the scenes for me that I don't even know about. I endeavor to cast all my cares onto the Lord and let Him care for me.

Is it easy? No, it was very hard work, at first, to get a hold of my emotions and allow God's Holy Spirit to help direct my steps through the situation. He's a Good Father God, a best friend, and is always there for me when situations come my way.

This is what's called a personal relationship with God. I talk to Him out loud, and He talks back with me through my spirit. His Spirit living inside me leads me by His peace and His grace.

Now, I'm *not* living my life in the spin cycle, the ever-revolving circle of selfishness and frustration. My husband isn't either. He's not living with confusion and condemnation. We are endeavoring to live our lives according to the gifts and callings inside us, led by our Good Father God. My hope is that our stories will help you recognize patterns in your life to help reveal if you are on *your own* merry-go-round. (And *how to get off of them and on with your life!*)

Part Three: Allowing Light In

All those years of not following our hearts were like having a big spotlight shining before us, showing us the path of life, but continually ignoring it! Our real breakaway from *survival mode* began to come as our pastor taught us a lot about *walking according to the understanding we currently have.* He showed us in the Bible that if we ignore light (which is God's truth) long enough, we will stop seeing light and go back to being in the darkness. This is what we had repeatedly experienced, which had caused our main marriage issues.

STOP THE SPIN!

There are probably things going on in your life that you may not have identified or considered as a merry-go-round—patterns of fleshly behavior that you want to change but have not been successful at, yet. Here are some examples, and most of them I have personally dealt with over the past 57 years. Maybe you can identify with one of them:

- *Letting self-centeredness run your life*
- *Expressing negative and fearful first responses*
- *Unrealistic high expectations of yourself and others*
- *Bad time management and running late wherever you go*
- *Shopping before paying bills*
- *Choosing laziness and procrastination over activity and immediate movement*
- *Staying up too late and being exhausted the next day*
- *Being easily offended and needy for man's approval*
- *Never making the time to diligently study God's Word*

We must first identify these habits before we can move forward in getting the help we desire. This might be a good time for you to stop and evaluate your own life and write down some things that come to your mind—things you recognize as being like a revolving door, or a merry-go-round. Then, decide whether you are ready to say, "Bye! Bye! Merry-go-rounds!"

> Then Jesus said to them, "Yet a little while the Light is with you. Walk while you have the Light, lest darkness overtake you. He who walks in darkness does not know where he is going. While you have Light, believe in the Light that you may become sons of Light" (John 12:35–36 MEV; emphasis added).

Part of walking in the light means we are *doing what we know to do.* Walking in darkness is when we don't do what we know to do because of fear and unbelief. When we trust God, we will walk in the light of what we know He has told us to do because we trust His love for us. Walking in darkness will cause us to create our own merry-go-round, which is a set-up that will stop our dreams from coming to pass.

> For you were formerly darkness, but now you are light in the Lord. Walk as children of light— (Ephesians 5:8 MEV).

We must *"walk as children of **light**"* to immediately recognize when that rotation (spinning on the merry-go-round) starts to happen. We must identify it as a merry-go-round about to start. The merry-go-round is the repetitive cycle of doing the same thing (over and over) because of not believing that we have any other options or because we fear that God won't help us, etc. When fear settles in our hearts, darkness comes.

Living in the dark is paralyzing and doesn't allow us to move forward.

Are you putting off anything you know in your heart that you are supposed to do?

Are you frustrated enough yet to hear, *"Do something or die?"* We were. So read on! Maybe our story can help you.

Part Four: Do Something or Die

This story of the four lepers has a very personal meaning to David and me. It is a story that gave us a needed kick in the pants when we heard it applied to our situation. It caused us to get off our merry-go-round and finally go do what we thought about in our hearts every day.

> There were four leprous men at the entry of the gate, and they said to one another, **_"Why are we sitting here until we die_**_? If we say, 'Let us enter the city,' the famine is in the city, and we shall die there. But if we sit here, we die also. Now come, let us fall into the camp of the Arameans. If they spare our lives, we will live, and if they kill us, we will die."_
>
> _So they rose at twilight to enter the camp of the Arameans. When they came to the edge of the camp of the Arameans, there was no one there. For the Lord had caused the Aramean camp to hear the sound of chariots, horses, even the sound of a large army, so that they said to one another, "Listen, the king of Israel has hired the kings of the Hittites and the kings of the Egyptians to come against us." So they got up and ran away in the twilight and abandoned their tents, their horses, and their donkeys. The camp remained just as it was, and they ran for their lives._
>
> _When these leprous men came to the edge of the camp, they went into one tent. They ate and drank, carried off silver, gold, and clothes, and went and hid them. Then they went back, entered another tent, and carried off things from there and went and hid them_ (2 Kings 7:3–8 MEV; emphasis added).

Consider the portion that says, _"Let us enter the city."_ Then _they rose to enter in_. That was the moment they got _off the merry-go-round and on with a new way of living_. They chose to do something about the dreams that were never coming to sight.

By now, you've read many of our stories and the results of the merry-go-rounds of our lives. In this section, I'm skipping ahead thirty-two years and all the merry-go-rounds in between to re-emphasize that we found ourselves fully frustrated in the middle of our lives. We never got around to doing what we had in our hearts to do when we began our marriage. This frustration was dangerously wearing on us, our marriage, and our children.

Financially, we were still in no place to just up and go full-time to Bible college. Still, David finally decided to take some Bible school correspondence courses. It was a compromise, but better than not doing anything at all. David quickly discovered that working at least sixty hours a week and then studying (and actually getting something out of it) was almost impossible. Understandably, he only got through eleven courses in two years. I was praying about it constantly—seeking the Lord for the answer, knowing in my heart that David was supposed to be full-time in Bible school.

Our pastor of twelve years, and his wife, regularly shared with the congregation how *it is never too late to do what God has put in your heart to do*. I remember our pastor's wife even teaching one Friday night, using a whiteboard to illustrate the life of Joseph in the Old Testament. She showed how it *looked like* he had gotten off *the path of purpose* and how God got him back on. She also encouraged everyone that God could do it for all of us. *After years of hearing our pastors cheering for us, David and I began to deeply believe it.*

In February 2015, my family and I attended a conference sponsored by our church. Our pastor spoke each night. That week, I thought he was much like Braveheart[9], bold and courageous in delivering a pivotal message for our lives. His dynamic messages began to stir up childhood dreams inside of me again. We attended services at night, and we had time to reflect on them during the day. I'll never forget this. On one of those days, I was walking on the beach at Anna Maria Island, Florida, reflecting on the messages, when I had this conversation with God:

"Father God, I'm asking you for a business of my own, one that You specifically give me. I will take the business and do with it whatever you tell me. The only stipulation is that it helps people and brings all the glory back to You.

I'm willing to build a business of my own as long as I know it's from You." Well, immediately in my spirit, I heard what the business should be. I took a deep breath because it is a business in an industry I hated. I said, *"Father, am I hearing this correctly?"* I heard Him say, *"You don't have to."* I immediately said, *"I will do it and do it only how You tell me to."*

Right away, I began working on the research and development of a business in an industry I hated—but only because I knew it was from God. My clear direction is to help change the culture of this industry by introducing it to God's heart and His way of doing things. I have been steadily working on that since then. Coming soon, my friends, is the business I know the Lord gave me. That business is a BIG DREAM that is about to come to sight!

That was a giant step *off the merry-go-rounds and on with our life!* We were *going from spinning to winning as our new way of living!* But God had even more in store. As we walked in faith, taking action, we soon discovered even greater things than these we would see!

In June 2017, we took ten days and went to Colorado to Charis Bible College Business Summit. I was on the road to starting a business, so this seemed like it would be a good help to me too. David was already taking the Charis Bible College first-year correspondence classes at home. So we thought we would also just meet with an admissions counselor and gather some information. Our thoughts were, possibly *in the future, MAYBE, if we could figure it all out*, we might attend on-campus … somehow. We met with the admissions department on Tuesday, and we both began to *come alive* inside our hearts. The campus was beautiful and right at the foot of Pike's Peak—America's Mountain—but so far away from our children, family, and friends. We didn't know one single person who attended there. Our minds were working overtime, trying to figure out how to make it work so David could take classes on campus. Nothing seemed to make sense as to how we could do it.

Wednesday of that week, David was struggling. But I was praying and asking God, *"PLEASE COME TO OUR RESCUE! Please, show David this is the answer to relieving the years of frustration just <u>wandering around in the wilderness</u>!"*

Before we left for the meetings that night, I asked David this question: *"If money was not an issue, and if you never had to even think twice about money, what would you do?"*

He didn't answer me.

That evening, we got to the business summit early. We saw Andrew Wommack standing up at the front, just talking to anyone who came up to him. I said, *"Come on, let's go talk to Andrew!"* Neither of us knew that what was about to happen would change our lives forever! God is so fun! Andrew Wommack shook our hands, and we proceeded to tell him how David had been taking the correspondence classes and loving them. We told him how we were gathering information about classes on campus for the future. He just kept looking at us in the eyes ...

And then he said, *"If money was not an issue, what would you do?"*

(WOW! Hello?! How much clearer does it have to get? It was the exact same question I had asked earlier that night.)

David answered him, *"I would come."*

Tears started streaming down my face, and I was shaking inside. David was choked up and speechless. Next, even though we were relative strangers, Andrew said something so boldly that it caught us off guard:

"I don't even know you two, but the story in 2 Kings 7, about the four lepers who sat at the gate just waiting to die, keeps coming to my mind. They were starving, and there was a famine going on. They had a choice to stay there and die or go and surrender to the Syrians, who might kill them but who also might feed them. But if not, they were going to die anyway. So, they chose to do something different, and they lived."

Then Andrew said directly to us, *"**You better do something or die.**"*

Was Andrew referring to us maybe dying physically? Not necessarily. But David and I both knew enough about the direction we had been heading to understand that death was beginning to happen in other ways. Our health was going downhill, our passion was decreasing— the death of vision and purpose drove us to move forward. Definitely, the early death of our bodies would have been the eventual end result of not moving forward into the promised and prosperous plan God had for us.

The stronghold of fear gripped David as he was still trying to figure out how all this could work and if he truly would even do it from his heart. Then, Thursday morning's speaker nailed it on the head! He talked in David's language. He talked about preaching the Gospel in and through culture and our area of influence, which spoke directly to David's heart's desire. The speaker talked about how the Church should be the major influence in government, and this is how the Kingdom of God works in every area of culture. He then knew that he knew. This was the place he would learn from and become equipped to do it. We made the decision that day to do whatever it took to get him on campus to start school by the first of September 2017.

Because God is always helping us, He gave me a dream on Saturday morning right before we woke up to leave Colorado and go back home. I saw David and myself in our black truck (in the dream), all packed up and heading back home. It seemed very real and *in the moment,* like it was actually happening. We were heading down a road along the mountainside, and a corner was coming up. Suddenly, what looked like a river of black lava came around the corner. I screamed for David to stop the truck and stop heading for the black lava river! His eyes were glazed, and he kept looking forward and driving toward it. I saw a dirt road coming up on the right. It was a way for us to get out of the path of the black lava river.

I yelled for him to turn down that road. He wasn't even slowing down! I was yelling, "God, why won't he stop the truck? Why won't he turn down the road?" Then to him, "David, please stop the truck and get out! Why won't you get out of the truck?!"

He just kept heading toward the black lava, and as he passed the dirt road, I jumped out, tumbling onto the ground. He kept going and went into the black lava river. As the truck sank into the lava, it turned sideways, and I saw David's face staring at me—like a blank stare. Then, he and the truck were swallowed up into the black lava river as I stood there, helplessly watching.

When I woke up, David saw the state I was in. He listened, with all ears open, to my dream. Afterward, he and I both knew that what Andrew unknowingly said was a warning to us, *"Do something or die!"* David knew how serious this was that we do this. He knew that missing this school year on campus could be the last open door for us to do what was in our hearts to do. David says it was as if the Lord was telling him, *"This is it, Son!"*

We began the drive twelve hours back home to Missouri from Colorado. David knew he needed to start telling people about his decision to quit work, leave our family and friends, and come to Charis Bible College. Before he started making phone calls to our children and his boss, we got it settled that I was *also* supposed to attend as a full-time student. We were finally going to do what we each had in our hearts before we were even married.

There we were, in our fifties, when we finally decided to step out and follow our heart's desire. We were going to Bible school together to study God's Word. The summer we took that step, we talked off and on about living on a merry-go-round of frustration for thirty-four years simply because we never stepped out to do our dreams. We talked about all the reasons why we didn't do it earlier. It often boiled down to this: David perceived that everything he did was being watched under a magnifying glass and family opinions had great control over him. He felt condemned for anything he did, even the good things. It seemed to David that others, especially his family, never felt David did anything right. It seemed that he never had his family's approval for what he had on his heart to do. David still had a strong desire to preach the Gospel, just as he did when he got saved at seventeen. Every day that went by while not acting on the dream was like torture to David. He was totally stuck and didn't know how to get unstuck.

One day we were talking about it, and he said, *"Why would I have this huge dream and desire to learn God's Word and preach the Gospel if I wasn't going to be able to do it? It feels like God made a mistake and put me in the wrong family. My family has never supported my wanting to do this and has always ridiculed me for trying. I feel like my family screwed up my whole childhood and is still trying to interfere with my life! Why would God put me in this family?"*

Sadly, his family didn't support his wanting to preach the Gospel at seventeen, and they still weren't supporting him as a fifty-six-year-old man. The persecution and condemnation he had previously received had piled up in his heart and were pressing in big time. Then, as we announced our plans, we received fresh persecution from certain family members. Some even told us how irresponsible they thought we were by doing this at our age. *This time*, even feeling ridiculed for doing it, *he and I kept to the plan.* We were committed to getting off the merry-go-rounds of our past and getting on with our lives. At the end of August 2017, we packed up our truck, shut the door to our newly bought home, and said goodbye to our children, family, and friends.

The dream about the black lava reminded me of the many years I had watched my husband not go forward. My heart had been hurting for him, yet frustrated with him. Once we moved to Colorado to start classes, we soon saw that *condemnation had been holding him back.* It was trying to kill any vision and passion he had in his heart. We realized the black lava river in the dream was a picture of condemnation trying to bury him alive.

Armed with this insight, David dealt with that condemnation, *once and for all.* It was exposed. And *David was set free by hearing the truth about God's love for him* daily at Bible college. This, along with the twice-a-week morning worship services, was a part of the many enriching activities we got to be involved in while being students on campus.

Immediately when we arrived at Bible school, we felt translated into a different culture and world. *It was a dream come true!* There was an atmosphere like we had never experienced. Every day we drove onto the school property and walked into the building, teary-eyed and so thankful to be there. It seemed we could physically *feel* peace and love in the air and among all the staff. The praise and worship service we had every Monday and Wednesday morning was heavenly. Most of the time, we just stayed teary-eyed because we sensed God's presence and heard Him speaking to our hearts during these praise and worship times.

And further, we sensed healing taking place in our minds and received healing in the emotions heaped up over the years on the inside of us. David would tell you he was the one in whom God was doing the deep cleansing and healing. But equally, I was taken to a new level with God. God was loving on us both so much.

It was beautiful to watch my husband's heart begin to transform immediately after arriving. During praise and worship the first week we were there, David and I sang and worshiped God along with the entire student body. I had my arms raised up in the air, and I looked over at David and saw his arms up toward God. I saw tears coming down his face.

Right then, as I closed my eyes, it was like I began to watch a mini video. I saw what seemed to be a shape floating in the air, almost like the shape of a football. I saw Who I recognized to be Jesus, and He was dancing all around this little floating shape. The shape looked like a large water balloon and moved as it was floating. Jesus was moving his arms all around as He danced, and then, suddenly, He stopped. He cupped His hands up under His mouth and blew a deep breath toward the floating shape. When He did that, the image of the floating water balloon went forward and disappeared. The very next thing I saw (in my mind's video) was David's mother and father standing together. They were smiling.

I had a knowing; I could tell the floating water balloon shape had gone to *them, David's parents.* I gasped and began to cry because I knew it was David whom I had seen as the shape near Jesus; it was David into whom the Lord breathed and sent into his mother's womb. I saw Jesus singing and dancing over David before He sent him off to Earth to be raised by his parents. God breathed the breath of Life into my husband. That breath was filled with the hope that David would one day invite Jesus into his heart, find his God-given purpose and path and, when the time was right, go back to Heaven to live for eternity with Him.

I knew for certain. This vision was God's Spirit revealing to my spirit the answer to my husband's question, *"Did God make a mistake?"* I shared the vision with David to encourage him that *God did not make a mistake* by giving him to his parents and this family. The passions and dreams David had in his heart were God-given for his enjoyment while here on Earth.

That was one of many special encounters with God and life-changing experiences that we had while at Bible college. I should tell you, however, that just because it was the best thing we ever did as a married couple, it wasn't the easiest thing we've ever done. Every day we would wake up and look outside with joy, excitement, and tears of only thankfulness, but at the same time, *our faith and trust in God were tested.* Yes, we had faith before, as much as we knew. But now, it was time to see if that faith would stand the test before us.

David says he hardly slept due to the fear that was trying to harass him and keep its hold on him during the first two weeks of school. We paid our tuition upfront but still had to pay a mortgage and bills at home, plus over $1,300 a month rent plus expenses while living away from home. Thoughts from the enemy of us not having the money to stay at school were terrible. Thoughts were coming at us about how friends and family back home would think we missed it and didn't really hear from God if we ran out of money and couldn't finish school. Yet, we knew we were supposed to do *what* we did *when* we did it. God was trying to help us trust HIM and only HIM and let go of trying to figure things out ourselves. He was trying to help us learn what trusting Him looked like, instead of in our own efforts working a random job.

During morning chapel and praise and worship, there were numerous times when David would be all teary-eyed. Then he would turn, look at me, and tell me that he just heard the Lord say, *"David, I've got this,"* or *"David, do you trust Me?"* It wasn't until February when our savings was gone and we were down to under $40, that *we finally broke free from the fear.* Laying in bed in our little apartment, crying, holding hands, we said, *"If we have to sleep in our truck, we will not quit school!"*

That settled it! We had drawn a line in the sand. We were free, and to our surprise, we had a leading to look for work the next day. Sure, we could have been working a job in fast food or anything before this, but every time we started to get a job, we didn't have peace about it, and it was as if a big stop sign was in front of us. That seemed weird to us, considering work is what we have always done and were very willing to keep doing it. David admits that working is what he had always trusted in for provision. Not God.

God needed *us to know* <u>how bad we wanted this</u> and what we were willing to do to fulfill this deep yearning in our heart—like, sleep in our truck if we had to, for example. Because we spent years running from the call and purpose in our hearts, it was necessary that we *prove to ourselves* that we were not going backward, no matter what.

We also needed to know whether we really did trust God or not and if we would try to step in and begin to provide for ourselves again outside of God's leading. It's easy to trust God when everything is all hunky-dory (quite satisfactory, fine), but wouldn't you rather know if the trust is real? We would.

David says that God was after his WHOLE HEART, and he had to *learn* how to trust Him, not just *say* he was trusting Him. God didn't want David to fake it anymore—saying he was trusting God but honestly wasn't. He wanted him to live his Christian life honestly. I'll skip all the details, but the next day we finally got a buyer for the car we were trying to sell back home, and that money was in our hands in just a few days. It had been crickets until then like no one even saw the ad.

Also, the next day, I thought to call and ask for a refund from the publishing company I paid in advance for the book I was almost ready to publish *this book*. [Smiles.] I was told it would take six weeks to get the $3,800 refund, but we received it in less than two weeks. This money got us through until we started receiving a paycheck for cleaning houses and vacation rentals. That step eventually turned into our own business that was so blessed and prosperous that it paid our next two years of tuition and expenses for school. (As you can tell, I got another opportunity to get my book published, and it's better than it would have been at that time.)

Not knowing how everything would work out, but still determined to go for the full three years, we made the commitment to continue to step out and trust God. We proved to ourselves that we wanted it enough to do anything and that we could honestly trust God. David gave God his WHOLE HEART. We finished our Bible school training with almost perfect attendance and grades.

Looking back, because of the global pandemic of 2020, we now know that if we had missed going *that first year*, we would have missed getting the best of the best on-campus third-year experience. We are so thankful we could graduate from Charis Bible College in 2019. Then we went on to graduate from our third-year programs in 2020. I graduated from the Charis Business School, and David graduated from the Charis Practical Government School. We both are so thankful!

Here's the thing … *what God has done for us, He will do for you!* I so want you to hear this in all of our examples: God loves us so much He will speak personally to our hurts, confusion, and heart's desires. He wants us off our own merry-go-rounds more than we do.

With God's help, I stopped believing in and living in survival mode. David stopped believing that God had made a mistake by putting him in the family that He did. We **started believing** that all the gifts and talents inside us were placed in us to be used, not just during our childhood and teen years but also as adults.

Of course, the devil never wanted us to figure out and expose this circus of lies. Like a carnival merry-go-round ride, you can *get off the merry-go-round* and have an amazing dream-fulfilled life. The enemy never wanted us to allow the gifts and passions inside us to ever come out. But God put those inside each of us, you too, to help advance God's Kingdom!

The enemy never wanted David to recognize condemnation as a lie, coming from the father of lies. He wanted him stuck on that merry-go-round until he left Earth—never wanting the message in David's heart to come out and be shared with you and the world. But, with God's help, the message is coming out! His big dreams are being fulfilled and coming to pass! My big dreams are coming to pass too!

Our enemy's dreams and goals are that we advance *his* kingdom. It was a sad day for the enemy of my soul when I woke up and became aware of my merry-go-rounds! David and I stil have BIG DREAMS, but now our dreams have God's heart and purpose attached to them. Our dreams are so big it will take God to make them happen. *But HE IS!*

You, too, have things on the inside of you that have been stifled and not *allowed* to come out and be used for God's Kingdom. Like all of us, you have had something traumatic, in one degree or another, happen to you in your past life that made those things come to a screeching halt. That can change!

I believe that you are beginning to desire to recognize and face your life's merry-go-rounds. I believe you are getting stirred up RIGHT NOW to **let go** of your past (which was one minute ago) **and start letting God** loose the gifts

and callings in you that have been bound up. *No matter your age—it's not too late if you still have breath!*

It's time to get off the merry-go-round and on with your life! Get back on the path and get to work on those BIG DREAMS!

Our Own

Let's examine the components of *Our Own Merry-Go-Round*:

- ❖ The Center Post: Ignoring the light (knowledge and revelation) that you do have because you do not believe change can come will keep you perpetually spinning.

- ❖ The Base: Familiarity supports the lie when you keep relying on your established responses, always doing what you've always done, spinning and spinning, getting nowhere fast.

- ❖ The Decorative Fixtures and Handlebars: You keep holding on to negative patterns in self-centeredness and condemnation, thinking it will turn things your way.

- ❖ The End Result: You live frustrated, putting off the dreams you desire in your heart to do. The little merry-go-rounds on your life path lead to bigger ones.

ELEVEN

STOPPING THE SPIN

JESUS SHOWED US how to stop the spin by declaring, *"It is written ..."* and *"It is finished!"* Now, we just need to understand what He meant and how it applies to us today. I have often thought about having these two sentences tattooed on each of my lower arms, the same place Wonder Woman wears her wrist shields. It is more important that I have them tattooed in my heart and mind, ready to release and declare in my everyday life situations.

Before any human being ever knew what a *life-event merry-go-round* was, God made a way for us to avoid them. And if perhaps we failed to avoid them, He made a way to get off of any we might ever start riding. He declared, *"It is written!"* and through Jesus' sacrifice on the Cross, He also paid the price to declare that *"It is finished!"* These two declarations address our born-again position versus the devil and the Curse, so let's talk about them.

First, let's talk about the devil—just for a minute—and his influence on our life actions and decisions. I think most people can admit there is evil and darkness all around us, and it is constantly trying to influence us. If you've been in church for a small amount of time, you should have been told about the devil. The Bible talks about the devil and his evil works of destruction and how he is a liar and has no truth in him. So pastors and teachers should be boldly teaching about this. But you should have *also* heard the flip side—because of what was accomplished when Jesus went to the Cross, the devil is all bark and no bite! *For believers*, our enemy, **the devil, has been defeated**. Now he can only go about "as a roaring lion" (1 Peter 5:8). He can't do anything to us unless we let him.

The next important thing to know is … if the devil cannot do anything to us unless we let him, how do we *let* him? We give him place in our life by believing his lies and fears! Or we can give him place in our life by submitting our fleshly, emotional, carnal, old habits and desires to him for evil works (James 4:7).

But we don't have to! Jesus paid the full price for our freedom and declared, "It is finished!" So, we can let ourselves get free from this old way of living by immersing ourselves in the truth of God's Word. This is renewing our minds to who we are *now* spiritually and then living according to our new identity.

Part One: It Is Written!

Jesus was our example for responding to the devil and his lies. Didn't Jesus use and speak God's Word against satan when He was tempted in the wilderness? *Yes.* Didn't He tell satan, "It is written …" followed by the truth from the Word of God? *Yes.* Isn't Jesus our example? *Yes!* Watch how this works:

> Then Jesus was led up into the wilderness by the Spirit to be tempted by the devil. And He had fasted for forty days and forty nights, and then He was hungry. And the tempter came to Him and said, "If You are the Son of God, command that these stones be turned into bread." But He answered, "**It is written**, 'Man shall not live by bread alone, but by every word that proceeds out of the mouth of God.'"

Then the devil took Him up into the holy city and set Him on the highest point of the temple, and said to Him, "If You are the Son of God, throw Yourself down. For it is written, 'He shall give His angels charge concerning you, 'And 'In their hands, they shall lift you up, lest at any time you dash your foot against a stone.'

Jesus said to him, "**It is also written**, 'You shall not tempt the Lord your God.'" Again, the devil took Him up on a very high mountain and showed Him all the kingdoms of the world and their grandeur, and said to Him, "All these things I will give You if You will fall down and worship me." Then Jesus said to him, "Get away from here, satan! **For it is written**, 'You shall worship the Lord your God, and Him only shall you serve.'" Then the devil left Him, and immediately angels came and ministered to Him (Matthew 4:1–11 MEV; emphasis added).

When satan tempted Jesus, it was at a time when Jesus was most likely *physically* weak for denying His flesh food for the past forty days. Although certainly physically weak, He focused on things above and nailed down His identity and purpose. He was definitely spiritually minded and able to withstand the temptations the devil threw at Him.

The devil tempted Jesus with food—tempting Jesus to meet His own physical needs by using His supernatural power as the Son of God. The devil also attempted to make Jesus doubt His identity as the Son of God. Don't be surprised that this is how the enemy tempts us, also. The enemy wants us to cave into physical desires, doubt who we are IN CHRIST, and doubt the power and authority we have available to us because of Jesus.

If the enemy can get us to doubt that we are a child of God, *then* he can get us to give in to his temptations for sin and failure. We are heirs of Salvation who have authority over him. Don't let the enemy tell you who you are. He may try to do that through darts (thoughts) in your mind or through other people's words. Don't listen, don't believe it. **Let God's Word tell you who you are,** and *then* YOU TELL the devil and everyone else what God said!

Suppose people or the devil can get us to doubt God's love for us and doubt God's good, true nature. In that case, we are likely to believe the religious lies that say God is hooked with the devil and is letting bad things happen to us to teach us something. He is not!

Our best defense against the snares and traps of the devil is <u>to know God's Word and who we are as born-again believers</u>. It will take effort from us to renew our minds and get this TRUTH established in our minds and thoughts. But it is worth it when we can **confidently** say to the devil, "It is written …" followed by inserting the Word of Truth, "so SCRAM!" And, of course, he does!

I've added a large list of Scriptures (in the appendix) full of "IN CHRIST" and "IN HIM" promises to equip you. These are filled with loads of truth about who you are as a born-again believer in Jesus Christ. (This is actually a short version of the list I received from my church almost fifteen years ago. Other Scriptures on the list had to do with what we can now do and have "through Him/Christ" and would be a great word study for you to do also. When I received the two-page list, I immediately got out my Bible at home and looked up each and every one. You can read in the pages to come how my life was changed by these. I am confident if you take time to look at each of them, yours will be too!)

I'll drop a few of them here to give you a pattern—see if any of these instances sound familiar and how to use scriptural truths to replace those old mindsets. For example, *have you ever had thoughts that made you wonder if you really are a Christian? Or have you questioned whether you will really go to Heaven when you physically die?* When those thoughts come, like they usually do to new believers, remember what God says in John 3:15–16 (emphasis added):

> … <u>that whoever believes in Him should not perish but have eternal life</u>. For God so loved the world that He gave His only

begotten Son, that <u>whoever believes in Him should not perish but have everlasting life</u>.

If you believe **IN HIM** (Jesus), you have the promise that you will not perish, and you will have eternal life. Confront the thought and evaluate it with the Scripture. Do you believe that God gave His Son Jesus for you to believe in and have everlasting life when you do? Have you done that? If you have, then, no worries, boldly stand firm on this Scripture.

When you *recognize* thoughts bombarding you, condemning thoughts, you can refer to Romans 8:1 (emphasis added):

> There is therefore now no condemnation to those who are **IN CHRIST JESUS**, who do not walk according to the flesh, but according to the Spirit.

First of all, you are no longer condemned to Hell if you are born again. You will spend eternity in Heaven because you have received Jesus as your Lord and Savior. If the devil can't get you to believe you have lost your Salvation every other day, he will try to at least get you to think you are always doing something wrong.

Years ago, I had to refer to this Scripture more than any other. Condemning thoughts and feelings of condemnation were a regular thing for me—until I learned how to deal with them correctly. *I had to teach myself to stop and evaluate.* Is my conscience telling me I stepped over one of my own boundaries? Or, is this the devil trying to make me *feel* condemned and guilty for doing something wrong? Were the "yucky" feelings coming from my own conscience or the devil?

Back then, the crazy thing was that the condemning thoughts would come to me at the grocery store while I was buying groceries! I would have thoughts of spending too much, that I couldn't afford the good hamburger meat, or that God would only want me to buy the off-brand of food, not the name brands. Otherwise, I would feel like I would be wasting money. *Those were all lies.* I remember just leaving my cart in the aisle and walking out to the car to clear my head on one such day. That's how bad it was! So, I trained myself to pick it apart and then get it straight: those thoughts were nothing but condemning lies, and I wasn't a bad steward with my grocery money!

At times, I still must pick the thoughts apart and determine whether they are condemnation or correction. The good news is that it has become much easier. I check my heart's motive for doing or saying something. Was it pure and God-led? If I can answer yes, but I'm *still* feeling condemned for doing it or saying it, then I know it is false condemnation. The devil is just trying to make me think or *feel like* I did something wrong or even intentionally tried to hurt someone. If I realize that I was NOT walking in the flesh but was led by God's Spirit, I know I have full rights to use this Scripture to tell the devil to SCRAM! And he does!

Once condemnation is recognized, and I deal with it scripturally, those thoughts and feelings leave. I notice that condemning thoughts don't harass me nearly as often as they used to because now the devil knows I am recognizing them as coming from him!

So, don't just receive every thought that comes to you, readily accepting it as if God gave it to you. Identify them, find out where they came from. Condemnation, condemning thoughts, will become more recognizable when you begin to stop and confront those thoughts head-on and evaluate your actions and heart motives. They will stop coming as often because the devil will know that you know the truth about this and that you intend to reject those lies.

Here is another example: *Do you ever begin to doubt that ALL God's promises are for you?* When doubt comes into your heart or mind, find and read 2 Corinthians 1:20 (emphasis added):

> For all the promises of God **IN HIM** are Yes, and **IN HIM** Amen, to the glory of God through us.

God gets glory when we receive His promises. He *loves it* when we believe He meant it when He said His promises are YES and AMEN! (Amen means, "So be it.") Believe that God loves you more than any really good and generous earthly father. His promises are *for you* and anyone who believes.

Have you ever been afraid to ask God for something? Here is a Scripture (1 John 5:14–15; emphasis added) that helped me get over that:

> Now this is the confidence that we have IN HIM, that if we ask anything according to His will, He hears us. And if we know that He hears us, whatever we ask, we know that we have the petitions that we have asked of Him.

The key here is to believe you are IN HIM. Once you have that down, next, you must know that you can confidently ask Him for things that line up with His will. How do you know His will? The Bible says that life more abundantly is His will. It also says that Jesus showed us the Father's will. Everything Jesus did is God's will for us also! I hope you are getting as stirred up as I am right now as I share this with you!

I've only shown you a few examples. But I believe as you dig into God's Word for yourself, you will find that you can apply the IN HIM, IN CHRIST, THROUGH CHRIST Scriptures to your personal situations. Remember, there is a list of these Scriptures included in the appendix to help you. Dig into them for yourself. Your relationship with God will blossom as you do!

Part Two: You've Got This! (Or Do You Really?)

As we begin to learn about our new identity IN CHRIST, by faith, we choose to believe it. When we choose to live our lives according to that new identity, we stop with the "self" attempts to live our lives victoriously in our own power. Believing in God's love for us causes faith to rise up in us to humbly let go of our self-willpower. We can release the self-motivations that we used in the past before being born again. We will begin to live by the strength and faith of the Son of God living inside of us. We can stop being afraid and start standing up to the devil!

But to do that, we must first evaluate our own actions. We must check to ensure that we are not relying on our "bossy self" and human willpower. We should use the Word of God and not foolish words that man came up with, which deceive us into believing we are making forward progress when really, we aren't.

READ IT!
John 15
Authority and Ability Comes from
Abiding In Christ

When we stop walking in life alone or acting alone, we'll stop the spin. Read John 15 to see what I'm talking about. Even Jesus didn't walk apart from the Father while He was on Earth. *Why would we think we can?* It's pride to think we can. With that in mind, let's not thoughtlessly say things we've heard other people say! Some sayings make people look to themselves for help and away from God's help. There is one, in particular, that is popular but can really backfire—*Can I be transparent with you?* I share this with the hope it will help you.

I'm sure you have heard the saying, ***"You've got this!"*** I have seen a few people who declared this in life and death situations over themselves or other people, and it never worked out for them. Just relying on *self* to accomplish something will not produce long-lasting results. Our own willpower can't keep us going forever nor protect us from the works of the enemy. It just gives false hope because there seems to always come a time when we (in and of ourselves) *don't* "got this" and honestly come to the end of our own limitations.

The saddest part is when Christians say this. I have learned to never say this in cases where it would imply that someone can do something that only Jesus can provide! We aren't pointing anyone toward Jesus by saying, "You've got this!" Think about it. When we falsely convince ourselves that "we've got this" or tell others that "you've got this," and then what is being hoped for doesn't pan out, people blame God or say it must not have been God's will for it to happen. There is something pretty twisted about that.

If truth be told, they (we) should admit they didn't look to God or His Word for help and the right answer. We are not alone, so we should not be acting alone. **Anything we do to enforce our authority as believers must come from the foundation and revelation of Who Jesus is and who we are IN Him** (John 15:5). It has nothing to do with the "us" and everything to do with what Jesus already did and the new identity He freely gave us. We did not and cannot *earn* it. And we sure don't have "it" without Him!

When we believe and receive what Jesus did for us, we *become* the righteousness of God in Christ Jesus (2 Corinthians 5:21). That is how and when we receive the power and authority to enforce the victory Jesus handed over to us. **<u>If we don't stand up to the devil and enforce that victory, he will always try to illegally trespass into our lives and steal from us.</u> We do that by believing and speaking the Word of God.**

> Behold, I give you the authority to trample on serpents and scorpions, and over all the power of the enemy, and nothing shall by any means hurt you (Luke 10:19).

As long as we are here on Earth, the enemy will try to keep us confused about Jesus and about God's good and true nature. He wants to keep us deceived into thinking we have no power over him or authority to stop him in his tracks. He will always *try* to get us to doubt God's love for us and our new nature in Christ. He will *try* to keep us from loving God, ourselves, and other people. He absolutely hates love—Who is God! He absolutely hates believers because we have the Spirit of God in us and the ability to love people and enforce the victory over him that Jesus gave us.

We must recognize who is the one working against us and what his moves are. Do you agree? We know this philosophy is helpful and regularly used in business and competitions. Did you know that it also is a powerful Biblical principle? We must know how to stand against the crazy deceptive schemes of the devil and all his destructive works that come flying our way at times. We must know our Savior, and we must identify our enemy.

When I was young, I asked someone I knew about satan. I was told that we aren't supposed to do what satan wants, BUT we are supposed to respect him because he has a lot of power to use against us. Really? WOW! (And, no, that is not correct.) That statement never set right with my spirit, even as a young teenager ignorant of the truth! I don't even like to give the devil the satisfaction of capitalizing his name. Respecting him will never be something I do. I also never joke around about the devil or joke about him making me do something.

That old saying, "THE DEVIL MADE ME DO IT," is junk!

Friends, we sometimes give the devil way too much credit for the junk going on in our life. **No one is *making you* do anything!** It's not funny. The devil can't *make you* do anything, just like God won't *make you* do anything. The devil can only do things in your life that you allow him to do. And God has chosen to only work in you and live through you as much as you will allow Him.

Suppose you wake up every day and choose to be self-centered, emotion-led, and give in to every temptation the devil uses on your flesh and mind. In that case, you will live in constant turmoil—all the while thinking the devil is the one doing it. You, not the devil, are sabotaging your own victory. If you refuse to read God's Word and learn for yourself what it says, then you will continue to stay ignorant regarding the truths of His Word that are meant to help you. Your mind will never change, and you will always be thinking your old way. But you do not have to!

Part Three: It Is Finished!

In John 17, we can read the prayer Jesus prayed to His Heavenly Father. This was during the time we call *The Last Supper*. Jesus was with His disciples and they had just finished eating, and He had just finished washing their feet. In verse four, Jesus tells the Father, "I have glorified You on the Earth. I have finished the work which You have given Me to do."

On the Cross, right before His last breath, Jesus declared to everyone, "It is finished!" God sent Jesus to do a job and He did it.

When I first understood what Jesus meant when He said, "It is finished," it changed my thinking! I now understand better and filter things through the truth of "It is finished." But *what* is finished? And why is this important in my being equipped to get *off the merry-go-rounds and on with life?*

What is finished? The constant struggle to win the war on sin and eternal judgment for our personal sin. God's focus is no longer sin, and ours should not be either. We no longer have to be *sin-conscious*. We are now the righteousness of God, IN CHRIST! If Jesus said it, then I believe it! **Because I believe it, I now choose to stop the spinning and begin to live my life winning**! Why? Because through Jesus, our life has a new purpose and destiny—which is to be a winner!

This doesn't mean hard things won't come our way, and it doesn't mean changes come overnight. It does mean that when we allow our thinking to change, we are not on the losing team anymore! I've changed sides, and you can too! **If we are born-again Christians, then we are born winners, according to this Scripture:**

> For whatever is born of God overcomes the world. And this is the victory that has overcome the world—our faith. Who is he who overcomes the world, but he who believes that Jesus is the Son of God? (1 John 5:4–5)

Years ago, I was introduced to a game. I think I only played one round of this game and then refused to ever play again. It was called *Loser.* All I really remember about the game is what happened if you answered wrong or did the wrong thing—you were booed. Everyone held up their hand, making their fingers look like a big "L." I hated that game! You might think I'm being a little ridiculous. Still, it made you feel like a loser when everyone shouts out, "Loser!" to you, holds the big "L" in your face, and laughs. I never wanted to confess I was a loser or call someone else a loser. What a horrible game! I prefer to hold up the "W" sign (which is my three center fingers) and shouting "Winner," or the "V" sign (which is my two fingers like a peace sign) for "Victorious!"

But all games aside, when we come into this world, we actually *are* born losers. The sin and fall of mankind caused us to *lose* our authority here on Earth. It caused us to lose fellowship with God. We lost all the blessings of God and no longer had dominion over the things God originally gave Adam at His creation. We lost all freedom and became under the Curse and the Law.

BUT! Jesus went to the Cross and paid the penalty for *all* the sin of *all* mankind for *all* eternity. Through Jesus Christ, everything was restored back to us. The relationship with God was restored back to us. Whether we believe it or not, and whether we receive it or not, that's what Jesus did for us. He paid for our freedom from the Curse that came upon mankind. It is finished. To possess it, all we must do is believe and receive it. We are literally born again as winners when we are born again through faith in (believing and receiving) Jesus Christ's *finished* work on the Cross. Now, we don't have to live from miracle to miracle. We can live every single day in the Blessing given to us in Christ Jesus.

> Christ has redeemed us from the curse of the law, having become a curse for us for it is written, "Cursed is everyone who hangs on a tree," that the blessing of Abraham might come upon the Gentiles in Christ Jesus, that we might receive the promise of the Spirit through faith (Galatians 3:13–14; emphasis added).

As born-again believers, if something isn't working right in our Christian walk, it isn't God who has failed us. God is love, and love never fails. **His love will take us across the finish line and into the "It is finished" life that we can now receive through Jesus if we allow it.**

Yes, I said *if we allow it*. Remember, when we spiritually realize, mentally understand, and come into agreement with God's perfect love for us, fear leaves. So, if something isn't working right, it is most likely because we haven't *come into agreement* with His Word and still have more fear than trust in God. It could also be that there are just some things we don't understand *yet* in our human way of thinking, because our natural minds are not yet fully renewed. For instance, some may not yet know and believe in their hearts that God has planned an awesome life for them. We all must believe that what Jesus did for us on the Cross allows this plan to bring a winning life to us *now*.

Because He loved us and wanted a personal relationship with us, Jesus did what was needed to set us free from ALL the power and works of the kingdom of darkness. **We are no longer slaves to sin and destined for Hell**. Why continue to live under the power of that dark, losing kingdom? Jesus said, "IT IS FINISHED!" *Agree with God!*

> After this, <u>Jesus, knowing that all things were now accomplished</u>, that the Scripture might be fulfilled, said, "I thirst!" Now a vessel full of sour wine was sitting there, and they filled a sponge with sour wine, put it on hyssop, and put it to His mouth. So when Jesus had received the sour wine, He said, "<u>It is finished</u>!" And bowing His head, He gave up His spirit (John 19:28–30; emphasis added).

Jesus finished it! He did what it took to bring us back into right standing with God. He repaired the relationship gap between Him and us after Adam sinned. God no longer holds our sin against us and requires a sacrifice for our sin. Jesus became that sacrifice, once and for all.

> … that is, that God was in Christ reconciling the world to Himself, <u>not counting their sins against them</u>, and has entrusted to us the message of reconciliation (2 Corinthians 5:19 MEV; emphasis added).

I want to make it clear. People don't go to Hell because of unconfessed sin. They go to Hell for eternity (separated from God) because they do not receive and confess Jesus as the sacrifice for their sin. They don't believe in Jesus and what He did. Jesus said, "It is finished!" because sacrifices for sin are no longer required. Sacrifices aren't a "thing" anymore, but *believing in Jesus is!*

Jesus *already* did what was needed. **He fought for us and won!** Jesus *already* took back from the devil what Adam and Eve lost to the devil. He redeemed us from the Curse brought on us all when Adam and Eve doubted God's love and goodness and believed a lie instead.

I was a cheerleader in my youth for our school wrestling team. There was a wrestling cheer we used in high school that went like this: "R-E-V-E-R-S-E! Reverse! Reverse!" If it wasn't looking too good for our guy, we cheerleaders would start yelling this cheer. Well, we can do that now in everyday life! If things aren't looking so good for us and we are totally under attack from the enemy, we can remind the devil what Jesus did on the Cross! We can say, **"Listen, satan, the Curse has been reversed! I'm NOT CURSED! Jesus restored the Blessing back to me!"**

I personally choose to believe the Curse has been reversed through the <u>full redemptive work</u> of Jesus through His death, burial, and resurrection. I am choosing to come into agreement with Jesus and say, **"It is finished!"**

> Christ has redeemed us from the curse of the law, having become a curse for us, for it is written, "Cursed is everyone who hangs on a tree" (Galatians 3:13).

READ IT!
Galatians 3
BLESSED NOT CURSED

The authority to rule and reign here on Earth was given back to mankind when Jesus rose from the dead. He <u>defeated</u> satan and the power of his evil works right then! His last words were declared, **"IT IS FINISHED!"** Meaning, **it's over, devil**!!

> [Jesus] having wiped out the handwriting of requirements that was against us, which was contrary to us. And He has taken it out of the way, having nailed it to the cross. Having disarmed principalities and powers, He made a public spectacle of them, triumphing over them in it (Colossians 2:14–15; emphasis added).

If principalities and powers are disarmed, then *why are they still able to do their destructive works in our lives, even as Christians?* Because of the ignorance of God's children. We allow these things to happen because we do not know we can resist them and enforce the victory Jesus gave us! Look at this verse:

> My people are destroyed for lack of knowledge because you have rejected knowledge . . . (Hosea 4:6).

God's people were being destroyed because they lacked knowledge—they rejected knowledge—about God in their lives. We need to know and acknowledge God, His help, and what Jesus has done! As we do, we will stop falling into the destruction from the enemy. We will stop perishing because we stop rejecting the help we have been given in God's Word! Look at Proverbs 29:18 (NIV):

> Where there is no revelation, people cast off restraint; but blessed is the one who heeds wisdom's instruction.

Looking back at these Scriptures, we can see that God gives us a head's up! He tells us exactly how to prevent being duped by the enemy—receive the knowledge and revelation from God's Word!

Part Four: My Bossy Self

God's Word shows us how Jesus handled the enemy and how we're supposed to deal with the enemy. ***He already won the war*** that some Christians are still trying to fight! What war? The war on sin and the Curse that came because of sin. When we read and study God's Word, we will see that we should be resting in the victory Jesus gave us.

Because I didn't fully understand my right standing with God, I resorted for years to using my bold "bossy self" to declare the Word of God to the enemy. Doing this made me *think* I was genuinely making headway in the battle. Using my own human strength and stubborn willpower to try and take down the enemy just about burned me out. It seemed like I was really doing some damage to the powers of darkness and running off the devil, but I wasn't. If the enemy can keep the spin going with lies and man-made actions that have no real results, then he can keep us from getting back the victory he stole from us. I really hope this chapter brings understanding to help you.

Here's an example of my attempt to stand up against the enemy's works. But I had only my BOSSY SELF as my help:

For years I was confused about using my God-given authority to keep the devil's works at bay and enforce my right to life more abundantly. I would say, "It is written, devil ..." but, I basically only made noise.

I used my "bossy self" and self-willpower and confused it with my right to have authority as a believer in Jesus. I knew what I was doing was not genuinely effective because I didn't get actual results most of the time. Something was missing. However, I continued to do it, hoping that I'd hit the jackpot one day if it worked.

Yes, I would say, "In Jesus' name ..." before or after bossing the devil around. And yes, I was quoting Scriptures to him. Yes, that's what we are supposed to do. (Remember, that is what I taught you to do earlier in the chapter?) So why didn't it work for me? What was I missing?

Here is what I was missing: *I* was doing it. I was acting *alone,* in my own power. My declarations were not based on anything except that I did know I could speak the Scripture just like Jesus did when He said, "It is written." So, I made a bunch of noise and wore myself out, but that is about all. I never really got real results until years later.

How about I help you skip that part and hand you a shortcut? Real results only came after I began to really **KNOW (have deep revelation)** about the righteousness of God in Christ. Remember that list of "In Him" and "In Christ" Scriptures that I mentioned earlier? Find them in the appendix! When I looked up every one of them and read them, I embraced the new identity that I received when I accepted Jesus Christ as my Lord and Savior. That is where I found what had been missing! And you will too!

Now when I am hit with something trying to steal my right to abundant life as a believer, I remind the devil of who I am IN CHRIST! If he's messing with me, he's messing with a Child of God who knows she has been set free from the Curse! I let the devil know that I AM THE RIGHTEOUSNESS OF GOD IN CHRIST JESUS!

I **submit my *SELF* to God.** I declare that Jesus is my Lord. I'm not acting in my own authority; I'm acting on **His authority**, having been deputized, so to speak. I start there. I build that foundation first. I look up to Jesus as my Source, and I place myself under Him.

That is when I can now unleash the rest of God's promises given to me by being a child of God! I notify the enemy of the foundation I am standing on and Who's got my back! Then, the devil realizes he's been caught as a thief, and he doesn't have any right to steal from me! He knows it's not just my bossy self speaking now. I've had real results since I stopped trying to enforce *my* authority and started enforcing Jesus' authority that we have been deputized to use.

The Bible says our weapons are not carnal weapons. We do not wrestle against flesh and blood, meaning we don't need to focus on the people the enemy is using but on the real enemy. We need to use the right weapons to hit the

READ IT!
Ephesians 6:10-18
The Full Armor of God

right target. God did not leave us unequipped without weapons! He supplied the right weapons to protect ourselves *and* help us walk in our freedom as a believer. God is not a bad shepherd—He's a Good Shepherd!

Here are some truths for your spiritual fighting bag that you must believe and use to enforce the victory Jesus gave us:

Assuredly, I say to you, whatever you bind on earth will be bound in heaven, and whatever you loose on earth will be loosed in heaven (Matthew 18:18; emphasis added).

But thanks be to God, who gives us the victory through our Lord Jesus Christ (1 Corinthians 15:57; emphasis added).

He has delivered us from the power of darkness and conveyed us into the kingdom of the Son of His love (Colossians 1:13; emphasis added).

Since, therefore, [these His] children share in flesh and blood [in the physical nature of human beings], He [Himself] in a similar manner partook of the same [nature], that by [going through] death He might bring to nought and make of no effect him who had the power of death—that is, the devil (Hebrews 2:14 AMPC; emphasis added).

… as His divine power has <u>given to us all things that pertain to life and godliness</u>, through the knowledge of Him who called us by glory and virtue, by which <u>have been given to us exceedingly great and precious promises</u>, that <u>through these you may be partakers of the divine nature</u>, having escaped the corruption that is in the world through lust (2 Peter 1:3–4; emphasis added).

It's clear to me that Jesus did what it took to allow us to have everything we need to live an awesome, Godly life. He gave us the right fighting equipment and protective gear! If *junk* is going on in our lives, and we accept it as God's will for us, then we are not doing what Jesus told us to do. God's Word clearly tells us what to do when attacks from the enemy come.

Even though it is not our Good Father God's desire that any should perish (on Earth physically or spiritually for eternity), He will not force us to change. He will not force us to let loose of the reins so that He can allow His good and perfect will to come into our life. This is a decision we are so blessed to be able to make each and every day when we wake up.

<u>Real results can happen for you. Failed attempts can become less and less, and the spinning can stop</u>. Listen, even if you've done it wrong for years. Even if you have yielded to your own merry-go-round for years with failed attempts to stop the spin because of doing it wrong, it's not impossible for God to get you off. We are never too far gone for Him! You must believe that your ongoing, negative situations and relationships *can change* and that you really *can get off* the merry-go-rounds in your life. This book is full of help if you want it. I know God wants to help you!

Is anything too hard for the Lord?

That is in Genesis 18:14, and the answer to that question is no! Nothing is too hard for the Lord. You can do this **through Christ our Lord**!! You can show the world there is help and that freedom can also happen for them. Show them a *different* way of doing things. It starts with you personally doing things differently. Things change and real results come when you stop with the religious wrong thinking and actions that have no results and begin to follow the instructions given in God's Word.

I have entered the peaceful rest of "It is finished!" I use God's Word and say, "It is written!" So, I now walk in faith, and I can cast the cares of my life onto the Lord a lot easier.

We can let our lights of faith, peace, joy, and all the fruits of God's Spirit released in our lives shine out there ON the darkness. Our bright lights can so shine on the darkness that it exposes the lies, fears, and traps other people are in bondage to. The light, love, and freedom we live by will bring truth and stir up hopes and dreams in people for their future while here on Earth. Don't you want to be a part of that? I believe you do.

It's not too hard for the Lord to stop the spin in your life first! Do you believe it?

TWELVE

PREPARE TO WALK OFF

Part One: Line Up!

Life's merry-go-rounds are all around us, but have no fear! After reading this book, I know it will be easier to recognize and avoid them. These repetitive movements and lifestyle familiarities do not have to interfere with God's plan for us.

Let's get you prepared to walk off your merry-go-rounds! In this chapter, I want to help you get lined up correctly so that you can walk straight out and into His good plan. Knowing the real fight, the truth about the new you, and the amount of help God has lined up for you are all part of His equipping you to move forward.

In previous chapters, I mentioned that I was a cheerleader for the high school wrestling team. Did you know that the Bible uses a wrestling illustration in Ephesians 6:12–13? It reminds me of this cheer: "**When you fight, you win! You've got to fight to win!**"

What kind of fight are we talking about? Some people think there is no fight because their thinking is like this: "Jesus didn't fight on the Cross. Instead, He endured it and let it happen to Him." Indeed, Jesus did *not* fight against going through the sacrifice of the Cross. However, this way of thinking is not true in that Jesus *did* fight for us by enduring the suffering of the Cross as *He kept His eyes on the prize,* that being us. The <u>endurance was the fight of faith</u>—Jesus was holding on to something in faith. He was holding on to us. His faith in the end result of the Cross is what kept Him going. The same way Jesus fought for us on the Cross, with us in mind, is the same way we fight to stay off merry-go-rounds, with Him in mind. I think this Scripture sums it up well:

> Let us look to Jesus, the author and finisher of our faith, who <u>for the joy that was set before Him endured the cross</u>, despising the shame, and is seated at the right hand of the throne of God (Hebrews 12:2 MEV).

Our fight is not about the Cross or us carrying OUR cross—it's a fight to keep our eyes and minds focused on what He did for us *on the Cross.* It's about defending what Jesus gave us because He didn't fight to stay off the Cross. We need to know the truth about what happened on the Cross. We aren't supposed to be taking hits from the enemy, thinking we are being like Jesus. He took those hits so we wouldn't have to!

Let's get the truth straight about this fight I'm talking about. **The fight is not about trying to get something and win the game. This is a fight to KEEP holding on to what Jesus already won for us and gave to us. He got the victory and then gave us the reward He received.** (This might sound repetitive, but you must be clear on this.) Fighting to *stay off* a merry-go-round is much easier than fighting *while on* a merry-go-round or fighting to *get off* one.

Like a championship wrestler who defends the title (the new identity as a champion), our fight now is *defensive.* A champion, a winner, already has the win and defends the win.

Fight the good fight of faith, lay hold on eternal life, to which you were also called and have confessed the good confession in the presence of many witnesses (1 Timothy 6:12).

Let us hold fast the confession of our hope without wavering, for He who promised is faithful (Hebrews 10:23).

The fight is to remain steadfast, to keep our *faith* and trust in God—we defend our faith in the win—we hold fast to His promises for us until they are seen with the natural eye. The fight is about resisting the temptation to cross the line of absolutes and moral standards we've set for ourselves based on our new identity.

The fight is about standing our ground and holding that line when the devil tries to break into our lives and steal from us. It's a fight to resist our fleshly, old desires that want us to collapse under pressure and be unable to go forward. We fight to keep peace and joy flowing out of us—especially when it seems like everything is against us. It's a defensive fight to keep the win! There's only one right way to fight correctly. We must get lined up straight and then stay in line—God's way.

Do you remember when the teacher would say, "OK, Everyone, line up!" in elementary school? We all quickly got in line so she could lead us to the lunchroom or recess. If some of us were out of line, she would instruct us to stand or walk in a <u>straight line</u>. Walking in a straight line is difficult for a child, but a good teacher will help the children stay focused and not frustrated. A good teacher has their students' attention and respect. They will speak softly, without yelling or sounding condemning, and the students will love to obey them. A good teacher will make it almost enjoyable and cause the children to *want* to follow their lead in that line.

I remember having a sense of accomplishment every time our class followed our teacher in her well-structured line. With smiles on our faces, we would get to the designated area feeling safe, together, and well looked after. This type of teacher is someone we can trust. They have our interest in the center of their heart and motives. A good teacher will let you get to know them because they have nothing to hide. They want to earn your trust so you will receive truth, knowledge, and understanding from them. This is a good example of how it works with God's way of doing things.

> <u>Trust</u> in the Lord with all your heart, and lean not on your own understanding; In all your ways, know, recognize, and acknowledge Him, and **He will direct and make straight and plain your paths** (Proverbs 3:5–6 AMPC; emphasis added).

Knowing God and who we are because of Jesus causes us to trust Him—you can say that it lines us up correctly! God made us so that if we stay lined up, looking to Him as our good leader, everything in His plan for us moves along correctly. We make it to our designated area as planned. By this, I mean we will avoid the pitfalls, traps, and merry-go-round rides that are out there to distract us from following our good leader. Staying lined up as we walk our lives out here on Earth will keep us off the merry-go-rounds that are all around us.

Most Christians don't know the correct lineup, though. You know? They are *out of line*. You are not on your path if you are out of line like I was for most of my Christian walk. (No worries, though, because the Good Teacher can help you, just like He did me.) When we became new creatures in Christ Jesus, we should have been discipled right away and taught correctly. We should have been instructed on living *lined up* with God's design for us. But, since most of us didn't get good foundational instruction when we were born again, we must stay willing to learn more now. If we ask the Lord to show us anything we haven't seen before, and if we ask Him to show us everything He has made available to us, HE WILL!

There's a good chance that some of you have never heard how God made us three-part beings, the same as He made Adam: spirit, soul, and body. Did you know that the *real* you is a spirit? You live in a body, and you have a soul. (I Thessalonians 5:23) Your spirit, on the inside, is the real you. Your spirit is who was born again and is where God's Spirit now dwells, not your body and not your soul. Your soulish realm is your mind, will, and emotions. Victory happens in our life when we get our soulish (mental and emotional) realm to line up to the truth and come into agreement with our new, born-again spirit.

Before Adam sinned, God's Spirit lived inside Adam. After he sinned, God's Spirit separated from Adam's spirit and left because the dwelling place was no longer a holy place for God to dwell in. Every human, born after the separation took place in the Garden of Eden, is now physically born but spiritually dead because we are separated from Life (God). Suppose our physical bodies die while our spirits are not reunited to Life. In that case, our dead spirits will live eternally separated from Heaven and from the life of God. That's why Jesus said, "You must be born again" (John 3:7). Once we are born again, we no longer have dead spirits headed toward eternal death and darkness. We are alive IN CHRIST and reunited with Father God, and we will live eternally in Heaven.

Now, understand that we don't *become* God's Spirit when we are born again. We become a holy dwelling place *for* God's Spirit to *live inside our spirit.* We still have a human spirit, but it is no longer dead. It is alive with the life of Christ living inside. Guess what? His Spirit will **FOREVER** live in us (John 14:16), starting right when we receive Jesus.

For the born-again believer, God's Spirit doesn't *come and go* any longer as He did in the Old Testament. This is an important distinction. We don't (or shouldn't) have any reason to pray and ask Holy Spirit to *show up* in our church services, and we don't have a reason to ask Holy Spirit to go home with us. Why? Because He LIVES INSIDE US NOW (John 14:17). **When we show up, He shows up**. Wherever we go, He goes. It's true! Now that you've heard this over and over in my book, I hope you begin to let the life of Christ live *through you as you walk* through each day.

Actions resulting from our old nature, fleshly habits, or old mental belief system have no more right to stay in our soulish realm. We are brand new creatures! The old ways are useless to us now. We don't need them. We aren't living this life by our flesh any longer. If they are still hanging out in our thoughts and being seen in our actions, they are taking up space meant for our mind renewal and righteous living. This is where our problem comes in—we keep following those old living patterns. Instead, we can now let ourselves become transformed by renewing our minds to who we are in Christ. In our spirit, we are now different. Our human actions are supposed to be led by His Spirit IN us, not the other way around.

READ IT!
John 14, 15, & 16
The promise of the Spirit and Who He is

When we became born again, it was because we heard the seed of God's Word, and it was planted in the soil of our hearts. Holy Spirit activated the seed, and it became alive. *We* became alive! We became alive after we believed the truth of Jesus as our Savior. God's Word is truth, and hearing that truth and choosing to believe it caused us to become born again.

Sanctify them by Your truth. Your word is truth (John 17:17 MEV).

Now, we must continue to plant the seed of God's Word into our heart so our mind becomes renewed to the truth about the transformation that took place. Our thoughts need to be spiritually washed from the residue left behind from our old dead sin nature. We <u>must believe</u> His Word in order to align our mind (soulish realm) with our new spirit. They must come into agreement. God will not force this to happen. We are different now and not even the same person *on the inside*. Our new nature doesn't do things the same way our old nature did.

For example, if someone comes up to us and kicks us, our fleshly, old nature wants to kick them back. Not our redeemed spirit, though. Our spirit wants to treat them in a way that would introduce them to Jesus and His love for them. Do you see the difference? Getting our mind, will, and emotions lined up with our born-again spirit is the most important factor in our Christian life. Yet, most Christians have never heard this before.

Once lined up, we must stay lined up *correctly* with God's Word and truth as our leader. His truth will help us <u>hold that line</u>—resisting the enemy's offensive moves! If we use a wrestling analogy, we can say that the time clock counts down for the enemy. He will be kicked out of the ring when the buzzer goes off! He's already lost not only this round, but he has lost the entire match! He is just trying to see if he can pin us down (get a few spiritual holds in on us) before he is fully ejected from the ring. Are we going to let him? NO! And NO! Let's not let him get one over on us. We can get in line and not move!

One of my very favorite Scriptures is Psalm 62:6. I often speak this out of my mouth when I feel life-event earthquakes happening. It keeps me mentally stable and unmoved when my emotions are quaking:

> He only is my rock and my salvation; He is my refuge; I will not be moved.

How do we prevent the enemy from making a few points against us? We find out what's been made available to us as believers in God, redeemed through His Son, Jesus. First, we must take responsibility for getting to know God and hearing His Word for ourselves and not just rely on a preacher to teach us. We tend to think because someone stands behind a pulpit, they must know everything. My most recent pastors and teachers of the Bible have all said we should not take their word for it, but *we should look it up for ourselves.* That's exactly why I have included so many Scriptures in this book and extra reading for you!

We will stay on our path and make it to our designated area by knowing how God lined it up for us! *Everything we need to help and equip us to live a victorious Christian life is given to us when we are born again.* Some of you may have never heard that before reading this book. Ok, so how do we access everything we need, then? We access them by gaining knowledge about them—by finding out what Salvation really means and all that was given to us by Him.

We must get to KNOW HIM intimately for ourselves, so we will trust Him and follow Him!

How does trust in God come? By faith. Romans 10:17 says that faith in God comes by hearing the Word of God. Trust is an action of that faith. The more revelation we have from the Word of God, the more we know God, and the more we trust Him.

> Grace and peace be multiplied to you **in the knowledge** of God and of Jesus our Lord, as His divine power has given to us all things that pertain to life and godliness, **through the knowledge** of Him who called us by glory and virtue, by which have been given to us exceedingly great and precious promises, that through these you may be partakers of the divine nature, having escaped the corruption that is in the world through lust.

> But also for this very reason, giving all diligence, add to your faith virtue, to virtue knowledge, to knowledge self-control, to self-control perseverance, to perseverance godliness, to godliness brotherly kindness, and to brotherly kindness love. For if these things are yours and abound, you will be neither barren nor unfruitful **in the knowledge** of our Lord Jesus Christ. For he who lacks these things is shortsighted, even to blindness, and has forgotten that he was cleansed from his old sins (2 Peter 1:2–9; emphasis added).

> But **grow in the grace and knowledge** of our Lord and Savior Jesus Christ (2 Peter 3:18; emphasis added).

> … that the God of our Lord Jesus Christ, the Father of glory, may give to you the spirit of wisdom and revelation **in the knowledge of Him**, the eyes of your understanding being en-lightened; **that you may know** what is the hope of His calling,

what are the riches of the glory of His inheritance in the saints, and what is the exceeding greatness of His power toward us who believe, according to the working of His mighty power (Ephesians 1:17–19; emphasis added).

… that Christ may dwell in your hearts through faith; that you, being rooted and grounded in love, may be **able to comprehend** with all the saints what is the width and length and depth and height— **to know** the love of Christ which passes knowledge; that you may be filled with all the fullness of God (Ephesians 3:17–19; emphasis added).

Receiving knowledge and revelation about God's true nature (and how I can access the life He has planned for me) caused me to love Him even more. It caused me to truly trust Him with my life. Getting off our own merry-go-round(s) will require us to put our trust in God. Remember the story I shared in chapter ten about David and I finally stepping out and going to Bible school? We were in our fifties with kids and grandkids! We had to learn to trust God in a new measure while doing this. For most, it's normal not to trust someone we don't know. David says he could only trust God to the extent of which he knew God and His unconditional love for him. The more deeply we got to know Him through the Word taught at Bible college, the more we trusted Him.

Ephesians 3:20 says that *God is able* to do exceedingly, abundantly above all that we ask or think. If you don't stop there, it continues to say that <u>it's according to the power that works in us</u>. Well, if we don't *know* about the power working in us, God will be limited to what He can do in our lives. In chapter three, we talked about the different types of unbelief. What He can personally do for us is limited to what we know and believe about Him.

God didn't put all those Scriptures about knowing Him in the Bible for no reason. The Good Teacher is saying, "Line Up! Get to know Me! Trust Me! Don't be moved! I'm here to lead you, guide you, and comfort you as you walk to your designated area."

Part Two: Help Is IN You!

If you think you can walk right off any of your life's full-speed merry-go-rounds, maybe you can. However, it would not be wise nor give permanent results without the help God provides for us. *God is our helper.* God is the best life coach you could ask for! No, God is not like the people you may have met; God is not like an egomaniac with a hero complex, needing to *feel* like He is the only one who can come to our real rescue. God IS THE ONLY ONE who loved us enough to have *already* come to our rescue. He gave us the victory when we received Jesus, and He is the only life coach Who will lead us to that victory. Yielding to the coaching and leading of <u>His Spirit inside us</u> will cause us to genuinely move forward in our life and never go back to repeated wilderness living. He can coach us to the goal and across the finish line without any interferences, fouls, or time-outs when we allow Him. He will make sure the victory Jesus has given us is not stolen from us. As we go on, if I could name a Scripture as the theme of this chapter, it would be Romans 8:11.

> But if the Spirit of Him who raised Jesus from the dead <u>lives in you</u>, He who raised Christ from the dead <u>will also give life to your mortal bodies</u> through His Spirit that <u>lives in you</u> (Romans 8:11 MEV; emphasis added).

I want to share three of the biggest helps found in the Bible, next to Jesus Himself. The first help I'll talk about is <u>Holy Spirit</u>, who is the supernatural power of God. The second help is <u>grace</u>, the supernatural ability that comes through Jesus. The third help is <u>truth</u>, which is what makes us free.

It's odd to me how we have been supplied with these helps through Jesus, yet it seems the Church as a whole does not teach about them. Most Christians don't know about the power of God's Spirit, grace, and truth made available to them. Most denominational doctrines don't include these Full Gospel, Good

News teachings, so the shepherds are not teaching about them to their sheep (congregation). In turn, the *sheep* stay ignorant about them, as I did for years.

Before moving on, I would like to share my experience with what was once, for me, an unfamiliar subject: The Holy Spirit Who is THE Helper. I want you to experience the same help I received over forty-one years ago. I told you in chapter one how I got off my high school merry-go-round and went ALL IN with the Lord the last semester of my senior year in high school. After graduating in 1982, I spent the summer without going to parties or hanging with friends. I mostly spent it at home and alone. I was about to head off to Bible college in the fall, so my time when I wasn't at work was spent developing my personal relationship with Jesus. The Lord was preparing my heart to leave my family and familiar surroundings to venture into unknown territory outside my small town of 300 people. That summer, mostly at night after work, I would ride my bike around town.

One night, during a bike ride down the main street in my little town, I clearly remember a conversation I had with God. I told Him that I was fully giving my life to Him and open to receiving anything He had for me. I had been half in and half out (lukewarm) in my relationship with God for such a long time. Now I was making it clear to Him that I was ALL IN.

Right after I told the Lord this, tears began rolling down my face as I shared my heart with Him and sensed His love for me. Then, seemingly out of nowhere, as I was worshipping Him, I began to have a prompting to sing out words that sounded foreign to me. I began to sing them out. They were like Spanish or something, except I knew enough Spanish words to know this was not Spanish. I just let it come out! I continued singing these unknown words in a tune from my heart and out of my mouth to the Lord.

I remember feeling like I was falling in love with Jesus and people *more and more as I yielded.* I knew something was happening inside me that I had never experienced before. It was beautiful. It was peaceful. And I could tell it was precious to the Lord. At the same time, I was hoping nobody would hear me singing in the unknown language because I thought they would think I was weird or something. This went on for several minutes.

Suddenly, a guy on a bike popped out of nowhere and started riding alongside me. It was the guy in our small town who was well known as "the perv." None of us girls EVER wanted to be around him or ride our bikes past his house. We had heard many stories about this man in his twenties. I knew him to be very angry. I heard stories of how he would hurt anyone (girls or guys) without even thinking twice about it. I abruptly stopped singing and said, "Hi" to him. He asked me what I was doing riding my bike in the dark. I told him I had just gotten off work and wanted to go for a bike ride. He said, "It doesn't seem very smart to me. You know I could rape you and kill you right now, right? Aren't you scared of me?" I said, "I know you could, but I'm not scared of you." I said, "Besides if you did, I'd go straight to Heaven, so that wouldn't be so bad!"

I did something I had never done before. I was bold and stood up to the town's perverted bully! You know what? He respected me, right then, and from then on! I honestly think he sensed God's love coming through me for him, and his mean desire to hurt me left! This guy thrived on putting fear in people. Well, it didn't work on me that night as he had planned by creeping up behind me on his bike and saying his normal threatening lines. When he realized it didn't move me, he just started talking about other things and rode bikes with me for a while. I was even able to talk about Jesus with him. Then, he said goodbye and went home. If the encounter with this guy had happened before my singing in the Spirit experience, I know I would have been petrified with fear. I often wonder if the things I was so brave to tell him that night about Jesus stuck with him.

Something beautiful happened that night. I received a level of love and boldness I never had before, along with that unusual song full of words I'd never heard before. Looking back now, I realize that night is when I was filled with God's Holy Spirit. It was just like on the day of Pentecost when the disciples of Jesus were filled with power, and they began to speak in other tongues. The Bible says this happened when the Holy Spirit came upon them. The power was for them to be witnesses.

But <u>you shall receive power when the Holy Spirit comes upon you</u>. And <u>you shall be My witnesses</u> in Jerusalem, and in all Judea and Samaria, and to the ends of the earth (Acts 1:8 MEV; emphasis added).

READ IT!
Acts 2
Filled with the Holy Spirit

I felt empowered to witness that night to the strange, scary guy who talked and rode bikes with me. Because I had never been taught anything about it, I didn't even know what was happening. I only knew that something definitely *was* taking place. The Holy Spirit had come upon me, and He also came inside me. I didn't stop it from happening outwardly, and I didn't interfere with what was going on in me inwardly, either.

And I will pray the Father, and He will give you another Helper, <u>that He may abide with you forever</u>—the Spirit of truth, whom the world cannot receive, because it neither sees Him nor knows Him; but you know Him, for He dwells with you <u>and will be in you</u> (John 14:16–17; emphasis added).

I unknowingly invited Holy Spirit in when I told the Lord I was fully surrendered to Him and wanted to receive anything He had for me. All I knew was that I wanted to be ALL IN with Him, and I was totally open to whatever He had for me. Well, that night, my ALL IN got deeper.

In Him you also trusted, after you heard the word of truth, the gospel of your salvation; in whom also, having believed, you were sealed with the Holy Spirit of promise, who is the guarantee of our inheritance until the redemption of the purchased possession, to the praise of His glory (Ephesians 1:13–14).

Over the next twelve years, religious thinking and actions settled deeper into my innocent heart and mind, darkening any light I had about Holy Spirit. I call this period *my dark ages*. God's Spirit in me became mostly quenched, and my hearing of God's Spirit became *dull*. It first began when I attended Bible college in the fall after graduation and continued as I stayed within my denominational circle. The mindsets and actions I developed during this season changed me. They became strongholds in my mind and patterns in my actions. I put limits on God based on denominational teachings. I mentioned a portion of this in chapter one, but I feel to share a bit deeper here. I became super-legalistic and sin-focused on myself and everyone around me. I was not pointing people to the true Gospel of Jesus. Instead, I (unknowingly) pointed them toward religious methods that caused them to use their own self-works and efforts.

The experience I had with Holy Spirit that night on my bike ride soon became a forgotten memory. Remember me telling you how I went street witnessing with the group of Christians from a different denomination during my year at the Bible college? How some of these people were softly praying words I didn't understand? Well, that's how *dull* I had become. I didn't even recognize what they were doing, even though I had done the same thing just a few months before. What I heard just went right over my head.

My relationship with my Helper, Holy Spirit, stayed shallow during those next years. I never grew further in the boldness and power because I had no teaching about the baptism and infilling of the Holy Spirit. I was like most Christians who were ONLY fed what the Bible calls "the milk of the word." I was what the Word calls "unskilled in righteousness" and was never given solid food to mature my thinking and renew my mind. Because of this, I couldn't recognize the evil that I had become infected with ... *man-made religion*. **Now,**

I can recognize that man-made religion is evil and deceptive. <u>Living out of my new identity in Christ is pure and good.</u>

> Everyone who lives on milk is unskilled in the word of righteousness, for he is a baby. But solid food belongs to those who are mature, for those who through practice have powers of discernment that are trained to distinguish good from evil (Hebrew 5:13–14 MEV).

Still, even after my mind became infected with man-made religion, I would sing to the Lord every so often in this unfamiliar language (that seemed like it was Spanish but wasn't). It always happened during my intimate and alone times with the Lord. I would get promptings—on the inside of me—to start talking or singing with these words I didn't recognize. I had no clue that I was talking and singing from my spirit in an unknown tongue to the Lord, but I still did it. Look how these next Scriptures make it clear that my experience was lining up with God's Word. (Paul was explaining how to correctly use tongues and prophecy.) I was doing both, <u>singing and praying with understanding</u> and **singing and praying in the spirit**.

> For if I pray in an unknown tongue, **my spirit prays**, but my understanding is unfruitful. What is it then? I will **pray with the spirit**, <u>and I will pray with the understanding</u>. **I will sing with the spirit**, and <u>I will sing with the understanding</u> (1 Corinthians 14:14–15; emphasis added).

> <u>God is Spirit</u>, and those who worship Him must <u>worship Him in spirit and truth</u> (John 4:24 MEV; emphasis added).

John 4:24 expresses that God seeks people who will worship Him in spirit and truth. That night on my bicycle, I was worshipping Him out of my spirit.

I was not a spectator, as man-made religion later taught me to be. Religious people only worship God out of their heads and not their spirit.

In the fall of 1994, David and I stepped out of our denominational circle. We attended a conference at a church in Little Rock, Arkansas. That weekend, I learned about being *baptized in the Holy Spirit* with evidence of speaking in tongues. When the invitation came from the speaker to receive this gift from God, I felt my heart go pitter-patter, and I knew I was supposed to go up. The lady speaker laid her hands on my head and told me not to think about anything except what words were coming to me. She said to just *let* whatever syllables I was thinking about just come out of my mouth. I had a short phrase with three odd words come to my mind, and I spoke them out of my mouth. I did it! I spoke unusual words out of my mouth, but it was the first time I had ever done this around anyone else. I heard others speaking also, and it didn't seem weird anymore. I sat back down, and later that night, laying in the motel room bed, I began to say that short phrase over and over again. I was thanking the Lord that more of this unusual language was coming out of me.

Suddenly, I felt a warm, fiery sensation all over my body. I began to speak more and more phrases. I woke David up and told him I was getting more and more phrases coming to me to speak. He looked at me and noticed the tears of love running down my face and even noticed my skin tone looked dark pink. He said, "Well, SPEAK IT!" Then he rolled over and went back to sleep while I lay there almost all night just crying and speaking in this unknown language. It felt like I had just been empowered to love again, just like that night of my special bike ride.

I was encountering another beautiful love experience with the Lord, except I understood what was happening *this time*. I pressed in even more to receive. This time, there is NO WAY any wrong teaching or religious person could ever snuff this out or tell me this was not from God! About six months later, David had a similar experience. David asked the Lord to help him receive the baptism of the Holy Spirit. As David asked for this, he received a short phrase that later became a whole language. To this day, he and I both speak our spiritual language every day to stay edified in ourselves.

Years later, I put the puzzle pieces of my Christian life together (thus far), and I figured out what happened that night on my bicycle ride through town. I was baptized in the Spirit that night at age seventeen and spoke in tongues. It made sense to me that I felt stronger, more peaceful, and clearer-headed every time I spoke out or sang the unknown language from my spirit. My experience that night, and off and on over the next twelve years, lined up with God's Word—which is truth. I'm so thankful that God gave us a way to stay edified and built up in our MOST holy faith so we can make it through this life easier.

Here are the Scriptures I'm referring to:

> He who speaks in an unknown tongue <u>edifies himself</u> (1 Corinthians 14:4 MEV; emphasis added).

> But you, beloved, <u>building yourselves up</u> in your most holy faith, praying in the Holy Spirit (Jude 1:20; emphasis added).

Before man-made religion got a hold of me, my experiences lined up with God's Word. Later, when I did the same thing every other religious person does, I mistakenly tried *to make* God's Word line up with my experience. Of course, the devil wants us to stay ignorant about this help—our Helper—through God's Holy Spirit. He doesn't want Christians knowing about this HUGE thing that is supposed to also happen after receiving Jesus as our Lord and Savior. He doesn't want us to know about this free, empowering gift that God has made available to **all of us**. He hopes all Christians continue to argue about this and stay in the dark, so they stay powerless! Well, that's why God is leading me to bring this subject out into the light.

Even though I may receive persecution from some fellow Christians, I will obey God and not man and share this truth to help you. I'm familiar with being persecuted for the Word's sake. I know that any persecution I might receive for speaking in tongues will come from those who <u>don't</u> speak in tongues. They are the ones who are trying to make God's Word line up with their experience of not receiving. How do I know this? Again, I know because I used to do it, right alongside other Christians in the same denominational circles. I vividly remember saying this sentence out of ignorance, "Tongues are of the devil!" (I bet I'm not the only one who has ever said that.) My dark ages were the years I stayed on the denominational merry-go-round, never moving forward out into deeper waters of meatier revelation from God's Word.

Speaking in tongues is not ONLY for certain people or denominations. And it hasn't passed away. You might ask me, "Then why do we only hear about it happening in certain denominations?" Or, you might say, "I have never heard of this!" Remember, faith comes by hearing the Word. If a denomination you are a part of won't preach this truth, you will stay ignorant about it and therefore won't have faith to receive it. The Bible is clear regarding the baptism of the Holy Spirit with evidence of speaking in tongues; it is for any Christian who believes it and receives it. It's just like forgiveness of sin and any other promise from God.

Receiving the baptism of the Holy Spirit was the best and most empowering thing that has ever happened to David and me! *It can be for you, also.*

I need to explain something, though, if you wonder about this. In the previous chapters of this book, I give a lot of examples of my own merry-go-riding. These all took place even <u>after</u> David and I received the empowering gift of the baptism of the Holy Spirit with evidence of speaking in tongues. You might wonder, "Why did you continue to spin on those merry-go-rounds if you had this help and empowerment on the inside of you?" Well, the truth is that **it totally helped me as I was growing up emotionally. It helped me get my mind renewed to more truths in God's Word and begin to live from the inside out by my new Christlike spirit**. It DID NOT help me anytime I went at it alone without relying on His leading!

At first, it was a process for me to recognize the spin of the merry-go-rounds. (I didn't have this book filled with examples of someone else's life-spinning experiences to help me <u>as you do</u>.) After that, it was a process for me to learn to stop myself from handling the negative circumstances alone and begin using the power available to me by God's grace and Holy Spirit.

Are you interested in hearing more about being baptized in the Holy Spirit? I have some Scriptures at the back of this book (in the appendix) that will help you. Everyone OK? Let's go deeper and talk about grace now.

<u>You are not alone! Help is here!</u>

You aren't helpless anymore. God's grace is available to you to help you get free, get *off the merry-go-round, and on with your life*. Maybe you were like me and were not discipled correctly after receiving Jesus. Maybe you have never heard that you don't have to struggle in your *own* strength, just trying to be the best, faithful child of God you could possibly be. All the while, you've continued for years just spinning instead of winning, riding different merry-go-rounds year after year. Sound familiar?

Some of you might be asking, "What is grace?" And, "How does that grace help me?" Let's look at Titus 2:11–14 (with emphasis added), where you can see that Jesus **is** God's grace sent from God to bring Salvation to all men:

> For the <u>grace of God that brings salvation has appeared to all men</u>, teaching us that, denying ungodliness and worldly lusts, we should live soberly, righteously, and godly **in the present age**, looking for the blessed hope and glorious appearing of our great God and Savior Jesus Christ, who gave Himself for us, that He might redeem us from every lawless deed and purify for Himself His own special people, zealous for good works.

Let's look specifically at verse 11: "For the grace of God that brings salvation has appeared to all men." *Did grace bring Salvation?* Yes. God provided grace—Jesus—for you. Jesus brought Salvation to you through His death, burial, and resurrection. Jesus is your help—your Salvation. WOW!

Everyone needs Salvation. This is something man could not do for himself, so God provided Jesus as our Saving Grace. God, through Jesus, did what man could not do for himself. Thanks to Jesus, now you have everything you need to live an abundant life here on Earth. You can walk in God's good plan for you, be successful, victorious, and free from the bondage of sin and defeat *because of Salvation.*

Here are some more verses that show you the grace of God you have in Jesus. As you look at these, read them in the light of "Jesus *is* God's grace."

For <u>by grace you have been saved through faith</u>, and that not of yourselves; it is the gift of God (Ephesians 2:8; emphasis added).

Let us therefore <u>come boldly to the throne of grace</u>, that we may obtain mercy and find <u>grace to help</u> in time of need (Hebrews 4:16; emphasis added).

And He said to me, "<u>My grace is sufficient for you</u>, for My strength is made perfect in weakness." Therefore most gladly I will rather boast in my infirmities (weaknesses) that the power of Christ may rest upon me" (2 Corinthians 12:9; emphasis added).

You therefore, my son, <u>be strong in the grace</u> that is in Christ Jesus (2 Timothy 2:1; emphasis added).

But <u>by the grace of God</u> I am what I am, and <u>His grace toward me</u> was not in vain; but I labored more abundantly than they all, yet not I, but the grace of God which was with me (1 Corinthians 15:10; emphasis added).

And <u>God is able to make all grace abound toward you</u>, that you, always having all sufficiency in all things, may have abundance for every good work (2 Corinthians 9:8; emphasis added).

I remember the impact it had on me when I began to be taught different-ly about God's grace. For most of my Christian life, I was only taught that grace was God's unmerited favor toward me. Before that, I never even knew that God's grace (help and ability) was what *enabled me to get through my life,* winning instead of always spinning. But when I heard and received revelation about God's grace *empowering me for good works,* it caused an excitement about this **truth** to rise up in me! Now, no religious man can steal this from me!

Hearing about God's grace sent me on a journey to study God's Word for myself and learn everything I could about Jesus and the <u>new me</u>. I finally had hope! I finally had an attainable goal because I have grace—God's provision for everything in my life that I need—on my side! I finally could see myself as, one day, *off the merry-go-round(s) getting on with my life!* I came to know that I *can* go forward into my Promised Land, right here, right now, on Earth!

READ IT!
Hebrews 13:5, Deuteronomy 31:6,
Jeremiah 29:11
God will never abandon you.

God never wanted us to walk alone through this life. He restored His rela-tionship with us through Jesus so we can now personally talk to Him and tap into <u>His</u> wisdom, help, strength, and guidance every day. In Hebrews 13:5 and Deuteronomy 31:6, we are told God will never leave us or forsake (abandon) us. In Jeremiah 29:11, He tells us He has good plans for our lives. Okay, so if God has a good plan for us and He said He would never leave us (because He now dwells forever inside us), wouldn't it be wise to believe it? Wouldn't it be wise to follow His lead to move forward *into* that good plan? I mean, since He *is* the One who knows the plan and all ...

This all sounds like GOOD NEWS to me. Does it to you?

God gave you all these *good-news* truths in His Word to be a good steward with. Throughout this book, the truth you are hearing is the truth that will help *all men* come to repentance. *It must be shared!* It will change the way people think about God and themselves—they will go from believing lies to believing the truth. Material blessings are the goodness of God when they come from God, and He is given the glory. But the *best* goodness we can share with people is the grace and truth that came through Jesus. This next verse is another favorite of mine:

> For the law was given through Moses; <u>grace and truth came through Jesus Christ</u> (John 1:17 MEV; emphasis added).

If you live out grace and truth in your own life, **you will be sharing the Gospel of Jesus** with everyone in your circle of influence. You will be sharing the GOOD NEWS. You will be living it out in public. Once you realize that God did not leave you alone and helpless to fend for yourself out there in the dark world, you'll also want other people to know that truth.

Grace and truth. That is another example of God's giving because He is so good and loves us so much. We don't need to go searching for it. It's right here in His Word for us to study and see.

As if Holy Spirit and grace and truth aren't enough, God also gave us the example of how Jesus walked out His life while here on Earth. We should never feel alone, helpless, or walking in darkness anymore. He's such a Good Father God to go overboard on giving us help. The Bible is full of examples of people who we can learn from, but Jesus is our ultimate example to follow because He is light and truth and so much more. He showed us how He spent intimate alone time with the Father to hear His daily assignments.

<u>Jesus is our number one example of how to get help!</u> Jesus Himself was full of God's Spirit and walked in power, setting the captives free by sharing the truth. He had faith and said He only did what His Father told Him to do. You can live this way, also. You can have faith, hear from God in your spirit, and then *only* do what He's leading you to do. (You aren't supposed to be *hitting* *and missing* every decision you make. That's why He gave us His Spirit to lead us and guide us.)

If you ask God for answers and direction and haven't taken the time to intimately know and hear from Him, you will just be guessing what to do. If you guess wrong, you might think God told you to do it, and it failed. Perhaps the truth is, He never told you to; you just guessed and didn't really hear from Him—because you didn't ask or get quiet long enough to hear clearly from Him. It's called a relationship *for a reason.* Two people going through life talking with each other and listening to each other is a healthy relationship. Let Father God help you and guide you like He did Jesus. ***Even Jesus, while a man on Earth, spent hours with the Father, praying and hearing from Him, getting direction for His next steps.***

> For I have not spoken on My own authority; but the Father who sent Me gave Me a command, what I should say and what I should speak. And I know that His command is everlasting life. Therefore, <u>whatever I speak, just as the Father has told Me, so I speak</u> (John 12:49–50; emphasis added).

> Then Jesus answered and said to them, "Most assuredly, I say to you, the Son can do nothing of Himself, but what He sees the Father do; for whatever He does, the Son also does in like manner. For the Father loves the Son, and <u>shows Him</u> all things that He Himself does; and He will show Him greater works than these, that you may marvel (John 5:19–20; emphasis added).

> At that day you will know that I am in My Father, and you in Me, and I in you (John 14:20).

That last Scripture (John14:20) tells you that Jesus is in His Heavenly Father, you are in Jesus, and He is in you. AWESOME!! That means you can hear what the Father is saying also, right? Don't you love that?!! I do.

STOP THE SPIN!

Get up on your Heavenly Father's lap and learn of Him. Fellowship with Him. Sit quietly, listening, not just telling Him things He already knows or asking Him questions He has already answered. If you are quiet and listen, you will hear.

Once you hear, then get down off His lap and go do the things you heard Him tell you. Regularly get back up on His lap, like a listening child, spending time getting to know Him more and hearing what else He is saying. I call this hearing and doing, hearing and doing. It's one of my favorite things to do!

Listen, I must confess I don't have all this perfected in my life—nobody does. It's a progressive journey. Sometimes I have even gotten off track and out of line. Sometimes I haven't relied wholly on God's help. But, the revelation (spiritual light) of *grace and truth* I've received has brought me out of my dark ages. This revelation has helped me more than all the religious *man-made-up* teachings I have received over my fifty-eight years and counting.

We can't get off a *life circumstance or bondage merry-go-round* without God's help. Equally important is to understand that it's not wise to walk our everyday journey hoping to avoid them on our own. We are *supposed* to be relying on His help. He gave us Jesus, His Spirit, His grace, His truth, and His voice as examples to follow in His Word. These are ALL in us. It's all about His goodness toward us. He did not leave us alone!

Let's, together, share this GOOD NEWS!

THIRTEEN

SIX STEPS TO GET OFF THE MERRY-GO-ROUND AND STAY OFF

Now that you've seen the lineup God designed for you and how His help is IN you, can you see that getting off of your merry-go-rounds, and staying off, will get easier and easier?

Do you see that God loves you so much that He designed you to be so connected with Him from the moment you are born again?

Now, all you need to do is LET HIM love you and LET HIM lead you through your life.

As you begin to know the love God has for you, it will become easier to trust Him. You will begin desiring to let go of your old ways. You will begin changing things *from your heart*—instead of only because you are being told to (which rubs against human nature). Once you have identified bondages and merry-go-rounds in your life, you can get off and stay off by changing how you think about them and line up your thinking with God's Word.

Getting off a merry-go-round *doesn't always* require you to quickly JUMP OFF. In fact, it's quite dangerous just to up and jump off a playground merry-go-round! You should slow down the spin before you leap. In the same way, getting off your life's merry-go-rounds will be a slow-down process that will require steps. These will be daily step-by-step choices you will have to make, similar to the slowing down process of a physical merry-go-round.

As you read through the Bible, you will soon find that there are usually STEPS to take when God is involved.

> The steps of a good man are ordered by the Lord, And He delights in his way (Psalm 37:23).

> My foot has held fast to His steps; I have kept His way and not turned aside (Job 23:11).

> Uphold my steps in Your paths, That my footsteps may not slip (Psalm 17:5).

> He also brought me up out of a horrible pit, Out of the miry clay, And set my feet upon a rock, And established my steps (Psalm 40:2).

> Direct my steps by Your word, And let no iniquity have dominion over me (Psalm 119:133).

> A man's heart plans his way, But the Lord directs his steps (Proverbs 16:9).

> ... but who also walk in the steps of the faith which our father Abraham had ... (Romans 4:12).

> I urged Titus, and sent our brother with him. Did Titus take advantage of you? Did we not walk in the same spirit? Did we not walk in the same steps? (2 Corinthians 12:18)

For even hereunto were ye called, because Christ also suffered for us, leaving us an example, that you should follow His steps (1 Peter 2:21).

We see from these Scriptures that God is a big fan of STEPS. *After* you genuinely decide that you will do whatever it takes, you are ready for these next six steps. He will help you as you choose to replace your current lifestyle with a new lifestyle that reveals who you are now as a born-again, new creation in Christ Jesus. Living out of your new identity is what pleases and honors God.

This may sound like it will require a lot of effort on your part, but if you stay lined up, most of the effort will be consistently following God's lead by His Spirit inside you.

Remember, this isn't just a to-do list or a honey-do list that always feels burdensome. These six steps can be some of the easiest and most peaceful things you've ever done, especially in getting free from bondages and receiving life victories. As you do these, remember **you don't walk alone. And, you are well-equipped**, as we've already talked about. Doing these steps without relying on God's supernatural help won't bring lasting results. Works of the flesh are never productive and lasting. You have the Greater One in you to help you!

Step #1. EXPOSE IT!

One of the best ways to stop something from affecting you is to expose it. The worst thing you can do is hide it because you *fear* that someone will find out what you are dealing with. Fear is a *self-fulfilling* prophecy. You will draw the fear to you by constantly thinking about it and letting it control you. Have you ever heard that your fears come upon you?

For the thing I greatly feared has come upon me, and what I dreaded has happened to me (Job 3:25).

Face this thing _unafraid_ and conquer it!! Shine the light on the thief! Stop letting it control your life! If you give in to temptation, admit it right away, out loud, to yourself and to someone else.

> But all things that are exposed are made manifest by the light,
> for whatever makes manifest is light (Ephesians 5:13).

Don't let it get by! (My pastor of twelve years taught me that.) Suppose you have a habit of lying or exaggerating. In that case, the best way to make yourself stop is to immediately say something like, "Well, I take that back. That was a lie. That was an exaggeration. That wasn't exactly how it happened." It loses power when you do that.

_Hiding the problem or not admitting the problem will keep you _in_ the problem._

The devil would be thrilled if you believed you could permanently get over a problem yourself without anyone knowing what you are going through. But that is simply not true. Get off the merry-go-round of fear where you are too scared to admit you need God or anyone's help. _Be a tattletale_—only on _yourself_, though. [Smiles.]

Step #2. STOP FEEDING the speed of the merry-go-round.

Stop feeding the speed—by doing something different. Try this exercise: Picture yourself alone on a park swing with no one there pushing you. With no one pushing you, it is your decision to go faster or slower. If you want to slow down, then the first thing you must do is _stop doing what makes the swing continue_ moving back and forth. You would stop thrusting your legs up and your body outward, right? This will eventually stop the faster movement. It is exactly the same with the swings in life! For example, if you want to stop being depressed, stop thinking about how depressed you are. This will stop the depression from becoming stronger. If you want to stop looking at pornography, then _stop letting yourself_ think about pornography. Think about something else.

I heard this from my pastor, and it helped me:

Your mind is your mind! You can think about whatever you want to think about!

This is where the real battle is! If you don't think about things you shouldn't, you won't get off track. In life, the way we see ourselves and what we think about is where we'll go. The Bible tells us many times to "take no thought." Sounds like we really do have an option and ability to control our own thoughts, right? It's not supposed to be hard. As we train our minds to think differently, according to Philippians 4:6–9, we will begin to live free from merry-go-rounds:

> Be anxious (careful) for nothing; but in everything by prayer and supplication, with thanksgiving, let your requests be made known to God; and the peace of God, which surpasses all understanding, will guard your hearts and minds through Christ Jesus. Finally, brethren, whatsoever things are TRUE, whatsoever things are NOBLE, whatsoever things are JUST, whatsoever things are PURE, whatsoever things are LOVE-LY, whatsoever things are of GOOD REPORT, if there is any virtue and if there anything praiseworthy <u>meditate on these things</u>. The things which you LEARNED, and RECEIVED, and HEARD, and SAW in me, these do and the God of peace will be with you (Philippians 4:6–9; emphasis added).

Stop feeding the speed—by believing something different. What do you believe to see? *I grabbed ahold of this verse over twenty years ago regarding my husband and second-born daughter.*

> I would have lost heart unless I had **believed that I would see** the goodness of the Lord in the land of the living (Psalm 27:13; emphasis added).

We can believe whatever we choose to believe! We have the ability to believe something or not believe something. It is NOT GOD'S WILL for you to be stuck repeating things over and over, never becoming a productive person in society or in the Kingdom. You must first believe that it is wasted time just riding a merry-go-round and never accomplishing anything in your life.

> Jesus said unto him, "If you can believe, all things are possible to him who believes" (Mark 9:23).

You were made to succeed! Jesus came to give you life more abundantly! Anything you are doing that is robbing you of *life more abundantly* is not the will of God for you, and you definitely have a choice to stop doing it. It doesn't matter if it is lying, depression, substance abuse, excessive gambling, pornography, sexual addictions, junk food addiction, etc. You must believe *in your heart* this IS NOT the life you were allotted by God, your Creator.

You might be thinking, *"Well, if God wants it to stop, He will stop it, so if I'm going through it, it must mean He wants me to."*

That is not Biblical teaching. Religious people who teach that God wants us to go through all that junk to teach us something have actually talked us out of putting up a fight. <u>They have talked us out of believing we can be free.</u>

You get to choose. We have been given a choice to choose life or death, blessing or cursing. God even tells us which one to choose! He said, "Choose life!" It's in *OUR* control!

> I call heaven and earth as witnesses today against you, that I have set before you life and death, blessing and cursing; therefore choose life, that both you and your descendants may live (Deuteronomy 30:19).

Many Christians haven't heard that we are blessed—*now*—because of our new, born-again identity in Christ. So, if we ARE blessed, why would we continue living our lives as if we are cursed—not moving forward into our promised land? If we are blessed, then why are we always trying to get God to bless us? Sounds like an <u>unbelief problem</u>. We honestly <u>can believe</u> that we have a new, blessed identity since we have been born again. And we honestly <u>can choose</u> to live according to this new, blessed identity. This is living *from the inside out*.

Step #3. SLOW DOWN what you are doing.

This might be the only time it is OK to drag your feet to do something. Put the brakes on, so to speak. This reminds me of the Flintstones cartoon. They used their own feet to stop their vehicles. (If you aren't familiar with that cartoon, you can search for the image. It will stay with you and be a great visual reminder!) You can use your own feet to stop the movement of your merry-go-round. *It will be up to you to make an effort to slow down and stop.* Why do we need to slow down? Because it helps us SEE things more clearly. If we are zooming around one hundred miles an hour, we are *zooming* right through our life. In Psalm 46:10, the Lord tells us to …

Be still, and know that I am God.

We could be missing what God wants us to SEE. Once we have a *clear vision*, it is OK to take off and start doing it. <u>Most of the time, we don't have a *clear vision*</u>. This is because we did not **slow down**, **turn down** the noise, **get away** from the clutter, and **open our ears** to hear what God is saying to us. Therefore, we are MISSING our answers and thinking God isn't talking. God has *the right answer* for how you can stop the merry-go-round you are on and get off permanently. Why waste time trying to figure it out yourself? *He knows you and your situation better than you do.*

If you take the time to get quiet and just meditate (think about and ponder) on Him and His love and goodness, you … will … hear. Meditating is not just opening your mind to anything that wants to crawl in. **Purposeful meditation on the Word of God** will strengthen you and cause revelation and truth to come to you.

You cannot get these revelations any other way. You cannot get them by *just* going to church, Bible studies, or reading books about other people's revelations (even good ones like mine in this book). **You** have to get the revelation for yourself, down in your own heart, for it to change your thought pattern and how you SEE yourself and God. Purposeful meditation on God's Word is the key! Try it and SEE!

Step #4. SEE YOURSELF OFF the merry-go-round.

Replace all your old, bad habits and behaviors with A NEW IMAGE OF YOURSELF DOING SOMETHING DIFFERENT.

Allow yourself to imagine. Allow God to put the new vision in you. Create a picture in your mind of you living free, off your usual, everyday merry-go-round. Imagine yourself waking up and doing something you have always wanted to do but have never done yet. Sit and just *imagine* yourself laughing so hard that you fall off your chair. Picture yourself walking, skipping, jumping, running ... ALL IN A *FORWARD* MOVEMENT. See with the eyes of Jesus. Change how you see yourself, and you'll change the direction you are going ... and reach your destiny.

Think of a circumstance you are in. Imagine that you do nothing about it until you have a direct word from the Lord and His direction regarding it. It can be a financial situation, a relationship issue, a work problem, etc. Imagine the excitement you'll have when you stop trying to figure something out on your own and mess things up, and instead, you sit back, trusting God, and watch how He meets your needs and directs your path.

Focus your thoughts on what you can do each day for someone else. See yourself as a giver and not a taker.

Picture yourself praying and joyfully waiting on the Lord to bring you the right spouse or friends with whom He wants you connected.

Picture yourself trusting Him and allowing His peace in your heart to lead you.

See yourself sitting down and planning your meals—being *in control* of what you are feeding yourself. See yourself *caring* about what you put in your body and envisioning yourself doing exercises because you want your body in good, physical shape.

Imagine yourself planning your next day, deciding when you need to go to bed to wake up refreshed and ready to go. Then, see yourself waking up refreshed. Picture yourself jumping out of bed right when the alarm goes off, singing a joyful song. See yourself calmly walking into work, church, or appointments because you got there early.

Imagine hearing a bad report and immediately casting the care of it onto the Lord. Imagine running to God's Word for instruction on dealing with it spiritually instead of just emotionally.

See yourself getting your paycheck, sitting down, taking out your giving first, and then paying every bill due that coming week. Then, you can head to the mall without feeling guilty for being there.

Picture yourself being a leader and motivating other people to reach their goals. Imagine what it would be like to *not be offended* or emotionally hurt if and when people don't agree with you or you don't get your way.

Picture yourself with a smile on your face, picking up your Bible, then sitting down and enjoying your time in God's Word.

Remember the ten spies of Israel? They never could *see* themselves as able to go into the Promised Land. They only *saw* themselves as grasshoppers because that's what they let themselves think about … and so they were.

> There we saw the giants (the descendants of Anak came from the giants); and we were like grasshoppers in our <u>own sight</u>, and so we were in their sight (Numbers 13:33; emphasis added).

If the Bible says we become what we behold, then let's choose to *see* the *unseen*:

> While we do not look at the things which are seen, but at the things which are not seen. For the things which are seen are temporary, but the things which are not seen are eternal (2 Corinthians 4:18).

The bottom line with seeing yourself *off the merry-go-round and on with living your life* is asking yourself these questions: What does <u>the process</u> of getting *off the merry-go-round* LOOK like to me? What does it look like <u>to be</u> (to live) *OFF the merry-go-round?*

You will know the effort and the process needed to get off the merry-go-round if you can visualize that process. If you can visualize it, you will be able to picture yourself doing what is necessary! These are powerful thoughts that equip you!

What you see on the inside is what you get on the outside!

> Then the Lord answered me and said: "Write the vision And make it plain on tablets, That he may run who reads it (Habakkuk 2:2).

Make a personal vision and goal list based on the desires God has *put in your heart*. Train yourself to SEE—imagine—*you* as everything on that list and accomplishing everything He wants you to do. Meditate on Scriptures that talk about who you are "In Christ"—your starter list is already prepared and in the appendix!

Remember—**Christ is in you now and everything about Him is available to you.** Everything He is, You are! All of His characteristics are now in the *new you!* So, see yourself as a child of God, like Jesus, and go for all of it!

Here is something that helps me, and maybe it will help you too: Imagine accomplishing your vision and heart's desires like a road trip to a certain destination. Think about the difference between using the small GPS map on your phone or a large paper roadmap to find your way. Personally, I like to use both the GPS and paper map when traveling because the paper roadmap gives me a full, big picture, sky-view perspective. The GPS only shows in part, like where you are currently. Once I have the full picture of the trip in my vision, I take a mental snapshot of it from beginning to end. Then, as I use my small GPS map for directions, the big picture makes sense.

Having your vision before you will help you see where you are heading and where you will end up, not just where you are currently. Visualizing the personal vision list and picturing yourself going the right direction and correct route mentally will cause you to physically go that way too.

Step #5. RESIST the urge to even think about going back to living your old way of life.

This will take practice *using* the self-control you already have available to you in your new spirit. If you rehearse the past, you'll stay in the past.

Look at what happened to Lot's wife in Genesis 19:17–26. The Lord told Lot and his family not to look back at their past life in Sodom and Gomorrah. If they did, they would be *consumed*. Lot's wife looked back, and she became a pillar of salt. (OOPS! Now that's one mistake you can't afford nor take back.) You might not turn into a literal pillar of salt, but looking longingly back at your past could ignite the habit again and suck you back into the life you just got free from. This time it will probably have a stronger hold on you.

You will NEVER get past your past if you constantly go over and over it in your mind. If you rehearse the painful issues of your past, and that is all you think and talk about, then you are keeping it spinning, never winning.

I encourage you to start thinking and talking about getting through it and on the other side. Getting hooked in a strong Bible-teaching church and involved with others who talk about the Lord and His goodness will help you. Ask a spiritually mature person to check in on you and hold you accountable. Allow someone you respect into your *inner circle* so they can speak into your life. Find someone you will honestly pay attention to when they give you Biblical instruction or correction. Then, <u>act</u> on what you hear.

> But be doers of the word, and not hearers only, deceiving your-selves. But he who looks into the perfect law of liberty and continues in it, and is not a forgetful hearer but a doer of the work, this one will be blessed in what he does (James 1:22, 25).

God will always send you laborers when He knows you will receive them. He sends them to help you through the hard times—as you resist the urge to go backward.

Take responsibility for yourself and your own actions. What happened to you might not have been your fault, but *how you responded and reacted* could have brought things on you that made the situation worse and even last longer. (If you believe in your *heart* that God wanted that bad thing to happen to you then you definitely won't resist it or fight to get through it. Let that wrong belief go. It is a lie.)

Let's talk about resisting for a minute. Will God do your resisting for you? According to these Scriptures, the answer is no, He won't. He gives grace to the humble, but He expects you to do the resisting in the power of His grace:

> But He gives more grace. For this reason, it says: "God resists the proud, but gives grace to the humble." Therefore submit yourselves to God. ***Resist the devil***, and he will flee from you (James 4:6–7 MEV; emphasis added).

> "God resists the proud, but gives grace to the humble." Humble yourselves under the mighty hand of God, that He may exalt you in due time. Cast all your care upon Him, because He cares for you.

> Be sober and watchful, because your adversary the devil walks around as a roaring lion, seeking whom he may devour. ***Resist*** him firmly in the faith, knowing that the same afflictions are

experienced by your brotherhood throughout the world (1 Peter 5:5–9 MEV; emphasis added).

God gave us these passages for a reason. We must follow these instructions when we are tempted to go back on the merry-go-round way of living. Merry-go-round living is *not* being sober or watchful. It's *not* letting God handle our cares. It's being prideful and not following God's leading in submitting to Him. As we submit to God's way of living, we are given the grace to resist the enemy.

According to these verses, God *resists* us if we are proud (prideful about something we have done or can do ourselves naturally). God gave us the responsibility to resist the devil—then he (the devil) will flee. He only flees once we have submitted ourselves to God.

Do we automatically get His grace to resist the urges of temptations the devil brings? We don't, according to these verses. We have a part, and God has a part. *Then* … the devil flees.

Here's our part in this: Submit to God. Be submissive to one another. Be clothed in humility. Humble ourselves under the mighty hand of God. Cast all our cares on Him. Be sober and vigilant.

Here's God's part if we DO NOT do our part: *He resists the proud.*

BUT, here's God's part if we DO our part: He gives more grace (provision and ability). He gives grace to the humble. He will exalt you in due time. He takes care of you.

And, here's what happens next … ***the devil flees from us.***

Have you ever done this? Have you ever humbled yourself, submitted to God, and resisted the devil <u>for yourself</u>? I act on these verses all the time and get the results the verses say I should get. Do you believe it?

I've also tried resisting the devil without being first submitted to God's help (His grace) and got NO REAL RESULTS. Get bold and rebel against the devil when he tempts you to leave your help (ignoring grace). Say, "How dare you, devil, even think you will get me to lose faith in my God through this attack on me!!"

Step #6. Time to Replace and Recover—and move on—YAY!!

A-C-T-I-O-N! Action! Action! Action! (That's another cheer I learned in high school.)

Replace PRIDE!	With HUMILITY
DOUBT the devil!	BELIEVE God's promises!
STARVE your doubts!	FEED your faith!
REBEL against the devil!	SUBMIT to God!
RESIST the lusts of your flesh!	WALK & LIVE in the Spirit.
CAST DOWN vain imaginations!	THINK ON things above!

If you make the required <u>effort</u> to stop the merry-go-round and then get off, *you will.* Let's just say you'll *be a happy camper!!* The required effort I'm speaking about is not about performing the *dos and don'ts* of man's religious traditions. It's about you doing what I stated in the previous list. Let God's Word do any *performing* that needs to take place.

> And being fully convinced that what He had promised He was also able to perform (Romans 4:21; emphasis added).

> Being confident of this very thing, that He who has begun a good work in you will complete it until the day of Jesus Christ (Philippians 1:6; emphasis added).

> I will cry out to God Most High, To God who performs all things for me (Psalm 57:2; emphasis added).

This doesn't mean that you sit back and *only* wait on Him and His Word to work—ignoring that you have a part in this. You must be trusting that God will perform His Word and His promises in your life. (He really is big enough.) Rest and peace will come over your heart, emotions, and thoughts when you do this.

Being proactive and in control of the steering wheel of your life course will be so <u>gratifying and rewarding</u>. As you pray and connect with God, asking Him every day for wisdom, direction, and strength, you will begin to see your life headed in the right direction.

READ IT!
John 10
Jesus is our Shepherd
We are His sheep

No matter what is happening around you or what you might see your fa-vorite people in the world choosing to do, you must choose to stay your course. Decide that you will not change your belief, course, or conviction based on the pull of temptations. Focus on the true knowledge about Who God is. Simply listen to your Good Shepherd's voice on the inside of you, and He will lead you right to where you need to go. The key is ONLY listening to your GOOD SHEPHERD and getting HIS WORD inside your *heart and mind*.

If you are afraid to do what it takes to stop the *same-ol', same-ol'*—the same thing that is always done or that always happens[10]—from continuing, then you will stay paralyzed because of it. Are you going to just sit back and let UNBELIEF and FEAR rob you from doing what's *in your heart?* **NO WAY!**

I know you desire to get rid of the fear and REPLACE it with faith in our Great God and His purpose for you. You can believe God to show you what steps YOU need to take for His plan, in your heart, to come to pass in your life! YOU ARE WELL ABLE TO TAKE THE LAND GOD HAS GIVEN YOU AND RECOVER!!

I have a wooden plaque hanging in my breezeway, and it says this:

"If the plan doesn't work, change the plan, but never the goal."

My husband and I have had to change plans many times in our life journey. But, we've never changed the goal of pursuing what's in our hearts to do with our lives.

I'm going to continue to GO FOR IT!! I hope you do too!!

FOURTEEN

THE RED CARPET WALKWAY

W<small>E'VE COVERED A</small> lot in this book and have come a long way, so let's do a quick review before going further. At the beginning of this book, I introduced what merry-go-round riding looked like and exposed several different merry-go-rounds I have personally ridden in my life.

I also shared the four major components of every merry-go-round, which are:

The Center Post is unbelief and lies. This is what keeps a merry-go-round spinning. Unbelief is the deadliest part of the ride because it is based on lies, the thief, and a killer of abundant life. Fear is what fuels the unbelief to keep it spinning.

The Base or revolving platform is what one sits or stands on while riding. It supports the spinning ride and is attached to the post of unbelief.

The Decorative Fixtures and Handlebars represent something attractive that someone holds on to as they spin on the merry-go-round. It's usually something one's flesh doesn't want to let go of. These things deceive, keeping the person from realizing they have been going in circles.

The End Result or consequence of riding a merry-go-round is that (after spinning for a while) the person doesn't like it. Still, now they are confused and don't know how to get off and move forward. They realize they've been stuck and spent years just going in circles and aren't sure how to walk straight. At this point is when they realize they have, so far, missed going into the Promised Land that God has available to them here on Earth.

We went on to see how to stop the spin of the enemy's work and lies and that it's not meant for us to walk off a merry-go-round alone by our own self-efforts. You now know how to first prepare for the walk-off and use the freely-given help God made available to us to continue living without spinning. I shared with you what I believe to be the three biggest helps, next to the example of Jesus; Holy Spirit, grace, and truth. I then gave you six steps to get off and stay off.

Now, let's talk about how God has already prepared our walkway—through His Word—to stop spinning and start winning, get *off the merry-go-round*, get on the right path, and *on with living our life!*

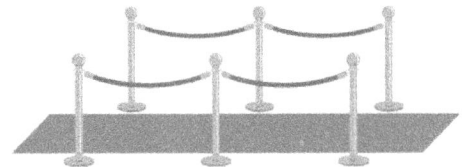

God has rolled out the red carpet of His Word for you to be able to walk on (and walk straight, at that). His *red-carpet walkway* is the only foundation needed under our feet for our entire life. On His red carpet, the only direction to go is FORWARD:

> But this one thing I do, forgetting those things which are behind and reaching FORWARD to those things which are ahead (Philippians 3:13 MEV; emphasis added).

Part One: The Landing Path Is Ready

Once you've decided to go forward, you'll see that God has a *previously prepared* way for you to step off the merry-go-round. Your steps won't look exactly like mine, and mine won't look like yours. **God has a path specific for each of us, and His Word is what will light our specific path.**

> Your word is a lamp to my feet And a light to my path (Psalm 119:105).

> But the path of the just is like the shining sun, That shines ever brighter unto the perfect day.

> My son, give attention to my words; Incline your ear to my sayings. Do not let them depart from your eyes;

> Keep them in the midst of your heart; For they are life to those who find them And health to all their flesh.

> Keep your heart with all diligence, For out of it spring the issues of life.

> Let your eyes look straight ahead, And your eyelids look right before you.

> Ponder the path of your feet, And let all your ways be established. Do not turn to the right or the left;

> Remove your foot from evil (Proverbs 4:18, 20–23, 25–27).

Stepping off the merry-go-round is comparable to how you would step off anything in the natural. Anytime you step off a moving and spinning object and onto the ground, you'll need to **make sure your landing is sturdy**.

You'll need a good, solid foundation for your first step. God has a solid foundation for you to step onto, and it's built by the revelation of His Word concerning who you are in Him. Once you have this solid foundation on the inside of you, you'll be able to continue stepping forward in the plan He has for your life. As you stay on this path, you will see that it will take you *around* the merry-go-rounds but never back onto the merry-go-rounds.

> For I know the thoughts and plans that I have for you, says the Lord, thoughts and plans for welfare and peace and not for evil, to give you hope in your final outcome (Jeremiah 29:11 AMPC).

When you flood your thinking with the truths in God's Word—the Bible—all the lies you've heard from the enemy and people will be exposed. Unbelief will begin to leave because the **truth** you receive from God's Word **will make you free** to believe. Getting your mind renewed to truth and getting God's love for you rooted in the soil of your heart should be your priority. If you seriously want to live life victoriously and in the plan that God has waiting for you, then you will do this.

So far, you've seen a lot of Scriptures throughout this book and heard a lot about **the REAL you** and the truth that makes you free. Now, I want to share with you more Scriptures that I personally use to keep me thinking clearly about Who God is, His love for me, and who I am in this world *because of His great love for me* (1 John 4:17). I know these Bible Scriptures can renew your mind and help you see Him *and yourself* differently. They can help you go from being ALL IN shallow water to being ALL IN deep water. *Are you ready to go deeper?*

Red-carpet walkways are used for royalty. As you step forward, picture yourself as who you really are: a child of the King! The walkway of Scriptures you are about to read will meet you at whatever merry-go-round you've been riding, escort you off, and get you onto your royal path. These Scriptures from God's Word will reveal to you your rightful seat! What seat is that? This is a spiritual seat we have been given as a child of God. It's a seat where each of God's children is seated, whether they know it or not. The Scripture in Ephesians 2 tells you that you are seated next to Jesus. Can you see yourself sitting with Him?

> But God, being rich in mercy, because of His great love with which He loved us, even when we were dead in sins, <u>made us alive together with Christ</u> (by grace you have been saved), and He <u>raised us up</u> and <u>seated us together in the heavenly places</u> in Christ Jesus (Ephesians 2:4–6 MEV; emphasis added).

When did this seating take place? It took place when you were born again, in your spirit. In your spirit, you've been <u>made alive</u>. In your spirit, you've been <u>raised up</u> and <u>seated together with Christ</u> in heavenly places.

The red-carpet walkway is a foundation built for Kingdom living. Kingdom living is where we operate by God's attributes: His love, His faith, His grace, His Word, His truth, His wisdom, His strength, His authority, and His victory. It's how you can walk through life resting in His peace and joy. I'm going to let the Word of Truth speak for Himself as these Bible Scriptures roll out for you.

Before you read these, ask God to soften the ground of your heart. Ask Him to cause you to have a hunger and thirst for HIS RIGHTEOUSNESS—the very thing that's already inside of you that *He wants you to acknowledge*. Ask Father God to heal your broken heart and make you free in your mind so you can see Him and who you really are in the light of His Word. As you do, agree with me that these Words (which came from the mouth of God) will go forth into your heart and mind.

Agree with the Word that His Word will do the work of transforming you from the inside out. As you do, they will cause you to live out of your new, born-again spirit—just like the transformation of a butterfly coming out of its cocoon.

> Do not be conformed to this world, but be transformed by the renewing of your mind, that you may prove what is the good and acceptable and perfect will of God (Romans 12:2 MEV).

I pray as each one of you read these words from the Bible about God's true nature and His love for you that you are filled with the knowledge of Him and the truth that makes you free.

Before you read any further, I pray that you stop here and ask Holy Spirit to QUICKEN YOU and make His Word come alive in you—even in your natural mind.

I pray that what's inside your spirit connects with your natural mind in a way you've never experienced before. I pray that the eyes of your spiritual understanding are opened to a new level. As this happens, faith will be released and rise up in you, causing you to walk forward.

Part Two: Meditating on God's Truth About You

If you meditate on these Scriptures consistently, you *will* experience your relationship with God—your Abba Father—becoming beautiful and rich.

> The LORD, your God, is in your midst, a Mighty One, who **will save**. He will **rejoice over you with gladness**, He will **renew you with His love**. He will **rejoice over you with singing** (Zephaniah 3:17 MEV; emphasis added).

> I will praise You, for I am **fearfully and wonderfully made** (Psalm 139:14; emphasis added).

How **precious also are Your thoughts to me**, O God! How great is the sum of them! If I should count them, they would be more in number than the sand; When I awake, I am still with You (Psalm 139:17; emphasis added).

Surely He has **borne our griefs** and **carried our sorrows**; Yet we esteemed Him stricken, Smitten by God and afflicted. But He was **wounded for our transgressions**, He was **bruised for our iniquities**; The **chastisement for our peace was upon Him**, And **by His stripes, we are healed**. All we like sheep have gone astray; We have turned, every one, to his own way; And the LORD has **laid on Him the iniquty of us all** (Isaiah 53:4–6; emphasis added).

The LORD has appeared of old to me, saying: "Yes, **I have loved you with an everlasting love**; Therefore with lovingkindness, **I have drawn you**" (Jeremiah 31:3; emphasis added).

And she will bring forth a Son, and you shall call His name JESUS, for He will **save His people from their sins** (Matthew 1:21; emphasis added).

And when He had called His twelve disciples to Him, He gave them **power over unclean spirits**, to cast them out, and to **heal all kinds of sickness and all kinds of disease** (Matthew 10:1; emphasis added).

But as many as received Him, to them He gave the right to become **children of God**, to those who believe in His name (John 1:12; emphasis added).

For **God so loved the world that He gave** His only begotten Son, that whoever believes in Him should not perish but have eternal life (John 3:16; emphasis added).

All things that the Father has are Mine. Therefore I said that **He will take of Mine and declare it to you** (John 16:15; emphasis added).

For the **Father Himself loves you**, because you have loved Me, and have believed that I came from God (John 16:27 MEV; emphasis added).

Now hope does not disappoint, because **the love of God has been poured out in our hearts** by the Holy Spirit who was given to us (Romans 5:5; emphasis added).

For as by one man's disobedience many were made sinners, so also by one Man's obedience many will be **made righteous** (Romans 5:19; emphasis added).

But if the Spirit of Him who raised Jesus from the dead dwells in you, He who raised Christ from the dead will also give **life to your mortal bodies** through His Spirit who dwells in you (Romans 8:11; emphasis added).

The Spirit Himself bears witness with our spirit that **we are children of God** (Romans 8:16; emphasis added).

What then shall we say to these things? If God is for us, **who can be against us**? He who did not spare His own Son, but delivered Him up for us all, how shall He not with Him **also freely give us all things**? (Romans 8:31–32; emphasis added)

Who shall bring a charge against God's elect? It is God who justifies. Who is he who condemns? It is Christ who died, and furthermore is also risen, who is even at the right hand of God, who also **makes intercession for us** (Romans 8:33; emphasis added).

Yet in all things we are **more than conquerors** through Him who loved us (Romans 8:37; emphasis added).

But of Him **you are in Christ Jesus**, who became for us wisdom from God—and **righteousness and sanctification and redemption** (1 Corinthians 1:30; emphasis added).

For 'who has known the mind of the LORD that he may instruct Him?' But **we have the mind of Christ** (1 Corinthians 2:16; emphasis added).

Do you not know that **you are the temple of God** and that **the Spirit of God dwells in you**? (1 Corinthians 3:16; emphasis added)

But he who is joined to the Lord is **one spirit with Him** (1 Corinthians 6:17; emphasis added).

Therefore, if anyone is in Christ, **he is a new creation**; old things have passed away; behold, **all things have become new** (2 Corinthians 5:17; emphasis added).

For He made Him who knew no sin to be sin for us, that we might become the **righteousness of God in Him** (2 Corinthians 5:21; emphasis added).

I have been crucified with Christ; it is no longer I who live, **but Christ lives in me**; and the life which I now live in the flesh I live by faith in the Son of God, who **loved me and gave Himself for me** (Galatians 2:20; emphasis added).

For you are all **sons of God through faith in Christ Jesus** (Galatians 3:26; emphasis added).

And if you are Christ's, then you are Abraham's seed and **heirs according to the promise** (Galatians 3:29; emphasis added).

But when the fullness of the time had come, God sent forth His Son, born of a woman, born under the law, to **redeem those who were under the law**, that we might receive the **adoption as sons**. And because **you are sons**, God has sent forth the Spirit of His Son into your hearts, crying out, "Abba, Father!" Therefore **you are no longer a slave but a son, and if a son, then an heir of God through Christ** (Galatians 4:4–7; emphasis added).

Just as **He chose us in Him** before the foundation of the world, that we should be **holy and without blame before Him in love**, having predestined us to **adoption as sons** by Jesus Christ to Himself, according to the good pleasure of His will, to the praise of the glory of His grace, by which **He made us accepted in the Beloved**. In Him, we have **redemption** through His blood, the **forgiveness of sins**, according to the **riches of His grace** (Ephesians 1:4–7; emphasis added).

In Him you also trusted, after you heard the word of truth, the gospel of your salvation; in whom also, having believed, **you**

were sealed with the Holy Spirit of promise (Ephesians 1:13; emphasis added).

And **you He made alive**, who were dead in trespasses and sins (Ephesians 2:1; emphasis added).

For by grace you have been saved through faith, and that not of yourselves; it is the gift of God, not of works, lest anyone should boast. For **we are His workmanship, created in Christ Jesus** for good works, which God prepared beforehand that we should walk in them (Ephesians 2:8–10; emphasis added).

But now in Christ Jesus, you who once were far off **have been brought near by the blood of Christ**. For He, Himself is our **peace**, who has **made both one** and has **broken down the middle wall of separation** (Ephesians 2:13–14; emphasis added).

That you put on the **new man** which was created according to God, in **true righteousness and holiness** (Ephesians 4:24; emphasis added).

And you, who once were alienated and enemies in your mind by wicked works, yet now He has **reconciled** in the body of His flesh through death, to present you **holy, and blameless, and above reproach in His sight** (Colossians 1:21–22; emphasis added).

And you, being dead in your trespasses and the uncircumcision of your flesh, He **has made alive** together with Him, having **forgiven you all trespasses**, having **wiped out the handwriting of requirements that was against us**, which was contrary to us. And He has taken it out of the way, having **nailed it to the cross** (Colossians 2:13–14; emphasis added).

You are all **sons of light and sons of the day**. We are **not of the night nor of darkness** (1 Thessalonians 5:5; emphasis added).

Not with the blood of goats and calves, but with His own blood He entered the Most Holy Place **once for all**, having **obtained eternal redemption** (Hebrews 9:12; emphasis added).

But the Holy Spirit also witnesses to us; for after He had said before, "This is the covenant that I will make with them after those days, says the LORD: I will put My laws into their hearts, and in their minds, I will write them," then He adds, "**Their sins and their lawless deeds I will remember no more**" (Hebrews 10:15–17; emphasis added).

[He] Himself bore our sins in His own body on the tree, that we having died to sins, might live for righteousness—by whose stripes **you were healed** (1 Peter 2:24; emphasis added).

His divine power **has given to us all things that pertain to life and godliness**, through the knowledge of Him who called us by glory and virtue, by which have been **given to us exceedingly great and precious promises**, that through these **you may be partakers of the divine nature**, having escaped the corruption that is in the world through lust (2 Peter 1:3–4; emphasis added).

Because you are strong, and the word of God **abides in you**, And you have overcome the wicked one (1 John 2:14; emphasis added).

But **you have an anointing from the Holy One, and you know all things** (1 John 2:20; emphasis added).

You are of God, little children, and have **overcome** them, because **He who is in you is greater than he who is in the world** (1 John 4:4; emphasis added).

For whatever is born of God **overcomes the world**. And this is the victory that has overcome the world—our faith (1 John 5:4; emphasis added).

Wow! What a red-carpet walkway! And this is just a teaspoonful compared to the rest of God's Word. I can tell your mind is being renewed right now! I bet your back straightened up and your shoulders went back as you read **these beautiful Scriptures that talk about you**. I bet there's a smile on your face and maybe a few tears in your eyes. Now you know how I feel when I read these myself. I have especially put them in this book for you to regularly read and meditate on. I hope you do.

Grabbing hold of one of these Scriptures—**meditating on it until it clicks with you**—is more important than memorizing tons of Scriptures that *only* stay in your mental realm. *Why?* Because the goal is that the Word of God that you do read, confess, and pray **will actually take hold in your heart**. This happens when your mind comes into agreement with your new, born-again spirit—which is where the mind of Christ is. When *that* happens, you have a *locked-down* revelation of truth that nobody can take from you.

As you start declaring that, as you read and meditate on these Scriptures, the image you have of yourself will begin to come into agreement with the image of Christ that *you became* when you received Jesus. It won't take long for you to start seeing yourself correctly.

Grab your megaphone and make this declaration if you believe it:

> "God's Word says I have been made righteous! I choose to believe it! I love the Lord my God with all my heart, and I love people. I love God's Word, and it is working in me, through me, and for me. When I speak the Word of God, His angels go out and help me because I am an heir of Salvation! I expect to see changes in my life because I only believe and speak what God's Word says!"

Now that's a good faith confession and a sure way to get off any merry-go-round!!

Part Three: Praying According to God's Word

I'd like to share another helpful way to meditate on God's Word. I use these (and other) New Testament prayers **when praying for myself,** my spouse, my children, or others. I personalized these prayers and started praying them over my husband and me years ago. I saw results right away as I humbly prayed (in faith) for changes in my own heart first.

I have given these to many people who have used them, and they have reported to me how these have helped them stay focused while praying for themselves and other people. I included all of these, but remember, it only takes a revelation of <u>one</u> of them to change your life in an area. Having faith in Scripture can give it access to work in your life.

As you walk through life, give voice to (use your voice to declare) **God's promises** (as seen in the red-carpet walkway) and these **scriptural prayers.** By doing so, you are declaring God's Word and confessing it over your life. I'm confident that as you do this by faith, you will be encouraged in your heart, and your mind will become clearer and better focused to keep the faith and not lose hope.

You can personalize the prayers by inserting your own name, your spouse's name, the name of a friend, child, or family member. Pray these from <u>your heart</u>, not religiously from your head, believing that His Word will do what it is sent out to do, through YOUR VOICE. These prayers in Scripture are not to be used like some religions use prayer (by only chanting them or using them daily to mark off their ritualistic routine). I give these to you as a reference and reminder that God's Word is here to help when we apply it personally to our life situations.

From 2 Corinthians 5:17

Thank You, Father, that through Jesus, I have been made new, and the past things I have done are no longer attached to me. I am new with Christ inside me now. Please help me to see myself as You see me.

Or you can personalize the same Scripture passage for others like this:

Thank You, Father, that through Jesus (*insert your spouse's name, the name of a friend, child, or family member*) has been made new, and the past things they have done are no longer attached to them. (Insert name) is new with Christ inside them now. Please help them to see themself as You see them.

From Ephesians 5:2

Father, help me to walk in love toward others and follow the example of how Christ loved me and gave Himself up for me.

From Psalm 147:3

Father, help me receive the healing Jesus provided for my broken and wounded heart. Help me extend mercy and grace toward others as You have done for me and help me to know that they are also hurting.

From Colossians 2:13–14

Father, thank You that, because of Jesus, I am no longer trapped in sin but am now made alive like He is. Thank You that I am forgiven, and my record of sin was canceled when Jesus went to the Cross. I choose to do what Jesus did—I forgive myself and others of any debt I feel is still owed.

From Luke 6:31

Father, just as I desire others to treat me a certain way, help me treat them that way.

From 1 Thessalonians 3:12–13

Lord, I ask that You help me increase and abound in Your unconditional love for myself and others.

From 1 John 4:8 and 1 Corinthians 13:4–7

Father, I know You are love. I choose to love others the way that You love them. By Your grace, I will express Your love toward others by being patient, kind, not envying, not parading myself haughtily, and not being prideful with them. I need Your help to not be rude and seek my own way with people, and I need Your help so that I'm not easily offended and touchy. I don't want to think evil thoughts of people. I don't want to be glad when people are caught in sin, but I want to be excited when they do right. Help me bear up with whatever is going on with others and believe the best in them, hoping for good, and enduring with them through whatever they are dealing with.

From Philippians 4:8–9

Father, help me to only think on whatever is true, whatever is honorable, whatever is just, whatever is pure, whatever is lovely, whatever is commendable, excellent, and worthy of praise. Help me practice choosing to walk in your ways with other people and thinking about others the way You think about me.

From 2 Peter 1:3–8

Father, thank You for granting me all things that pertain to life and godliness as I gain more knowledge of You and Your true nature of love. Thank You for granting me Your precious and great promises. I want to receive and walk in Your promises. With Your help, I want to make every effort to supplement my faith with virtue, virtue with knowledge, knowledge with self-control, self-control with steadfastness, steadfastness with godliness, godliness with brotherly affection, and brotherly affection with love. I ask that these qualities increase in me and keep me from being ineffective and unfruitful in the knowledge of You, my Lord Jesus Christ.

From James 3:17–18

Your wisdom is pure, peaceable, gentle, open to reason, full of mercy and good fruits, impartial and sincere. Father, help me use Your wisdom when dealing with other people.

From Ephesians 1:15–19

Father, I ask You to open up the eyes of my understanding. I ask that I would know the calling You are hoping for me to find, know the riches You gave me through my inheritance from You, and know the exceeding greatness of Your power working in me as I believe what You say in Your Word.

From Romans 15:5,6,13

Father, You are the God of patience and comfort and hope. I ask that You help me be like-minded toward other people, according to Christ Jesus, that I may glorify You with one mind and mouth. I ask You to fill me with all joy and peace in believing that I may abound in the hope You have for me by the power of Your Holy Spirit.

From Ephesians 3:14–19

Father, I ask that You strengthen me and that I would be rooted and grounded in the revelation of Your love for me. I know You are able to do exceedingly abundantly above all that I ask or think, according to Your power that works in me, so I ask You to help me allow Your power to work in me.

From Proverbs 3:5–6

Father, I ask You to help me trust You with all my heart and not try to figure things out on my own. Please help me include You in my decision-making and allow You to be the One I get my direction from.

From Colossians 4:12

Father, I pray that I may stand perfect and complete in all Your will for me, doing whatever You tell me.

From 3 John 1:2

Father, I pray that I would prosper in all things and be in health, just as my soul prospers.

From 1 Corinthians 15:57

Thank You, Father, for giving me the victory through the finished work Jesus did for me on the Cross.

Please remember that we aren't praying, confessing, or memorizing Scriptures and prayers thinking we will *make God* do something. He's given us these because He has given us everything that pertains to life and Godliness. Now, it is up to us to rest IN that and *only believe* that we have these things we are praying for. Rest is the keyword. Simply trusting in Him—that's what pleases Him.

You've just been given a lot of what I like to call *Truth Nuggets*. Put them in your treasure chest to grab later when needed. You may have started this book with only an ankle-deep revelation or knee-deep revelation of God's Word and love for you. Before reading this book, you may have known very little about your new identity in Christ as a born-again believer. Now, because of all the truth you've seen so far … there is no reason your ALL IN can't take you out to the deeper places with the Lord. This book is packed with truth and help for you. The stronger and more firm the foundation, the stronger and more firm you'll remain as you move forward.

The wisdom and revelation that the Lord downloaded to me over my Christian walk have been imparted to you. Will you value it? Will you keep hold of it like a found treasure? *Will you use it to help others?*

I don't know about you, but I choose to believe these Scriptures and stay on my path!

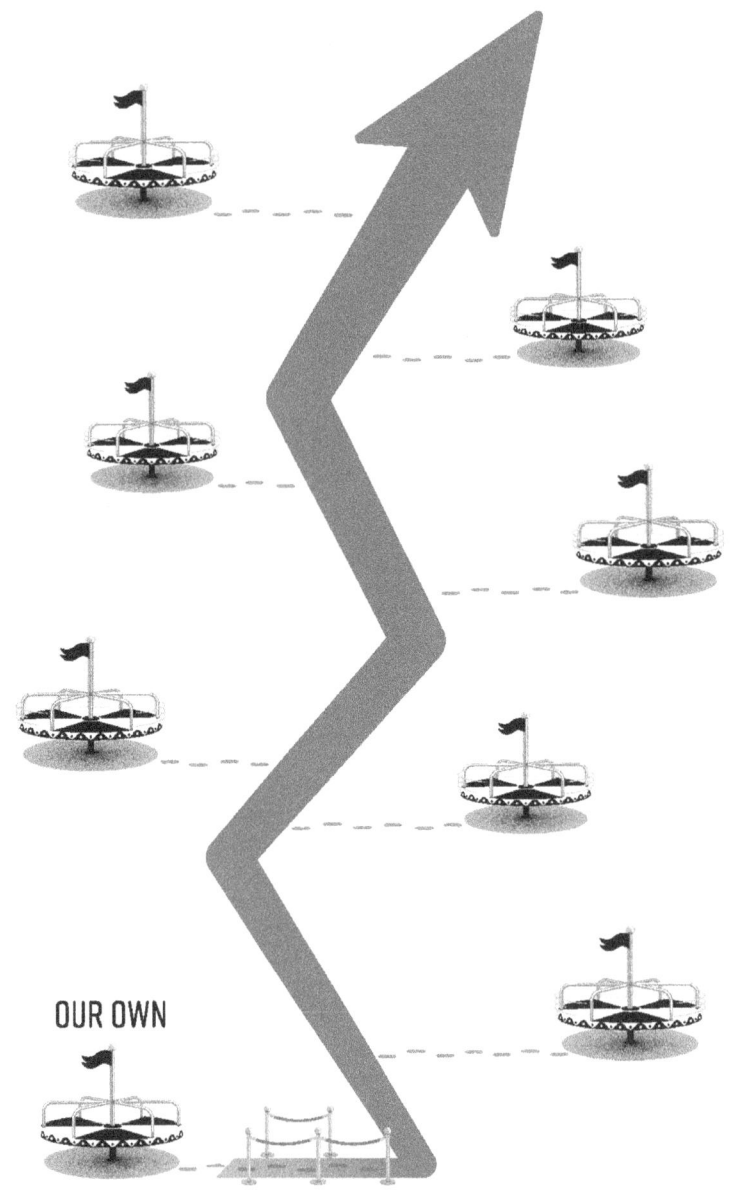

OUR OWN

350

FIFTEEN

A NEW WAY OF LIVING

NOW THAT YOU'VE just built your sure foundation and taken a stroll down the red-carpet walkway, my hope (with these final chapters) is to get you going on your new path. Not long ago, I saw this image in my mind, and then I had it created to share with you. Let's walk through it. To me, it's a great illustration of what our life here on Earth is supposed to be like:

Can you see how the red-carpet walkway of God's Word will meet you at the edge of your life's merry-go-round?

Can you see how it will escort you directly to your path of truth, liberty, direction, and purpose?

Can you see yourself getting off all the merry-go-rounds in your life and walking on the path God has for you?

His path for you will be IN THE WORLD and in your area of influence and life's calling. His path *won't* seclude you from the world, but it *will* keep you off the spinning merry-go-rounds of the world's influence *if you stay on the path*. Jesus wants us *in the world* so that we can reach the world with the truth of the Good News!

<u>They are not of the world</u>, even as I am not of the world. Sancti-fy them by Your truth. Your word is truth. As You sent Me into the world, <u>so I sent them into the world</u>. I in them and You in Me, that they may be perfect in unity, and <u>that the world may know that You have sent Me</u>, and have loved them as You have loved Me (John 17:16–18, 23 MEV; emphasis added).

Each of us needs to realize that getting off our merry-go-rounds and mov-ing forward in our new way of living does not mean we run away from the world and avoid the world. As Jesus said, we are in the world, but not of the world. **We are to avoid the world's merry-go-rounds, but not the world's people.**

(Christians who obviously *live in this world*, but believe they need to stay away from the people *of this world*, have misunderstood the Great Commission told by Jesus.)

Read these next Scriptures through the lens of *understanding God's heart for people* and not through the filter of religious teachings and man-made tra-ditions.

And He said to them, *"Go into **all the world** and preach the gospel to every creature"* (Mark 16:15; emphasis added).

Then the master said to the servant, "Go out into the highways and hedges, and compel them to come in, that my house may be filled" (Luke 14:23).

The two previous Scriptures have been widely misconstrued, giving the impression of meaning, "Go into the world and tell people to come to my church and get saved. Let's see how many people (numbers) we can get this next week." *Jesus didn't say that.* And He also did not say to preach the Gospel to only our little circle of friends. Did He? (I realize that would be easier and less uncomfortable than taking the risk of being persecuted and made fun of.)

But we see in these previous passages that He *did* say, "Go into all the world." And, the Word *does* say, "Go out into the highways and hedges." And, yes, the Word also says, "Compel them to come in, that my house may be filled."

I believe the *house* in this Scripture is the family of God—it is NOT a building and four walls. This isn't about looking at the number of people sitting in a church pew; it's about seeing *people,* truly loving them, and caring about their eternal life and future here on Earth. They are the *house. Go out* and compel them to come in … to Him, that they may be filled.

In almost every church I attended early on, the focus was to get people to *come to church.* This is the opposite of what Jesus (through these Scriptures) told us to do when He said *go to them* **in the world**. (If we can get them to come to us, we don't have to go to them, right? No, that's doing it backward!) It is man-made religion trying to take shortcuts and the easy way out instead of pure religion, which earnestly desires to reach lost and dying people. Man-made religion requires that they come to us and change their actions and appearances **instead of going** to meet them *where they are* and where their heart's level of understanding is.

God is not like an over-protective parent. He never wanted us to stay inside the four walls of our house or church, isolating ourselves. We are not purposed to just take in all the revelations and truths we learn and keep them to ourselves, our family, and our church family.

> Go therefore and make disciples of all nations, baptizing them in the name of the Father and of the Son and of the Holy Spirit, teaching them to observe all things I have commanded you. And remember, I am with you always, even to the end of the age. Amen (Matthew 28:19–20 MEV; emphasis added).

The Church (as a whole corporate Body of Christ) has been given instructions and a commandment by Jesus to go to the nations and disciple them. As the Church obeys this corporate commandment, it sets the example for the individual Christian, who makes up the Body of Christ—the Church, to go into *our world* and preach the Gospel of Jesus Christ. *Our world* is our area of influence. If we all do our part, the nations will be reached and discipled.

Church leaders and Christians who ignore what's happening all around them in the world are doing what I did for years (see chapter four), just living in my own La-La-Land. Suppose God wanted us to separate ourselves from society after receiving Salvation. Don't you think He would immediately "call us home" to safely be with Him and get us out of this wicked ol' world? Satan has deceived us! The enemy has whispered in the ears of many denominations and told Christians they need to get out of society, modern culture, and anything influencing the direction of society/culture. He has discipled THEM to believe that God does not want us involved. The enemy wants us so busy doing our own "Christian" things that many have unconsciously jumped right onto the religious merry-go-round.

Much of the Church is busy spinning with movement—appearing to impact people and culture—yet deceived. Christian churches (as a whole) are not yet making the impact we could be making, and quite honestly, we have sometimes caused people to run away from us. Christians who talk weird, walk weird, look and dress weird (like they are a costume party for their own group's fun time event) are running off the next generations left and right!

Especially in today's world culture, satan's desire is to convince all Christians that they must be shut-ins to be safe. He gets his way if we become shut-ins who can't function outside of our comfortable chairs, couch, bed, church pew, and protected surroundings! Let's learn how to change this. As we get freer and freer in knowing who we are IN Jesus (and off all merry-go-rounds), we must not become shut-ins. The red-carpet walkway of God's Word **equips us** to safely go outside and walk in the midst of the world. We can go outside, take a breath of fresh air, and see what our neighbor is up to. It's pretty hard to show love to our neighbors if we never leave our house!

When David's ninety-year-old stepmother became too scared to walk outside for fear of falling, he built a few ramps for her to safely get to three different areas *outside of the house*. He also added a handrail to the walkway of her porch. She was so blessed! She could now safely walk out to her barn **without**

tripping so she could go outside and do the very thing that she loved to do each and every day: feed the birds dried bread and table scraps. Too many people are prisoners in their own house or even their church building. They can't leave the security and familiarity of the inside environment because of fear that they will get hurt or fall away.

If I had to pick the most destructive merry-go-round of all, I'd say it is the Religious and Church-Going Merry-Go-Round. Why? Because we, as the Body of Christ and His Church, have often been doing it wrong!

I realize that is bold. Please don't get me wrong or get offended. I LOVE THE CHURCH, and Jesus loves His Church! That is the whole reason I bring this up. I believe it's why God showed me the illustration of this path. I know He wanted me to add it as a visual illustration. It is a powerful tool so that you can envision yourself walking off merry-go-rounds onto the red-carpet foundation He built for His royal family! Much like those ramps and handrails that David built his ninety-year-old stepmother, His Word of Truth will safely take you on the path of your victorious redeemed life here on Earth.

Meditate on God's unfailing, unconditional love for you.

Look again at the image of the merry-go-round. Do you recognize the radioactive symbol on the merry-go-round in all the illustrations?

I chose this because of the seriousness of life lived constantly riding on merry-go-rounds. The long-term effects of spinning life away can cause people to become weak and disoriented. Some are even dying before their time and missing God's wonderful path for them. We need to think of these life merry-go-rounds as something toxic trying to seep into our lives. Recognize them as poisonous, even radioactive!

STOP THE SPIN!

The Lord gave me points for us to remember as we walk on our path. Staying focused on these things will keep us from stepping off the path and back onto merry-go-rounds:

- *Keep your eyes off of self and look to Jesus first.*
- *Know who you are as a born-again believer in Jesus—know your new identity.*
- *Live a Spirit-led life.*
- *Meditate on God's grace and truth.*
- *Keep your right standing with God in mind.*
- *Remind yourself that you are now righteous and approved by God.*
- *Use the faith of Jesus given to you.*
- *Get to know Him. Your relationship with God should be intimate.*
- *Talk with Him! Ask of Him!*
- *Live according to the finished work of Jesus.*
- *Speak out the written Word of God and the prophetic personal words God gives you.*
- *Meditate on God's unfailing, unconditional love for you.*

The merry-go-rounds we rode on as a child were enjoyed because of the spinning sensation we got as we and our friends all laughed and screamed. It was great *until* we rode long past its thrill and started to become dizzy and nauseous. Remember my Silly-Silo experience at the county fair from chapter two? The merry-go-rounds of our adult life parallel to that same effect. The subtle, seemingly harmless thrill of that spinning ride we once enjoyed has now become a lifelong habit or compulsive behavior. At the very least, they produce hurtful actions, nauseating religious attitudes, or lives lived out just faking a good life in hopes we finally find one.

We could even look at these merry-go-rounds next to our path as <u>land mines</u>—one step onto them, and everything EXPLODES in our life in one way or another. Land mines are explosive devices hidden by an enemy of war in hopes you don't see them before you step on them to your own destruction. In the same way, our enemy hopes we don't see the destruction his devices can cause (the merry-go-rounds of life) before we step onto them. I don't know anyone who would ever *intentionally* walk on land mines if a path was available to bypass them. Do you? That's not normal. And, nobody likes being lost and wandering around in circles for years as the Israelites did. People *want* to stay on paths that take them safely to their end destination, right?

After reading this book, hopefully, you will recognize these merry-go-rounds are dangerous, like land mines, and start choosing to avoid them. If you accidentally do step on one, God won't hate you over it. God will HELP YOU off of it. Call out to Him. Get your Scriptures back out (like from chapter fourteen). Open the Word. He wants you to stop spinning and start winning. He wants you *to **get off the merry-go-round and on with your life**,* even more than you do! You've probably heard of *practice makes perfect:* The more you do this, the more it will be natural to you.

God gave each of us a life purpose and mission before we were born. **He gave us the ability to find that purpose as we follow Christ on the path where our passions are revealed**. The path of God brings excitement and fulfillment to our hearts. It's a winning path through life, designed especially for us, for you! I truly believe He has that for you. I invite you to join me on the winning way, a walk with the Lord, the Love walk—one where we love each other and extend love to others as we lead them to their own right path in Christ.

Guess what? Today is the first day of the rest of your life! It's a good day for a fresh, new walk if you decide to join me. What do you say? Are you ready for a brighter journey?

Today, you have a new opportunity. You can boldly and unashamedly walk through the world—off old merry-go-rounds and moving forward. With Jesus inside of you, you will be lighting it up! You can light up your world **so people can see the truth** about God!

How's that? How does one changed life light a whole world? Like little fireflies light the skies with joy on a dark night, our light will draw people out of the darkness onto the path God has for them. Let's love the dying, lost, and spiritually hungry people who live in the kingdom of darkness. As we show them *our new way of living*, they will be encouraged and hopeful for change in their own lives. When the people around us see our regular victories, they will want what we have, what *you* now have.

Let's show the people of this culture and time that God is good! God is Love! God is faithful! God already gave us the victory! God has a great reason He picked me, you, and them to be born for this time and season!

Your new foundation is waiting for you. It is safe and secure, not spinning. It is built on the Scriptures and testimonies of God's goodness shared in this entire book. Your bright path has been prepared. The light of the Gospel is shining on it now. Your way is lit, and you can see things more clearly and differently. Now, it's time to step *off the merry-go-round and get on with your life.* Step off the merry-go-round and onto the red-carpet walkway of God's promises and grace, which leads you straight to your FORWARD moving path. Then, start walking!

Here you go! I'll see you out there taking control of your life and walking *in this world, but on your path*. You'll be living your BIG DREAMS, using your God-given gifts, and loving God and people all along the way! I'm excited for you!

SIXTEEN

POP THE CORK AND GO!™

WE'VE SPENT THE past fifteen chapters understanding the dynamics and dangers of life's merry-go-rounds. I'm trusting that the seeds of knowledge and inspiration in this book have helped you decide it is your time to get off the merry-go-rounds and on with your life!

As I close up in this final chapter, I'm excited to share a couple of final life stories with you. As I do so, I will step away from the merry-go-round analogy. We can let this symbolize your past chapters in life closing and your own stepping away from those merry-go-rounds. Exciting days and powerful experiences are ahead of you.

Today you embark on a fresh spiritual walk, launching forward with God. So, I want to share two of the most powerful, spiritual experiences that ever happened to me after being born again and baptized in the Holy Spirit.

Do you remember the meme from chapter one? It read, *Be all in or get all out. There is no halfway.* Well, the first story is about me going ALL IN even deeper, as I received a deeper and more real revelation of God's love for me. The second story—which really rocked my world—happened soon after coming out of the denominational background. It was the first time I had ever experienced such a rich and beautiful time with the Lord after being baptized in the Holy Spirit.

These spiritual events between me and God, which happened about fifteen years apart, changed my life in so many ways. In both times, it was just what I needed to launch forward on my spiritual walk with God and into deeper waters, deep *flowing* waters.

I share them both, hoping that they will help you become more intimate with God as you allow Him to take you ALL OUT of religious lies and thinking and ALL IN to who you are IN CHRIST.

Part One: Let Him Love You

I have entitled the first story, *LET HIM LOVE YOU*. It expresses the difference between what man-made religion taught me and what God was always trying to teach me. From the time I got saved at age ten, I would express to God every single day how much I loved Him. I would acknowledge Him by saying, "I love You, God," "Have a good day, God," or "Can't wait to see You, God," just talking to God off and on. As I was going about my semi-messed-up childhood, my mind was on Him a lot.

Once I really committed and surrendered my life to Him in my senior year in high school, I began to worship Him and communicate with Him deeper. I began to develop a relationship with Him, thanking Him constantly for forgiving my sins and rescuing me from the direction my life was headed. I constantly told God that I honored and valued Him. I told God that I would do whatever He wanted me to do with my life—even be a missionary overseas. My heart for my Heavenly Father was pure because I really did believe He loved me. However, our conversation was shallow (not very deep) because I kept it one-sided most of the time.

I saw God as loving and forgiving, but at that time, I didn't really know that He saw me as His own child. I didn't know He looked at me the same way He looks at Jesus. I didn't know what His love actually provided for me.

Because I didn't understand that a change took place inside me when I was adopted into His family, I was not seeing God or myself correctly.

Eventually, there came a time when I realized I was not *letting* God show me His love in natural ways. I had not let myself meditate on His goodness (outside of forgiveness of sins) because of the religious teaching and thinking that was still in me. The traditions in man-made religion said, "Just focus on *you* loving God—but don't always *expect* His love or blessings to be expressed in natural ways." I thought that was fine because it *sounded right,* and I was not trying to get His approval. I genuinely loved expressing my love for Him and wanted Him to know how much I loved Him. I would even write Him love notes in my journal.

I was more comparable to a little puppy in my relationship with God. You know how puppies are, jumping upon the master's legs and lap, wagging their tail—just wanting to sit and lick all over the master's face as it expresses its love for him? I was like the puppy in that I wanted to be *emotionally held and coddled.*

I remember the feelings I had as a child of craving to receive affection and attention from my earthly father. I also craved the ability to express my love and affection to my earthly father but rarely got that opportunity. I knew my Heavenly Father loved the attention I gave Him, and I loved giving it. The only place I was truly expecting His love to be shown back to me was "in my heart." I never expected to be blessed with things, and I never would *ask* God for any-thing. I simply thought it was more important for me to constantly express my love to Him than for Him to ever express His love to me through tangible gifts.

One day, while I was thanking and praising Him, *in my heart* (spirit), I heard Him say to me,

> Stop for a minute. Dana, I know you love Me and will do whatever I ask or lead you to do. You've proven that. **I** am so thankful to YOU for how *your heart* has always been to serve Me. I have noticed your life. I have noticed you worshipping and dancing and singing to Me. It has honored Me. Did you

know that I rejoice and sing over YOU, though? I watch you, and I LOVE YOU! <u>LET ME</u> love you. <u>LET ME</u> bless you. <u>LET ME</u> show you off. <u>LET ME</u> give you gifts. <u>LET ME</u> take your cares from you, and <u>LET ME</u> care for YOU. You are precious to me, Dana. I have received from you for a long time. I gave My Son for you so I could have a relationship with you. <u>LET ME</u> have an intimate personal relationship with you. Now ... receive from ME.

After hearing this from the Lord in my spirit, I answered, "Yes, Abba Father." That is like saying, "Yes, Daddy."

This conversation with the Lord changed my life. It played a huge part in opening my eyes to see the religious thinking that was hindering me from being WHO I was IN HIM.

Now I have a great relationship with God as a father/daughter, except way better than any earthly father relationship could ever be ... *waaayyyy* better [smiles]. Now I see myself as *a daughter of my King* vs. *a servant to my master.* Nope—it's not a servant and slave relationship anymore. I serve Him and live my life for Him because *I WANT to.* I'm settled in His love for me. All the fear and unbelief I once had regarding His love for me are gone.

Before this *heart-to-heart* talk with the Lord about Him telling me to <u>*let Him*</u> love me, I had never meditated on the specific Scriptures that reveal His love. I can tell you I DO NOW—and it has changed my life. Now I meditate on Father God's truth and love for me all the time. It causes me to love people and myself more in the same way He loves me. I especially love Him more and more. I have found a place of rest in what Jesus did for me, and WOW! It is nice!

Now, I LET HIM love on me emotionally every single day, but I also expect His love to be shown to me through good things that come my way. I see them as gifts from Him. Even small things, like finding something unique at the store or getting the last one of something on the shelf that I've always wanted. It was like He hid it from others just so I could find it—stuff like that. He'll do that for you too!

Now, because of this conversation with the Lord and learning more in God's Word, I ASK Him for things. Yep, that's right! He loves it! He loves it the same way we love it when our children hand us their Christmas list. We *want to know* what they want. God wants you to express to Him what you want. He gives you desires in your heart, so why not ASK HIM TO BRING THEM TO PASS?

In early 1995, I got out my Bible concordance and did a study on the word *ask*. I was absolutely amazed at all the times God and Jesus say, "Ask" in the Bible. (*Instead of me giving you the whole line-up, I hope you do the same thing I did and put some effort into researching these Bible truths.*)

I learned that I could ask and receive. I learned that I could ask and it will be given. And I learned that I **have not** because I **ask not**. I saw so many Scriptures about asking. I also began to learn that God gives us the desires of our hearts. If He is the One who gave us the desire *for* them to begin with, then why wouldn't He GIVE US THEM? Silly people! He does!

READ IT!
John 14:13-14, John 15:7, and John 16:23.

Look up all the Scriptures in the New Testament where we are told to ask our Father God for good things! The Internet makes it easy to study this out. Specifically, I would meditate on John 14:13–14, John 15:7, and John 16:23. During my word study on "ask," I began to respectfully ask God to show His love to me through giving me the desires I had in my heart.

As I share my personal experience, please know that our faith in God for the things we ask is a personal journey specific to each of us. My journey does not look like yours, and yours does not look like mine, so it's important we don't compare. This next story is my personal testimony, but your testimony will look different.

I have always had a deep desire to have a boy child. I only had sisters growing up, and I remember wondering what it would be like to have a little boy in the family. Well, my first three children were all girls. I loved them like crazy and had so much fun with the girls. My girls were easy to buy for. At that time, girl toys and girl clothes were more available in selection than boys, so shopping offered lots of variety. But, I had a desire in my heart for a baby boy child. Just the thought of raising a boy to be a man was thrilling to my husband and me. So, one day, I went for a walk and a talk. I walked out in our field next to the house and had a conversation with the Lord. This is how it went:

"Father, I'm asking you for a boy. Can I have a baby boy?"

It was a quick answer back as I immediately heard in my heart, "Yes, you can!"

I sensed God smiling at me because I felt close enough to Him as my providing Father to ask Him. Please note that I didn't ask God just off the cuff for something random, like a baby boy. God had this desire working in me for quite some time. It had grown to a point where I was confident enough to bring it up to the Lord.

Well, guess what? Almost a year later, I became pregnant. Right away, I knew that I knew I was pregnant with the baby boy I had asked the Lord for a year earlier out in the field. I had no need to even have an ultrasound to prove it, but I knew David was still hesitant to get his hopes up. We ended up getting an ultrasound, anyway, so I ASKED the Lord to make it obvious to my husband that the baby was a boy. David nervously stood next to me as the lady tech smiled and said, "I have never seen a gender so obvious as this. There is no doubt this baby is a boy!" David and I looked on the screen and saw our son's gender sticking straight up in the air! His legs were spread apart, and there was a perfect shot of our boy! How fun is that?!

David got teary-eyed, and I was glowing with excitement for my husband to have a boy born to him. Our son Luke was born eight years after our last daughter! Side note: some of David's friends and family often joked with him that he couldn't make a boy, especially after three daughters. Even though they joked, it messed with his mind and thoughts. Me asking the Lord for a boy delivered not only a blessing for me, but this "ask" also turned into a blessing for my husband and our three daughters. We finally got our boy, and our family felt complete!

I am so thankful I found out God wants me to LET HIM show me His love in physical and natural ways. He wants all of our hearts blessed and our desires brought to pass. I hope you, too, will begin to let Him love you in ways you never would before. Go ahead and take the limits off God and LET HIM LOVE YOU!

Part Two: The Final Story

Now for the final story, and the reason why this chapter is entitled, *POP the Cork and Go!*

In the mid-1990s, we began attending a Full Gospel church. One week, they invited a special guest minister to come in and hold meetings. These meetings were powerful and spiritually and emotionally refreshing! I had never been exposed to anything like this before, yet I was open and receptive. I loved these meetings! There was one particular night that was extra special to me. The guest speaker walked around in the sanctuary and laid hands on different ones as the Spirit led him. While he was walking around praying for others, I became quite aware that my spiritual side was influencing my natural body and emotions. I began to shake—inside first, and then my whole body.

My seat was at the end of a row, on the left side of the church, along the window aisle. I knew the guest speaker was at the back of the church, walking up toward the front, along the left side, where I was sitting. I didn't open my eyes, though. I was talking to the Lord, just thanking Him for manifesting Himself to me, when I heard inside my spirit these words to me: **"I'm going to pop your cork!"**

Instantly, I pictured a bottle of champagne being shaken back and forth. It had so much pressure built up in the bottle that the champagne inside just started spraying out all over the place when the cork was popped. Right after I heard and saw this in my mind, this speaker came up next to me and laid his hand on top of my head. I felt my head get very hot, and then suddenly, it felt like a pop went off inside of me, and I began to laugh and cry uncontrollably.

(Well, I suppose I could have interrupted it and made it all stop. But, I yielded because I knew the Holy Spirit was doing spiritual work inside of me, and I needed to let the pressure I was feeling come out!)

What happened next amazed me.

This man said to the congregation, **"God just popped her cork!"** God is Spirit, and He communicated that same message to both the guest speaker and me in our spirits. *Again, how fun is that?!*

But that isn't the whole of it! The back story is that before this happened, I told God I wanted to know Him more. I gave Him permission to mess up my wrong thinking and show me things I've never allowed Him to show me before. He was faithful, and after that night, I did **begin** to see things differently. *Because God knows how much we can handle, He doesn't always give us a full understanding of what happened until years and years later.* It was progressive light for me. That night, I told "something" to leave me and never come back. At the time, I didn't even have a name for it, but it packed its bags and left! What left me? It was the man-made, messed-up, legalistic bondage of religion! The vanity of man's worthless religion left me. In its former place, God's pure, undefiled religion—grace-filled devotion—flowed freely … uncorked! (Just like we find in James 1:26–27.)

I realized later that this was the beginning of my freedom from years of having a *religious cork*, so to speak, which kept who I really was IN CHRIST all bottled up. This religious cork held the real me down with legalistic thinking, actions, and bondages. These religious lies and perversions were imposters—posing as the Gospel of Grace and Truth. They had me *bottled up* for years, stealing from the love relationship I was supposed to be having with Christ and the true Gospel.

I was so full of lies about God and His true nature, and I was confused by man's religious traditions. I couldn't even begin to see who I was IN CHRIST until all that junk was released. *But, thank God for that uncorked POP of free-*

dom! I began to see a whole new me a whole new me bubbling up and out and truly living free! I was now free to let my new nature, which is the true nature of God inside me, and all His wonderful characteristics burst forth and flow out of me!

It's been quite a process and journey since that night. This mental freeing process really began to escalate in 2009 when I started learning how man-made religion and true, pure Christianity are **two completely different things**. I learned that man's forms of religion are based on the lie that you cannot personally get close to God—because, in that system, He's untouchable. But true Christianity IS a relationship—an intimate, close relationship—with God through Jesus. Man's defiled idea of religion is all about *what we do* for God. Pure Christianity is all about receiving what *Christ did for us* and walking in it as a response! Man's form of religion teaches us constantly to do, perform, and show God how much we love Him. Christianity exists because *God first loved us!* It is first about God showing us how much He loves us and our response in *receiving it.* Religion (without Spirit) is us "getting more faith" (or more people to pray, etc.) to make God move on our behalf. Christianity (which means "like Christ," of His Spirit) is us <u>releasing our faith</u>—which He gives to us—to receive all that He *already gave us*, which even covers our heart's desires!

When that cork was popped back in the mid-1990s, it was the beginning of me getting the religious knots inside my thinking untied. It was the beginning of liberty in Christ I'd never known before. I immediately began to see things differently. No matter what trauma or drama surrounds me, *my mind* is now free to believe everything God has done for me!

Keeping those religious thoughts and actions from coming back to my mind took some effort—and it still does. It's probably comparable to how a person who used to live life with an addiction or compulsive behavior must stay alert and aware that it often tries to subtly creep back in.

What really kicked OUT the religious lies about God's love for me was when I began meditating on Scriptures about how He sees me and what He provided for me through Jesus. I have included many of the same Scriptures in this book, especially in chapter eleven, chapter fourteen, and the appendix.

Renewing my mind to truth is ongoing, and the transformation process is ongoing. But, at least now, there's no cork in the way, plugging up the flow or my forward progress!

Friends, if we Christians aren't waking up every day and loving life, we are doing it wrong. Living a Christian life is supposed to be the most relaxed and restful thing we will ever do. We have one job as Christians, and that's to LET the life of Christ come out of us unhindered and touch everyone around us.

Truth is what makes that possible and what makes you free. There's only one truth: God's truth found in His Word. Knowing God and living by the truth of your born-again identity is the most important thing you can ever do! Popping the cork will make room for truth, so you can begin to think right and believe right. Your new way of living is on the path of TRUTH, free from bottled-up lies and religious thinking.

We must keep our minds focused and make sure (by using the truths we learn in the Word of God) that the cork NEVER gets put back on! Living a *cork-free* life will ensure that Christ's truth and love for us and others can bubble up and flow out of us, unblocked and unhindered!

I live my life ALL IN and with the cork popped off! I fully expect God to reveal more and more to me as I no longer keep Him sealed off with a cork of religious lies and limitations. I fully expect my ALL IN to become a deeper way of life for me. This can be your new way of living too! Like a good bottle of champagne, it is full of celebration and needs to be released!

Isn't it time for you to wake up loving life? Let's get your religious cork popped off and release the REAL YOU. Allow all that is inside your born-again spirit to be released. Allow the real you (who you are in Jesus) to bubble up and start the deep waters flowing so all can see! What do you have to do? Be open to the things in this book, even if you've never heard them before—these things about God and Jesus and your new identity. When you *pop the cork* of your old, WRONG ways of thinking—and the religious lies you've believed for years—that junk will not hinder you anymore. That's what happened to me!

I have literally and gladly made my life an open book to you in hopes you see things differently about the situations in your life. God's awesome plan for my life (uncorked and free from merry-go-rounds) has been worth fighting for. My family is worth fighting for. Yours is too! Think of it! The limits will be off, and the living water will get deeper! This is God's invitation for you to walk ALL IN and further out into rivers of living water.

I love you and pray this book has blessed you. I pray this ***pops the cork*** right off of your wrong thinking. I pray that you allow God to remove all previous limits off your understanding of God and your life as a Jesus believer and Bible reader. My desire and cheer for you are that His light shines out of you into every dark place you walk through in this world. Father God, Holy Spirit, and Jesus are real, and They want a real relationship with YOU!

Your best Christian-life days are ahead if you desire it. By following the awesome path God has laid out for you, you can "*Go from spinning to winning as your new way of living!*" Do you believe it?

From my heart to yours, POP the Cork and GO!

Dana Marie Ecklund

369

APPENDIX

INVITATION TO RECEIVE JESUS
BAPTIZED INTO THE BODY OF CHRIST

I don't believe it's an accident that you have this book in your hand. I believe the Lord is reaching out to you, possibly answering a heart's cry you've had. I want you to know that God loves you and is offering you a FREE gift: the gift of His Son, Jesus. If you have never received His gift, today I'd like to offer you an invitation to do so.

Inviting and receiving Jesus makes you spiritually born again and a child of God, like millions of other people and me are. Jesus made it possible, and through His finished work on the Cross, your sins **have already been forgiven** over 2,000 years ago. You do have a part, but it's easy. Your part is to *believe* this, *by faith, receive* Jesus and what He did for you, and then confess Him as your Lord and Savior. Receiving Jesus means you don't only receive forgiveness for sin. You also receive all of God's promises and complete freedom from being stuck living a life of <u>sin and bondage</u>.

Today, if you have never received Jesus by making Him your Lord and Savior, and you want to—you can right now! God's Word says, "if you confess with your mouth the Lord Jesus and believe in your heart that God has raised Him from the dead, you will be saved. For with the heart one believes unto righteousness, and with the mouth confession is made unto salvation" (Romans 10:9–10). It also says, "Whosoever shall call on the name of the Lord shall be saved" (Romans 10:13).

Beginning in the next paragraph there is a sample of how you can **talk to God** about this. You can pray (talk to God) <u>and say this if you believe it and choose to</u>. (Hint: This is a *conversation* between you and God.)

Jesus, I confess that I need You as my Savior. You are Lord, and I believe in my heart that You took my sins to the Cross and died for me and that God raised You from the dead. By faith and believing in Your Word, I call upon Your name, and I receive Your Salvation and everything You did for me. Thank You for saving me and coming into my heart and life! I receive Your love for me and ask You to help me love others unconditionally, the same way You love me.

Jesus, I choose to make You my Lord, and I offer You my life—to make something out of it that points others to you. With Your help, I will follow You for the rest of my life.

Thank You, Father God, for giving me Jesus and a new spirit and making me clean from my past life of sin. Thank You for adopting me into Your family and making me Your child.

If you said this by faith for the first time, my friend, you now have been <u>made righteous</u> and have received Jesus inside of you. His Spirit won't leave you. Now, it's important to let someone know right away. Talk to the Lord and ask Him to lead you to the church He wants you to attend so you can join together with other believers, worshipping Him and being taught His Word, the Bible. Remember, your spirit is now different, but your mind, will, and emotions are not. They will soon change as you build a personal relationship with God and begin changing how you think. Renewing your mind (by reading what God's Word says) will line up your ways of living to His good ways and plan for you.

If you are someone who has walked away from letting Jesus live through you, then you can renew your commitment to Him right now! Start fresh today and move forward by getting on God's good path for you.

This may be the first time you've ever made Jesus your Lord, or perhaps you are just coming back to Him. Either way, you should immediately take action and move forward building a personal relationship with Him by getting to know Him. As you read God's Word, your mind will change, and your actions will be transformed and cleansed from your old way of living. You will learn more about His love for you and begin to recognize His voice leading you. As you tap into God's love for you and the grace He has given you, your harmful habits and old lifestyle will no longer be as tempting to your flesh. Your desires will change because your heart has changed. You will soon be living from the inside out—from your new, born-again spirit. You are now free to exercise control over the thoughts and emotions that once ran your life and kept you on *merry-go-rounds*.

Get a Bible and start by reading the Book of John, Romans, and the Book of First John—then just keep reading. Get some Word (Truth) in you right away!

Congratulations on your new beginning! If I don't meet you here on Earth, I'll meet you in Heaven!!

Dana Marie Ecklund

BAPTISM IN WATER

One more thing!

I encourage you to also be <u>baptized in water</u>, whole body *physically immersed*, by another believer. Water baptism allows your faith to be made public and not hidden from the world. You publicly show that you are now dead to sin, born again, and alive to God when you do this. You are identifying with Jesus' death, burial and resurrection. Going under the water identifies with Jesus' *death and burial*. It symbolizes how your old man is dead and buried with Jesus. Coming up out of the water identifies with Jesus' *physical resurrection from the dead*. It symbolizes how your new man is alive, and now Christ lives in you.

What a celebration the angels are having for you!

BAPTISM IN THE HOLY SPIRIT

When you called upon Jesus and confessed Him as your Lord, believing He is the Son of God, you became a born-again child of God. At that moment, **you were baptized** *(spiritually immersed)* **into the Body of Christ** by the Holy Spirit.

> For by one Spirit we were all baptized into one body—whether Jews or Greeks, whether slaves or free—and have all been made to drink into one Spirit. For in fact the body is not one member but many (1 Corinthians 12:13–14).

Your Heavenly Father gave to you Jesus, and you received the gift of Jesus. He also wants to give you the gift of His Holy Spirit—the supernatural power you will need to live this new life as His child. You can be baptized (spiritually immersed) in the Holy Spirit as a believer. When this happens, you will also receive a unique prayer language and will be able to pray out things that you do not know. Praying in this new language will edify and strengthen you. It will be a perfect prayer because the Holy Spirit inside of you will be speaking through your spirit. It will be your own voice, though, making the sounds and words. It will not make sense to your natural mind, and it is unique to each person. It's easy to receive, but just like with Salvation, it is *only for those who believe.*

> If you then, being evil, know how to give good gifts to your children, how much more will **your** heavenly Father give the Holy Spirit to those who ask Him! (Luke 11:13)

> But you shall receive power when the Holy Spirit has come upon you; and you shall be witnesses to Me (Acts 1:8).

> And they were all filled with the Holy Spirit and began to speak with other tongues, as the Spirit gave them utterance (Acts 2:4).

Here is a sample prayer (talking to God) that you can say when you are ready to receive.

> **"Father, I recognize my need for Your power to live this new life. I want all that You have for me. Please fill me with Your Holy Spirit. By faith, I receive Him right now. Thank You for baptizing me in Your Holy Spirit."**

Now, by faith, start speaking! Once you begin speaking in your prayer language, you can use it as often as you want. Just as a child develops his vocabulary by continuing to speak, you will develop your spiritual prayer language as you continue to use it.

Don't be discouraged if you don't speak out any syllables at first. You only need to ask once, just like it is in receiving anything from the Lord.

"IN CHRIST" AND "IN HIM" SCRIPTURES

Romans 3:24
Romans 8:1-2
1 Corinthians 1:2
1 Corinthians 15:22
2 Corinthians 2:14
2 Corinthians 5:17
Galatians 2:4
Galatians 5:6
Ephesians 1:3
Ephesians 2:10
Ephesians 3:6
1 Thessalonians 4:16
1 Timothy 1:14
2 Timothy 1:13
2 Timothy 2:10
Philemon 1:6
Romans 12:5
1 Corinthians 1:30
2 Corinthians 1:21
2 Corinthians 3:14
2 Corinthians 5:19
Galatians 3:26
Galatians 6:15
Ephesians 2:6
Ephesians 2:13
Philippians 3:13-14
1 Thessalonians 5:18
2 Timothy 1:9
2 Timothy 2:1
2 Timothy 3:15

John 3:15-16
John 1:4
Acts 17:28
2 Corinthians 1:20
2 Corinthians 5:21
Ephesians 1:4
Ephesians 1:13
Philippians 3:9
Colossians 2:6-7
Colossians 2:10
1 John 2:5-6
1 John 2:8
1 John 3:3
1 John 3:6
1 John 4:13
1 John 5:20
1 John 2:27
1 John 3:5
1 John 3:24
1 John 5:14-15

NOTES

1	Merriam-Webster.com Dictionary, s.v. "folly," accessed November 28, 2021, https://www.merriam-webster.com/dictionary/folly.

2	Merriam-Webster.com Dictionary, s.v. "foolish," accessed November 28, 2021, https://www.merriam-webster.com/dictionary/foolish.

3	Lexico.com Oxford English Dictionary, s.v. "merry-go-round," accessed November 28, 2021, https://www.lexico.com/en/definition/merry-go-round

4	We know from Scripture that 603,550 were numbered by Moses in the wilderness as the "men of war," and all but two of these died without entering the Promised Land. The priests, women, children under age twenty, and the elderly were excluded from the census (Numbers 1:46, Deuteronomy 2:13-16).

5	Merriam-Webster.com Dictionary, s.v. "blackballed," accessed December 7, 2021, https://www.merriam-webster.com/dictionary/blackballed.

6	Lexico.com Oxford English Dictionary, s.v. "ludicrous," accessed November 28, 2021, https://www.lexico.com/en/definition/ludicrous

7	Merriam-Webster.com Dictionary, s.v. "snow," accessed December 7, 2021, https://www.merriam-webster.com/dictionary/snow: deceived, persuaded, or charmed glibly

8	Croce, Jim, "Bad, Bad Leroy Brown" (1973).

9	"Braveheart," a nickname (and movie character) based on the epic courageous true stories of William Wallace and Robert the Bruce, both who were Scottish heroes; Sourced: Wikipedia contributors, "Braveheart," Wikipedia, The Free Encyclopedia, https://en.wikipedia.org/w/index.php?title=Braveheart&oldid=1065718201 (accessed January 18, 2022).

10   McGraw-Hill Dictionary of American Idioms and Phrasal Verbs. S.v. "same ol' same ol'." Retrieved December 15 2022 from https://idioms.thefreedictionary.com/same+ol%27+same+ol%27

MEET THE AUTHOR
DANA MARIE ECKLUND

Author. Speaker. Teacher. Businesswoman. Friend. Whatever role or venue you meet her in, you will soon discover that Dana's biggest desire is to lead people to Jesus and help them see who they are as a born-again believer. She is a cheerleader at heart and loves seeing people get off circumstantial merry-go-rounds and on to the path God has for them in this life.

Here's a lady who has gone through numerous trials and tribulations and has remained faithful, not just months or weeks, but in years. Her faith has been displayed and defined throughout her thirty-nine years of marriage as

she and her husband raised four children amidst impossible situations. Her various life experiences, which took her on one merry-go-round after another, cover the following areas and more: religious legalism, sexual-identity crises, pornography, sexual abuse, family members who struggled with substance abuse lifestyles (including prison and rehab time), her own marriage struggles, children with major health diagnoses, work, school, and more.

Through all of these things, Dana has proven that she can recognize merry-go-rounds and is not afraid to get off and go forward. No matter the circumstances or situations she faced, she never quit believing God and His Word. She held to the Word of God. It has been her Rock. It is evident that her foundation, Who is the Lord Jesus Christ, is strong! This is who she is, and her victories are fully displayed in her life.

In 2017, Dana and her husband, David, jumped off the merry-go-round of frustration caused by not moving forward into their hearts' desires. As they finally stepped out to follow God's plan for their lives, together, they attended Charis Bible College in Woodland Park, CO, on campus for the next three years. Dana graduated her third year from the Charis Business School, and David from the Charis Practical Government School, in May 2020. Determined to keep moving forward, she is building the business God dropped in her heart in 2015. She is also helping her husband express his God-given passions through his Good News Teachings of the true Gospel of Jesus Christ and the Church's role in culture.

Dana and David Ecklund began their marriage in Southern California in 1983. They moved to raise their family in the mid-west and are now back in Southern California. Dana is a mother of three daughters, one son, and a grandmother of seven so far.

To invite Dana Marie Ecklund to speak,
to find additional products and motivational tools, or
to purchase additional copies, please visit :

OnWithYourLife.com